COLLEGE WRITING AND BEYOND

COLLEGE WRITING AND BEYOND

A New Framework for University Writing Instruction

ANNE BEAUFORT

2007
UTAH STATE UNIVERSITY PRESS
Logan, UT

Utah State University Press
Logan, Utah 84322–7800

Manufactured in the United States of America
Cover design by Barbara Yale-Read

Library of Congress Cataloging-in-Publication Data

   ISBN-13: 978-0-87421-659-2
   ISBN-10: 0-87421-659-1
Library of Congress Cataloging-in-Publication Data

Beaufort, Anne.
   College writing and beyond : a new framework for university writing instruction / Anne Beaufort.
      p. cm.
   Includes bibliographical references and index.
   ISBN 978-0-87421-659-2 (alk. paper)
   1. English language–Rhetoric–Study and teaching. 2. Report writing–Study and teaching. 3. English
teachers–Training of. I. Title.
   PE1404.B37 2007
   808'.042071173–dc22
                          2006102845

CONTENTS

ACKNOWLEDGMENTS

Carla, a dedicated, sharp writing lecturer, and Tim, a smart, mature, generous young man, are the stars of this work. Without them, there would be no lines, no entrance or exit points, no script. And for this writer, no subject matter. For Carla and Tim to expose themselves to a researcher's scrutiny was an act of trust and graciousness and courage. I hope, for my part, I have been as trustworthy, and in some measure gracious and courageous. But they are the ones who had to take the bigger leaps of courage than I. To them I owe deep thanks for educating us in this messy business of succeeding to master the craft of writing.

I would wish that Tim had gotten better writing instruction throughout his university experience. I would wish that Carla was better paid and would have the opportunity for sabbaticals, for time to study further the scholarship on teaching writing, this incredibly complex task that none of us has yet mastered. From my outsider perspective, both continue to succeed admirably in their lives in spite of fewer advantages than I might wish they could have. Tim is a parent, successful engineer, social activist, and spiritual seeker. Carla is parent, successful teacher and writer, and social activist.

For the intellectual work done here, I owe a debt to many teachers: Shirley Heath mentored me well in the rigors of ethnographic research. Other fine scholars in composition studies whose work has preceded mine and informs it also must be praised: Lucille McCarthy, David Russell, John Swales, Amy Devitt, Stuart Greene, and David Smit are just a few. Third, those in related fields whose work has particularly helped to frame this study I also thank: Sam Wineburg, Gaea Leinhardt and Kathleen Young, Carl Bereiter and Marlene Scardamalia, Patricia Alexander, David Perkins and Gavriel Salomon, and Robert Sternberg in particular.

I am also grateful to those who granted research leaves in order to accomplish the work, while I was at Stony Brook University—James Staros and Kay Losey—and to colleagues at Stony Brook whose disciplinary expertise gave me "insider" perspectives on the data in Chapters 4 and 5: David Ferguson, John Kincaid, Ned Landsman, Helen LeMay, Sara Lipton, and Gary Markus. Thanks to doctoral student Dana Driscoll, who so quickly grasped the vision I had for a curriculum based on the work here and collaborated in giving it fuller development in Appendix A. And thanks to my colleagues in the Interdisciplinary Arts and Sciences Program at the University of Washington, Tacoma, who have ably demonstrated that it is possible to integrate writing throughout a curriculum if there is a will to do so.

And I am indebted to Michael Spooner at Utah State University Press for his strong encouragement during the long process of reviews and publishing; to my husband, Guy Wulfing, who keeps believing in my work; and to Merrill Carrington, a spiritual mentor, who led me to the fine treatise on scholarship as sacred vocation by Jaroslav Pelikan. As months became years in the preparation of this manuscript, Pelikan's perspective kept me going and gave me a goal to aim for. He says:

> The standards of the scholar . . . who has also become a mature person . . . include: patience, honesty, industry, a sense of humility, a vision of something beyond the tawdry and the broken . . . It is not the results, be they short term or long term, to which the scholar has a vocation. The scholar is called to a process of research, to an attitude of curiosity. (Pelikan 1984)

If this project has pushed me in the directions Pelikan identifies, then I am grateful as well to the work itself.

LIST OF FIGURES AND TABLES

1

THE QUESTION OF UNIVERSITY WRITING INSTRUCTION

Anne: What's your sense of yourself as a writer now, compared to four years ago?

Tim: Uh, well, shoot. Four years ago I would have said, you know, I've got . . . I don't know . . . Four years ago, before taking classes here, I would have said, well that's not really writing . . . realizing that . . . it's not like a particular genre that qualifies as writing. Okay, now you can use style or you pay attention to this, but it's like, you know, whenever you scribble something down, I mean anytime you sit down at the keyboard then that's writing. Even if it's one, two, three, four . . .

—Tim, senior year of college

Anne: Do think you grew as a writer?

Tim: In college? Oh yeah, yeah.

Anne: How?

Tim: Well, I grew to enjoy it and I think I enjoyed it because I was set free, and in being set free I think I found that I had some skill at it . . . I had occasions that were handed to me (laughs). Write! Well, might as well make this fun.

—Tim, two years after college

This book has two stories to tell: the story of Tim's somewhat limited growth as a writer (from this researcher's perspective) between the time he started a freshman writing class at a major US university until two years after he had graduated from school; and second, more argument than story, a case for a re-conceptualization of writing instruction at the post-secondary level. In an earlier ethnography, I examined the struggles of four writers to acclimatize themselves to the demands of writing in college and then in the workplace. Out of that work came a beginning articulation of the nature of writing expertises and a demonstration of why transfer of writing skills from one social context to another is a major issue as yet given too little attention in conceptions of writing curricula. In this work—a blended genre of both ethnography and argument—I draw on the data of a longitudinal case study of one writer bridging from high school writing instruction to freshman writing and then to writing in his two majors, history and engineering, to answer the fundamental question college administrators, college professors in disciplines other than composition studies, and business leaders ask: why graduates of freshman writing cannot produce acceptable written documents in other contexts? At the same time, for those readers who are well acquainted with the scholarship that answers that question, I provide additional empirical work and pragmatic suggestions (in the final chapter and appendices) that may aid the effort to build more coherent writing instruction at the post-secondary level. And for theorists and critics who have not focused on these issues, I hope to provide food for thought on the nature of writing expertise. I see the issues I raise here as relevant to all venues for college-level writing instruction: freshman writing programs, writing-in-the-disciplines programs, programs to train teaching assistants and tutors in teaching of writing, and writing center pedagogies.

We know that writing is a complex cognitive and social activity and that the mental processes involved as well as the contextual knowledge bases that must be tapped are enormous. Writing skill is honed over a lifetime. A ten or a fourteen-week college course in expository or argumentative writing is only a small step on the journey. But given that that step is costing universities in the US (and ultimately, taxpayers) billions of dollars in their collective budgets every year and that there are major industries (publishing, testing) associated with these programs, the question, more finely tuned is, "Could these expenditures of dollars and human capital be made more wisely?" What has recent research in literacy studies or composition studies told us about why Dick and Jane cannot write documents of use to employers or colleagues at the end of college? And how could this research be applied to re-conceptualizing writing curricula and teacher training and tutor training?

The biggest, most costly aspect of writing instruction at the post-secondary level is the compulsory writing course offered in the freshman year to most college students. Some in the field of writing instruction (Petraglia 1995) have already suggested that freshman writing as an enterprise in US institutions of higher education should just close shop:

the "products" (i.e. graduates of freshman writing) are unfinished, the gains are too minute to show up in most assessment processes, and the cost–benefit ratios are too small. I have a different view based on my research, my understanding of colleagues' research, and my reading in fields that speak to the transfer of learning problem. Freshman writing, if taught with an eye toward transfer of learning and with an explicit acknowledgement of the context of freshman writing itself as a social practice, can set students on a course of life-long learning so that they know *how to learn* to become better and better writers in a variety of social contexts.

You may ask what qualifies me to set such a bold agenda for a single book, based on a single case study. I make my argument humbly, with great respect for those many teachers (including those who taught Tim) who work arduously, with great dedication to their students' growth as writers, whose insights may render my views flawed and limited. But I base my views on my own teaching of college writers, my experience mentoring teachers of writing and directing two writing programs at two universities in the US with very different student populations, my work on state-mandated assessment of writers, and my research. In the spirit of numbering my days, I am willing to take the risk to write this now. I hope that teachers, researchers, administrators, and publishers will be willing to listen and continue working with me on the agenda I set forth in this book.

Here is a road map to what follows. In the rest of this chapter I will further explain the problems with teaching writing as it is typically con-structed in institutions of higher education in the US, drawing on the work of others who also name the problem in theoretical ways. I will point out the theoretical and practical implications of these problems as they extend to writing-in-the-disciplines and writing center work. In addition, I will lay out a conceptual framework for my argument and the case study analysis.

Chapter 2 describes the institutional setting for Tim's freshman writ-ing experience and looks at Tim's writing, his professor's comments on his writing and her comments on her teaching, and some of Tim's views of his freshman writing experience. In this chapter, I demonstrate what appeared to be the real discourse community of Tim's freshman writing class and what possibly caused some missed opportunities for furthering Tim's writing development. In Chapter 3, I do a comparative analysis of Tim's writing experiences in one hundred-level history courses he was taking at the same time he was enrolled in freshman writing courses. The comparison makes evident that the writing challenges in his history courses were greater than in freshman writing, as were the challenges of reading-to-write and critical thinking tasks. From the data presented in these first two chapters, the reader can begin to see why the enterprise of freshman writing, as traditionally constructed and commonly practiced, needs to be questioned further.

Chapter 4 moves further into Tim's writing experiences in his sophomore and junior years, as he completed his coursework for the history major. This case study within a case study highlights instances of negative transfer (i.e. applying principles of writing learned in one context inappropriately in another context) and Tim's very limited progress in learning to write in history due to a lack of any developmental path in his writing assignments from course to course. Chapter 5 offers an in-depth look at Tim's experiences with writing for engineering his junior and senior years of college and two years later, when he had had that much experience in a small manufacturing company with writing on the job. This transition from history to engineering discourse community norms was not smooth. It required not only learning new genres and new subject matter, but also encountering a host of new rhetorical situations, new ways of thinking, and new roles as a writer. The problems Tim encountered set the transfer of learning issue in bold relief.

In Chapter 6, I return to the problem of freshman writing and its main corollary enterprises—teacher training, campus writing centers, and writing-across-the-curriculum programs—and offer a proposal for revamping the roles of these writing initiatives in higher education institutions so that the "product" is students who are expert at learning writing skills in multiple social contexts, rather than expert writers in a single context. In the Epilogue, we hear from Tim's freshman writing teacher—her perspective on the data and what it means for her teaching now. In Appendix A, I offer some principles and curricula for teaching for transfer, i.e. helping writers to become life-long students of the craft and practice of writing. The activities and frameworks presented in this appendix, while chiefly geared to writing courses, could be readily adapted to writing-intensive courses and writing tutorial settings. Appendix B gives Samples of Tim's writing. Appendix C gives more detail about the research methodology. But first, I return to the problem with conceptions of writing instruction at the post-secondary level.

PROBLEMS IN UNIVERSITY-LEVEL WRITING INSTRUCTION

In France and England, when I say I teach writing at the university level I am met with puzzled looks. A common response is: "Writing? Don't university students in the US know how to write already?" Formal writing instruction in most European countries ends in high school. In the US, if I say I teach writing, the next question is, "You teach creative writing?"

And yet, I am part of an American tradition of teaching expository and argumentative writing at the university level that was started in US higher education in the late 1800s at Harvard. This enterprise now employs thousands of teachers (many part time), supports over 60 Ph.D. programs in which historical, theoretical, and classroom-based research on the teaching of writing is carried out, and represents a healthy percentage of the college textbook industry's revenues.[1] Academic writing is one of two courses generally required of all college students (the other, a math course). Many campuses also have an upper-division writing program or writing-in-the-disciplines program as well, and a campus writing center where students can seek individualized help on writing projects.

Periodically, journalists, or politicians, or scholars critique this compulsory college level writing course. I concern myself here with the critiques of other scholars, which have generally come from two perspectives.[2] The first critique they make is based on social constructionism and activity theory and the related perspectives of literacy studies, genre theory, and critical theory. From these theoretical vantage points, all acts of writing—and writing instruction—are viewed as socially situated human activities. Writing literacy is a form of political and social capital. Genres perform social functions. Writers assume subject positions and political positions through the genres they employ.

This leads to a critique of freshman writing that goes something like this: because it is a compulsory course, taught in isolation from other disciplinary studies at the university as a basic skills course, this social context leads freshman writing to become a course in "writing to produce writing" (Dias 2000), or to "do school" (Russell 1995). For the majority of students, freshman writing is not a precursor to a writing major. It is an isolated course, an end in itself, a general education requirement to be gotten out of the way. If taught within an English department, or by teachers who are primarily trained in English or comparative literature, students may perceive it as an English course, and yet the course is often a poor step-child to literature courses in English or comparative literature departments and usually suffers the same isolationist lack of intellectual and social moorings.

But why does this lack of institutional grounding for freshman writing matter? Because usually there is no overt linking of the course to any intellectual discipline (even the disciplines of Rhetoric or Composition Studies are usually not invoked in freshman writing), the over-riding social context for students becomes the institutional requirement of the course itself. So writing papers is perceived by students as an activity to earn a grade rather than to communicate to an audience of readers in a given discourse community and papers are commodified into grades, grades into grade reports, grade reports into transcripts, etc. This condition is a serious detriment to motivating writers and to teaching writers to be sensitive to authentic social contexts for writing. This condition also misleads students into thinking writing is a generic skill that, once learned, becomes a "one size fits all" intellectual garb. This in turn leads to misappropriation of principles taught in the course in other contexts where some of those principles are not helpful, or, as cognitive psychologists would say, negative transfer of learning occurs.

On the other hand, no course, no writing situation is without a social context.[3] Given the backgrounds of those who typically teach writing courses and their interests in literature, creative writing, or cultural studies, students in writing courses are most often schooled in the discourse community norms and genres associated with literary studies or cultural studies or journalism (especially the sub-set of creative non-fiction). If students begin to learn some of the literacy practices of these discourse communities, there is some benefit. But what leaves students short-changed as they move into other course work and fields is that the particular discourse community (or communities) in which the teacher is situating himself or herself is not made explicit. And this leads to the second issue with a generic skills course in writing: the transfer of learning issue.

Most teachers of writing think of themselves as generalists. The particular institutional context of their classes and the future endeavors of their students are of less concern than the challenges of equipping students with basic skills. But research in composition studies and linguistic anthropology and literacy studies in the last 30 years has shown there is really no viable commodity called "general writing skills" once one gets beyond the level of vocabulary, spelling, grammar and sentence syntax (and some would argue that even at the sentence level, writing is specific to particular discourse communities' needs).[4] McCarthy's landmark study documented how little a student may gain from a generic writing skills course. Others have repeatedly documented over and over the context-specific expectations about what counts as "good writing" (Bazerman 1982, Berkenkotter et al.1988, Brandt 1990, Canagarajah 1997, Fahnestock and Secor 1991, Faigley and Hansen 1985, Heath 1983) Writing standards are largely cultural and socially specific. And yet, novice writers usually get little instruction in how to study and acquire the writing practices of different discourse communities.

Russell (1995) explains the problem with the assumption that there exists a set of "general writing skills" by drawing a sports analogy: it is as if there were a course in general ball handling that were intended to teach skills applicable to playing jacks, tennis, baseball, and soccer. Given the way freshman writing is typically taught, graduates of these courses could easily think the standards for writing they have been given in freshman writing are universal. They are ill-prepared to examine, question, or understand the literacy standards of discourse communities they are encountering in other disciplines, in the work world, or in other social spheres they participate in. This can result in negative transfer of learning: what worked for a freshman writing essay is inappropriately applied to writing in history, or social sciences, or the sciences or in business. The student must learn, through failed attempts at such transfer of supposed "general" writing skills, how to adapt to the standards and purposes for writing in new discourse communities. And there is significant documentation of students' inabilities, unassisted, to grasp these discourse community differences that affect writers' roles and the texts produced.[5]

In addition to these overriding problems—the inexplicit, or isolated social context of most generic writing courses that teach one way of writing (useful in freshman writing, and somewhat in literature, journalism, or comparative literature courses), rather than teaching a set of tools for analyzing and learning writing standards and practices in multiple contexts, i.e. to facilitate transfer of learning—there are other concrete problems with the typical curriculum in freshman writing. As part of the lack of clarity about what discourse community or communities freshman writing is within or attempting to approximate, there is the problem of a subject matter to write about within the context of a particular discourse community's values and standards. Even textual or rhetorical or literary analyses of texts—common assignments in freshman writing—are often conducted without students having solid grounding in the subject matter of the texts being analyzed and the discourse communities these texts come from. So again, the writing is being analyzed without examining how subject matter, rhetorical occasion, and discourse community context interact. It is a commonly held belief that the only subject of generic writing courses is "writing," and yet students read and write on a variety of subjects without attention to the effect of a given subject matter on written expression.

Kaufer and Young (1993) point out, writing with "no content in particular" wrongly assumes "pretty much the same skills of writing will develop no matter what content is chosen" (p. 78). In contrast to this position, Kaufer and Young highlight what the relationship of subject matter to development of writing skills is: (a) a language act is a composite of form and meaning; (b) subject matter constrains writing, that is, it is not simply a passive environment; and (c) subject matter makes a significant difference in the particular writing skills that get learned (p. 83).

Some teachers of freshman writing offer a smorgasbord of readings on a variety of topics from week to week, which keeps the level of engagement with ideas and information more superficial (Dias 2002). Others let students choose their own subjects to research and write about across a semester. At best, if the curriculum is laid out in either of these ways, the teacher can only sit on the intellectual sidelines of the subject matter the student is exploring, asking questions a generalist would ask.[6] And if a writing course is theme-based, with readings focused on a single intellectual topic, as is the case in the data I will present here, it is not uncommon for the subject matter to be secondary to writing process instruction; or, the subject matter is presented to writing students as an object for rhetorical study in a sealed chamber of rhetorical perspectives that are divorced from the full-range of socially embedded dynamics in a given text.[7] Again, writing becomes writing for the sake of a writing class, rather than writing for the sake of intellectual pursuits. And the skills taught are without grounding in, or acknowledgement of, the effects of subjects and their social contexts on writing activity.

And there are problems beyond having an engaging subject matter that invites intellectual curiosity and exploration and teaches the interrelatedness of content and form in texts. Without serious intellectual engagement in the problems of a particular subject matter, standards of assessment are skewed toward writing process skills and superficial treatment of subject matter is "excused," which is a missed opportunity to hook students on intellectual pursuits and to stretch their critical thinking skills.

As Kaufer and Young mention, without a specific subject matter rooted in a specific discourse community, the genres assigned are not explicitly named as genres "belonging to" or part of the practices of particular discourse communities; they are what some have called "school genres." So students perceive what they write as either "universal" forms of writing, or forms idiosyncratic to freshman writing or school writing. Typical genres assigned in freshman writing in the US include the personal narrative (is this a genre akin to the literary essay, a sub-specialty within the broader discourse community of journalism? Or does it take a particular form peculiar to freshman writing?), the academic essay (a school genre that is a variation on the op ed piece in a newspaper if mostly opinion, or a variation on various essay forms found in different disciplines within the humanities—history, philosophy, etc.), and the "research paper." As Larson (1982) points out, "research paper" defines not a genre but a method of developing subject matter. Or some assign the "textual analysis," again, a school genre, variations of which could be located in any of the humanities depending on the type of texts being analyzed. These genres are taught as if they were universal standards for communicating in all disciplines and yet hardly any discipline outside freshman writing would consider these assignments authentic to the genre requirements of their particular discourse communities.

For example, here is a writing assignment developed by a novice freshman writing teacher. It is an assignment in search of a genre and discourse community to belong to.

> Choose as your topic a place that is significant to you. It can be a neighborhood, a favorite hangout, a monument, or a childhood home. Describe the place in your own words and explain its personal import to you. Combine your personal opinion with historical information which explains the site's significance to the greater population. I want you to use Annie Dillard as inspiration for this essay, but keep in mind the difference between memoir, which she writes, and the academic essay, which you will write.

Invoking Annie Dillard as the model for students to follow in executing the assignment suggests the journalistic discourse community Dillard writes in, and the genre of the literary essay. And yet, students are to write an academic essay. What is the relation between Dillard's work and an academic essay? And what disciplines in academe take as their subject matter neighborhoods and how would those disciplines be thinking about and writing about such subject matter? If the teacher had wanted students to follow in the journalistic tradition of Dillard, at least the target discourse community would have been clear. But the target "academic essay" is in need of a specific disciplinary anchor to be a well-grounded intellectual and communicative task for these students. And unfortunately, this assignment is not an isolated example. Look at the teaching apparatus in almost any college writing text and the writing assignments suggested will reveal the same problems.

RELATED PROBLEMS WITH WRITING-IN-THE-DISCIPLINES AND WRITING CENTER APPROACHES

At this point, readers no doubt think I am going to propose a writing-in-the-disciplines or freshman seminar approach to introductory college level writing courses. In this approach to introductory college writing instruction, teachers in a range of disciplines offer seminars on topics within their fields and work on students' writing intensively.[8] Smit (2004) proposes such a model with a three-course sequence across the majors: a first course, "Introduction to Writing as Social Practice" would begin to acquaint students with the ways in which language is socially situated. A second and third course would introduce students to writing practices of distinct discourse communities. At many schools, courses in the major are designated as writing-intensive, and in these courses more attention is given to students' writing as the course subject matter is taught.

Writing courses in the major bypass the problem of contextualizing writing instruction in a discourse community. But while a more overt disciplinary basis to the writing instruction can solve the problem of writing that is devoid of a well-identified social context within which the writing is grounded and motivated, research in these approaches to writing instruction has uncovered other problems. Dias points out: "Writing [can be] defined . . . in the disciplinary courses primarily as a way of displaying learning"(2000,) So teachers give assignments that lead students to feel they are simply demonstrating that they read the book or listened to the lectures rather than their engaging in the intellectual work of the discipline through writing tasks. For example, a historian asks students to compare a novel and several primary sources, attempting to (a) get the students more interested in the subject matter and (b) prevent plagiarism. But historians rarely would take on such a task. The student knows, and the teacher knows, the writing is for purposes of gate-keeping/grade-giving.

A second problem with discipline-specific writing courses, taught by disciplinary experts, is the experts' difficulties in making overt the knowledge about writing standards they have learned from a slow acculturation process, rather than by direct instruction (Kaufer and Young 1993). As Russell (1995) says,

> A discipline uses writing as a tool for pursuing some object. Writing is not the object of its activity. Thus, writing tends to become transparent, automatic, and beneath the level of conscious activity for those who are thoroughly socialized into it . . . `As a result, experts may have great difficulty explaining these operations to neophytes (p. 70).

Or, as Polanyi (1966) would say, the knowledge of disciplinary writing conventions has become tacit knowledge, beneath the level of consciousness. To instruct newcomers requires making that tacit knowledge conscious.

A third problem with writing instruction in disciplinary settings is the issue of teaching students to learn how to learn the conventions of writing in new situations they will encounter. As Kaufer and Young (1993) point out, a unified theory that takes into account general and context-specific writing skills is needed for executing a solid writing curriculum. If the writing instruction is context-specific and students are not given the kinds of intellectual tools and frameworks for being able to become astute at learning to be flexible writers, they will not be able to adapt to a variety of writing situations.

In addition to the need for individuals assigning and coaching writing appropriately in their respective fields, Young and Leinhardt (1998) point out a critical need for " . . . models for the systematic instruction of disciplinary writing." In spite of the writing-across-the-curriculum movement (WAC) in higher education in the US since the early 1980s, there is little documentation of successful disciplinary writing curricula that are systematic in their approach, i.e. offering a sequence of writing assignments and instruction that explicitly move students progressively toward more complex and more expert writing performances as they pursue their major fields of study.[9]

Writing center tutors have an even greater challenge: eliciting from writers who come for help what the context is for the writing task they want help with. Often, novice writers are not clear what the task requirements are and do not understand the discourse community expectations embedded in the writing task. Or, the writing assignment itself is vague or confusing, leaving both tutor and writer in a difficult situation. While no theoretical framework can solve some of the problems writing tutors may face, there is room for a more robust theory of writing instruction that could serve tutors and students well.

Much of the current scholarship in writing center practice (Boquet 2002, Briggs and Woolbright 2000, Grimm 1999, Harris 1998, Hobson 1994, Pemberton and Kinkead 2003) combines expressivist views (supporting the individual writer in finding his/her voice) and social constructionist views (meaning in written texts is often created through collaborative dialogue between writer and tutor) and writing process approaches (how to help the writer develop a more robust writing process). But the move in writing center practice away from being directive or product-focused leads to very general approaches to guiding writers in revising drafts. Stephen North's dictum to "work with the writer, not the writing" is often invoked. The advice to "review the essay with the writer for development and organization" (Ryan 2002) is typical of tutoring guides.[10] It is understandable that writing center tutor training guides treat superficially the context-specific aspects of writing and focus largely on a very general set of guidelines for academic writing. But, if tutors added to their approaches to coaching writers a framework for assisting students in understanding how to analyze the context-specific nature of writing activities, the tutors could better promote the kinds of learning-how-to-learn skills all advanced writers need. Furthermore, the oft-cited dichotomy between working to produce better writing versus producing better writers could be set aside, as both goals could be accomplished through applying a more robust theory of writing expertise to tutor practices.

These then are some of the manifestations I see of a less-than fully articulated conceptual model of writing expertise and a limited, seldom-invoked conceptual model for aiding writers to transfer learning from one context to another. What I offer in the chapters that follow is both a theoretical lens and a case study that may add further clarity—even urgency—to the need for important additions to the curricula in general writing courses, additions to approaches to writing-in-the-disciplines work, and also to writing center approaches to assisting writers. In the concluding chapter and appendices I offer practical guidelines for doing so. I explain now the theoretical model for writing expertise I have worked out, based on the data in this and my earlier research, that can provide us with greater clarity about the components of a successful approach to instructing writers who have advanced beyond issues of sentence-level fluency.

A CONCEPTUAL MODEL OF WRITING EXPERTISE

If there is no such thing as writing expertise, or "general" writing skill, but rather, individual expert writing performances, as Bazerman (1994) argues, then there is a need to conceptualize writing in a whole other way. While writing expertise does not transfer wholesale from one writing context to another, it is possible to identify the common knowledge domains within which writers must develop context-specific knowledge. The literature on expertise suggests that experts not only have very rich, deep, context-specific knowledge, but they also have mental schema, or heuristics, with which to organize knowledge and aid problem-solving and gaining new knowledge in new situations.[11] So the question becomes, what knowledge domains best represent the mental schema employed in expert writing performances? And what knowledge domains—or mental schema—do writers need to invoke for analyzing new writing tasks in new discourse communities? If we can articulate these knowledge domains and apply them to shaping curriculum, we can then contextualize writing instruction more fully and have a basis for teaching for transfer, i.e. equipping students with a mental schema for learning writing skills in new genres in new discourse communities they will encounter throughout life.

If asked what they teach, most teachers of university-level writing would probably articulate some or all of the following: writing process knowledge (how to get writing done, from pre-drafting to final draft), rhetorical modes (narrative, exposition, persuasive writing, etc.), audience awareness, voice, style, grammar and mechanics. Some might include genre knowledge or critical thinking or research skills. Conspicuously missing from the list is subject matter knowledge or discourse community knowledge. And also absent is a sense of a whole, a way of conceptualizing how the different aspects of writing are related and fit together. An examination of composition readers and rhetorics and writing handbooks would, for the most, part mirror our partial and fragmented views of writing instruction, with a few notable exceptions.[12]

The same fragmentation is true in the theoretical and empirical literature in composition studies. The only overviews in composition studies of writing expertise are Carter's (1990) Bryson's (1991), and Smagorinsky and Smith's (1992). They outline in broad strokes the nature of research into expertise and general versus context-specific ways of thinking of writing skills. Others have identified single components of the domain knowledge and skills associated with expert writers' performances: writing process skills (Flower and Hayes 1981, Perl 1979, Sommers 1980), subject matter knowledge and rhetorical knowledge (Geisler 1994), and types of rhetorical strategies specific to particular fields of expertise (Fahnestock 1986, Fahnestock and Secor 1991, Herrington 1988). What is needed is a more inclusive model that can account for the multiple knowledge domains activated in expert writing performances. As an engineer must understand certain laws of physics, chemical properties of materials, etc. to create the desired product, so too, the writer must engage a considerable body of writing knowledge in acts of composing.

As a starting place to take into account the domains of knowledge writers employ, I use the model of writing expertise theorized from the data in my ethnographic study of writers' transitions from academic to professional writing (1999). Briefly, the model consists of five overlapping yet distinct domains of situated knowledge entailed in acts of writing: discourse community knowledge, subject matter knowledge, genre knowledge, rhetorical knowledge, and writing process knowledge.[13]

As depicted in Figure 1 (next page), these knowledge domains, all integral to writing expertise, overlap and interactive with each other. Labeling a particular aspect of writing expertise as one or the other dimension is at times difficult, given their interactive functions (Prior 1994). Nonetheless, for purposes of teasing out as many of the knowledge domains that comprise writing expertise as possible in this study, the distinctions are maintained at the same time that the interactive aspects are depicted.

Here is further articulation of this conceptual model. First, the overarching concept: a theory of discourse communities. What writing expertise is ultimately concerned with is becoming engaged in a particular community of writers who dialogue across texts, argue, and build on each other's work. Discourse communities exhibit a particular network of communicative channels, oral and written, whose interplay affects the purposes and meanings of the written texts produced within

FIGURE 1

Conceptual Model: Expert Writers Draw on Five Knowledge Domains

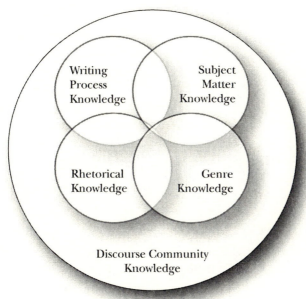

the community. Based on a set of shared goals and values and certain material/physical conditions, discourse communities establish norms for genres that may be unique to the community or shared with overlapping communities and roles and tasks for writers are appropriated within this activity system (Beaufort 1997). While some critique a theory of discourse community, I find the components of discourse communities I have isolated in my research to have great heuristic value.[14]

Besides the knowledge entailed in understanding and engaging the broader goals and activities of a discourse community, writers must engage a specific subject matter considered within the purview of a discourse community. In this aspect of writing, experts are both drawing on existing knowledge bases (i.e. background knowledge) and doing the critical thinking necessary for the creation of "new" or "transformed" knowledge (Bereiter and Scardamlia 1987, Bloom 1971) that is interactive with and is influenced by the discourse community. Such critical thinking includes knowing how to frame the inquiry, what kinds of questions to ask or analytical frameworks to use in order to "transform" or inscribe documents with new meaning(s).

Writers must also develop knowledge of genres whose boundaries and features the discourse community defines and stabilizes. Slevin's (1998) postmodern definition of genre[15] and Bawarshi's (2003) excellent exposition of the ways genres serve writers in the process of creating texts—are rich discussions of genres as a tool for writers and are a much-needed replacement to the limited theories of text types from classical rhetoric.[16] Some (Devitt 2004) would argue that genre knowledge is all-encompassing and a theory of discourse community is superfluous, but my research suggests both are necessary. I have found that genres such as the essay or the grant proposal vary greatly from one discourse community to another, and these variations become clear and understandable as one considers variations between discourse communities.[17]

In addition to discourse community knowledge, subject matter knowledge, and genre knowledge, writers must address the specific, immediate rhetorical situation of individual communicative acts (Ede and Lunsford 1984, Lunsford and Ede 1996). This includes considering the specific audience and purpose for a particular text and how best to communicate rhetorically in that instance. The rhetorical moment is also affected by the social context—material conditions, timing, social relationships, etc. within the discourse community. And finally, writers must have writing process knowledge, i.e. knowledge of the ways in which one proceeds through the writing task in its various phases. This procedural knowledge associated with writing process is also affected by the material, socially specific particulars of a given writing situation or "community of practice" (Flower 1994, Rogoff 1994).[18]

An illustration of one particular writing task familiar to academics may bring these abstract conceptions of the components of writing expertise into clear focus: let us examine the writing of an abstract of a journal article or book. An abstract is a *genre* (or sub-genre—part of another genre) read by those in several different *discourse communities*—researchers in the writer's field (biology, for example), librarians who need to build library collections and those who put bibliographic information on publications into databases, and editors of publications in the writer's field. Across these diverse discourse communities, there is a common *rhetorical occasion* that prompts the need for abstracts—namely, readers' need to quickly ascertain if there is "news" of interest in the longer work the abstract announces—or just how to categorize the *subject matter* of the piece is—and the writer's need to interest others in the new work. Like the first paragraph of a news or feature story in journalistic venues, or movie trailers shown in theaters before a film's release, the abstract must convey information succinctly, clearly, and with a sense of urgency, beckoning the reader to continue reading. Besides being well versed in all aspects of the subject matter being reported on, say, stem cell research, the writer of the abstract must know what the required content is for *the genre* of an abstract? Should it include a mention of research methods? The research problem? The main thesis? A sense of the subject's importance to this group of readers? Genre knowledge entails knowing what content is required, what is not; how best to sequence the content; what specific needs to readers will have, and how common or technical a vocabulary to use. And finally, the writer must find the best *writing process* for getting the abstract written: should s/he write it first, as a focusing device to guide composing the rest of the piece? Or should it be written last, after the writer has discovered, through writing, what s/he has to say? Should s/he just copy and paste from key lines in the body of the piece, or summarize the piece in a fresh way? These are the writing process decisions and know-how that complete the five domains of writing knowledge a writer draws on for this particular task.

Combined then, the five knowledge domains articulated here (including an expanded notion of subject matter knowledge that includes a critical thinking component) form the theoretical framework I will use for analyzing aspects of writing expertise Tim exhibited in freshman writing, in history, and in engineering over a six-year period. This conceptual framework will also inform the recommendations for restructuring university-level writing instruction in ways that will increase the likelihood of positive transfer of learning.

Such a position could be critiqued as positivist or foundationalist, i.e. as falsely implying that learning is a matter of "pouring in" knowledge to the blank slate of a person's mind and that the subject matter to be learned (i.e. writing knowledge) is fixed and stable. Those who would raise this critique might argue that knowing is only situational and dialogic—for the moment—and there are no fixed "categories" of knowledge. To those of this philosophical bent, I offer two comments: first, to conceptualize writing knowledge in distinct yet overlapping categories does not inherently imply either that those categories are fixed and discreet, or that learning is a rote affair, a matter of simply "banking" such knowledge. I would agree with Bereiter and Scardemalia, ". . . what counts with cooks and experts is what they do with the material in their pantries or memory stores (1993, p. 45)" Or, as they state more directly,

". . . we have to find [expertise] in the ongoing process in which knowledge is used, transformed, enhanced, and attuned to situations (p. 46)." Gaining writing expertise only takes place, I believe, in the context of situational problem-solving, or, as others have demonstrated, through legitimate participants in apprenticeship situations (Heath, 1982; Lave and Wenger1991; Prior, 1994). As Flower states, "The meaning of a literate act will not lie solely in the resources on which it draws, the conventions in which it participates, or the context to which it responds, but in the ways writers use and even transform their knowledge and resources to take action "(1994, p. 37). So a theory of writing expertise provides the schema that can guide a developmental process that empowers the individual writer, rather than place any limitations on writers.

To those who do not feel satisfied that there is enough of a critical, liberal agenda in this theory of writing expertise, I would say, yes, the theory is apolitical in the sense that no particular political agenda is being promoted and no one interest group is being catered to. But on the other hand, this view of expertise is crucial to the legitimate social causes of literacy, employment, and effective communication—to empowering all across gender, race, ethnic, and class lines to write effectively in a range of social contexts.

What I do is name the types of resources from which writers draw to create texts and a way of organizing a schematic for those resources. Again, to draw on Bereiter and Scardamalia's work on the nature of expertise, ". . . knowledge is not just one more factor . . . knowledge is a large part of what must be explained and not something that lies in the background" (1993, p. 44). Others have represented writing knowledge as a combination of content knowledge and rhetorical knowledge (Geisler 1994), or procedural knowledge and declarative knowledge (Berkenkotter, et al. 1989), or knowledge of text types and the linguistic features of written discourse.[19] What I am proposing here is a fuller accounting of the knowledge domains expert writers employ than has been given in other accounts, not to win some philosophical argument about the nature of truth, but rather, to try to get at a more fine-grained and unified sense of what is going on when we study writers' behaviors and a broader view of what we should consider in creating writing curricula.

THEORIZING THE DEVELOPMENTAL PROCESS FOR GAINING WRITING EXPERTISE

While the conceptual model I have described will enable a systematic look at skills Tim acquired during college and beyond, there is an additional perspective needed for purposes of planning and implementing a writing sequence within or across disciplines. In other words, we must also ask, how and when do writers gain expertise in a given knowledge domain? Is there a particular learning sequence for advanced writers that makes sense? The question takes on particular importance if, in fact, what Bereiter and Scardamalia (1993) state is true. They say,

> Writing violates the conventional wisdom about expertise on a number of counts. Conventional wisdom has it that practice makes perfect and that expertise is the natural outcome of years of practice. But few people become good writers, no matter how much they write. For many, the effect of years of practice is simply to produce increasingly fluent bad writing (p. x).

As in the case of trying to develop a composite of the knowledge domains writers draw upon, there is no comprehensive, empirically supported conceptual framework for the developmental processes of writers in gaining expertise at advanced stages of literacy that would enable us to better conceptualize delivery of writing instruction and assessment of learning in writing-intensive courses (Applebee 2000). There are a number of studies of students' progress from beginning to end of a single course (Carroll 2002, Herrington 1985, Walvoord and McCarthy 1990), and several longitudinal studies following university writers over several years that document general types of gains in critical thinking skills (Sternglass 1997), self-identity as writers (Herrington and Curtis 2000), and socialization (or not) into academic discourse communities(Herrington and Curtis 2000, McCarthy 1987). But these studies do not attempt a composite developmental model for writers at advanced levels of literacy development.

For most teachers, and even researchers, the time span available—one course, two, or three—for viewing a student's progress in developing writing skills is too brief to notice much change. We routinely hand out grades according to some predetermined standards. But rarely do we have the opportunity to measure, in meaningful ways, what has changed in a writer's work over a significant period of time. And, as Haswell points out, "Writing skill learned to pass a course but unused thereafter is learning that is not developmental"(1991, p. 5).

Assessing change or development in writing is also compounded methodologically by the fact that written products do not tell the whole story of what has transpired for the writer. Robust research methods are required to assess writing development. And exactly what it is we are looking for in terms of change or development may be unclear as well, given the absence of a theory of writing development beyond the stages of acquiring basic writing literacy. Although a building-block metaphor has traditionally been used to inform sequencing of writing instruction (moving from words to sentences to paragraphs, etc.), more recently composition studies has characterized the writer's developmental path in metaphorical terms as one of writers moving from outsider to insider status in particular discourse communities or activity systems and a more holistic, or communications approach to development has been the model for instruction.[20] However, most curricular guides for teaching writing at the university level use a developmental sequence based on Piaget's theory of child development, from egocentric (i.e. personal writing) to more audience-centered (i.e. argument) responses, even though there is no empirical evidence that this type of developmental sequence for writing tasks is better than another.

While there is no grand theory of writers' developmental processes, developmental processes in acquiring *particular* aspects of writing expertise have been articulated. These studies give us a start in looking for signs of development and a way to articulate a more comprehensive view of writers' developmental processes. For example, research has documented expert writers using a more robust composing process (Flower and Hayes 1981, Perl 1979, Sommers 1980) or employing a greater number of a genre's features (Beaufort 1999, Berkenkotter, et al. 1989, Eller 1989, Himley 1986) and having increased rhetorical skills (Geisler 1994, Herrington 1988). In addition, various studies have attempted to determine what sentence-level linguistic patterns of development are evidenced as students move through school (Beaufort 1999, Haswell 2000, Hunt 1965), suggesting that there is some correlation between advanced levels of literacy and the ability to use more complex grammatical structures. Others have pointed to a more sophisticated understanding of discourse community issues among more experienced writers, or to rhetorical fluency as a sign of advanced skills.[21] At least, these studies help to define the layers of knowledge in each of the domains comprising writing expertise.

To further complicate the challenge of articulating the developmental progress of writers, studies of literacy in early stages document numerous examples of students learning the complex dimensions of writing exper-tise not in compartmentalized fashion, but rather, holistically.[22] Even beginning writers must wrestle with writing process, with rhetorical/social contexts, and with genre demands, vocabulary, sentence structure, etc. These data reinforce the need to take into account all of the knowl-edge components embedded within literate acts, no matter what level or social context of writing development is being examined.

It is also not clear at what educational or age level certain writing skills are developmentally appropriate. A few studies have examined some of the features of writing development at specific grade levels.[23] For exam-ple, studies have documented that high school students in general are accustomed to writing reports (i.e. recall or summary of information in source texts) or advocacy (i.e. opinion) essays (Crowhurst 1991, Flower et al. 2000). In transitioning to college-level academic writing, students can experience difficulty bridging to more analytical thinking. But again, there is no composite view in the research so far of all aspects of writing expertise present (or not) at these developmental phases.

In the case of college writers, it is also important to consider issues of the development of critical thinking: to do the kinds of writing tasks expected in college and beyond requires increasingly complex forms of thinking. And, there is documentation of the jump in expectations from high school to college in terms of abilities to analyze, compare, synthe-size, and evaluate various forms of data (Freedman and Pringle, 1980, p. 580). Critical thinking skills go hand-in-hand with writing skills.

Bloom's (1971) hierarchy of critical thinking skills, which was an exten-sion of Piaget's schema of concrete versus formal operations and has been employed extensively in writing curriculum development, is a useful tool for analyzing writers' critical thinking skills and for developing assignment sequences, even though its ability to distinguish the fine points of critical thinking skills is limited. Even within different types of cognitive work (summary, seriation, classification, analysis, etc.) there can be gradations from simpler to more complex tasks (Kiniry and Strenski 1985), so what constitutes a "hierarchy" or progression from easier to more complex cognitive tasks is not so easily mapped out and more than one cognitive process may be employed in composing a single text. The domain-specific nature of critical thinking must also be taken into consideration.[24]

Yet in spite of various schematics of distinct types of critical thinking, generally there is agreement that indicators of more fully developed thinking skills as applicable to academic writing tasks include the ability to manipulate source texts in complex ways beyond simple restatement or recall[25] the ability to entertain more than one point of view, i.e. to do relativistic thinking on complex issues[26] and the ability to think metacognitively about one's own thinking.[27]

At this point, I would expect the reader's attention to want to wander. There are too many puzzle pieces on the table. Putting a developmental theory for writers with a theory of writing expertise is difficult. Alexander's work on the stages of development in accomplishing academic tasks, though not specific to writing tasks, can provide a useful starting point for examining developmental issues of college writers (Alexander, 2003). Rather than sharp distinctions between "novice" and "expert," she conceptualizes a continuum in three phases: 1) acclimation (the learner has limited and fragmented knowledge; 2) competence (exhibiting domain knowledge that is cohesive and "principled in structure"); and 3) proficiency (a broad and deep knowledge base and the ability to build new knowledge in the domain) (pp. 11–12). Alexander's framework can provide some of the signals for what is or is not developing as Tim responds to writing tasks over the college years and suggest a general measure of Tim's progress.

In this case study, I will also note what changed over six years in Tim's writing among all of the knowledge domains pertinent to writing expertise in an effort to contribute to theory-building regarding developmental processes of writers. To develop a composite of developmental processes at the university level could also contribute to our understandings of how to build curricular sequences in writing and how to design appropriate assessment standards.

AN OVERVIEW OF THE CASE STUDY

A case study offers the advantage of an in-depth examination of a particular situation. Given the goal in this study of examining a student's writing over a long time period through as many analytical frames as possible in order to determine what increased competencies in writing were evidenced, case study methodologies were ideal. While not generalizable, this case study offers the potential for refining a conceptual framework for writing expertise that could be tested in other settings. I describe in greater detail the methods used in the study in Appendix C, but here offer a brief overview of the methodology.

The study focuses on Tim, an undergraduate student at a major private university in the South from 1995–2000.[28] Tim had not taken AP

English, so took the standard two quarter sequence of freshman writing in his first year. He had a double major in college—history and engineering. He focused first on history. By the end of his junior year, he had completed all of his history requirements and began taking the math, science and engineering courses he needed. I met Tim while observing his freshman writing class for a pilot study on the issue of students learning to write in multiple contexts—academic and "real world." Tim had an interest in the project and an interest in examining himself as a writer, which he expressed to me on several occasions. As an outgrowth of the pilot study, data were collected Tim's freshman, junior, and senior years and two years after college.

There were seven data sources: (1) interviews with Tim (both general and discourse-based) over a six-year period, (2) samples of Tim's writing, (3) source materials Tim used for the freshman writing and history essays, (4) when available, evaluators' comments on his papers, (5) expert historians' and engineers' commentaries on Tim's disciplinary writing, which I solicited during the analysis of data, (6) observation of 12 sessions of Tim's second freshman writing course, and (7) interviews with Carla, Tim's freshman writing professor. These data sources were analyzed, coded, and read against each other, using the theoretical frames I have articulated here for the knowledge domains that comprise writing expertises, as well as heuristics for examining critical thinking. Time did not permit observation of classroom instruction in his history or engineering courses and it was not possible because of logistical constraints to interview Tim's professors in history or engineering.

Although a single case study, I will make strong assertions about the data and about the curricular changes the data suggest, in the hope of inviting teachers and researchers to give some pause and thought to their assumptions and practices. As Haswell (1991) says, "Will students gain ground if the teacher does not?" (p. 12).

2

THE DILEMMAS OF FRESHMAN WRITING

Like the playwright who gives stage directions so that the reader can imagine a living, breathing experience, or the composer who begins an opus with a prelude, I begin this chapter with excerpts of field notes and other documents gathered at the site of this case study—an English department at a prestigious private university in the South. These bits and pieces, together, form a backdrop to the discussion that follows.

The heavy wood door to English, in the middle of the quad, is like all the other nondescript doors on the quad—dark brown, with the department name in white lettering. Opening the door, one's eye is drawn to a wide, thickly-carpeted stairway with curling wrought-iron and wood railing leading to the second floor, where the department chair, his secretary, and the senior faculty have their offices.

In the first floor wood-paneled vestibule is a lighted glass case housing book jackets—those of books faculty have written. Next to the vestibule is a small anteroom that houses the faculty mailboxes, a love seat, and a coffee table. On it is a copy of The New York Times Book Review. *On a Wednesday morning, between 10 and 10:30, five men and one woman pick up mail. One catches snippets of conversation: "Did you attend the meeting on language and culture. . . . The way she situates the relationship of language to consciousness . . . models for a cultural context of violence and power." . . . Beside the mailboxes is a poster announcing a poetry reading in the afternoon.*

Next door, without carpeting or paneling or a lighted showcase, are the offices of creative writing (upstairs) and freshman writing (downstairs).

—researcher's field notes

***

Department chair: *. . . it's very hard to get people to volunteer to teach Freshman Writing.* It used to be routine, but there was a major change in the 1960s and 1970s. Since the 1970s research has been valued more . . . Over the years there's been involvement of the faculty in Freshman Writing. We want to reestablish it (emphasis mine).

Anne: Why is that important?

Department chair: The deans have demanded it. It's not the best use of faculty time and course distributions and they won't do as well as the lecturers because they've been out of the field. But here power flows from above. The penalty is no bucks. But on the positive side, some faculty involvement will show how good the program is.

After the tape recorder is turned off, the chair points to several textbooks authored by freshman writing lecturers on his desk and says. "These don't carry any status. They're not the books that get written up in *The New York Times Book Review.*"

> —*researcher's interview notes, January 24, 1995*

***

The freshman writing courses serve two educational functions. First . . . is to improve the skills of freshmen in writing, argumentation, and library research. The second is to give graduate students in English an opportunity to develop skills in teaching an undergraduate composition course. (A third function is to provide financial support for graduate students in English.)

We have reached the tentative conclusion that a significant fraction of students do not receive sufficient instruction in writing, especially of analytical essays that are widely required in various courses in humanities and the social sciences . . . For the two-term course, students are required to write a personal essay and to complete a series of rhetorical exercises in the first quarter, and to write a research paper in the second . . . A large fraction (more than two-thirds) of the freshman writing courses are literature. . . . the 5000 word writing requirement per quarter we regard as remarkably small . . . Indeed, several members of the review committee teach writing-intensive courses that require substantially more writing than this . . .

The key underlying policy issue is whether it makes sense to have a university requirement of this magnitude that is essentially ignored by the tenure track faculty . . .

> —*report of the ad hoc review committee for the freshman writing requirement, Committee on Undergraduate Studies, May 1995*

***

Despite the objections of some English professors, an "experiment" using graduate students from departments other than English as Freshman Writing instructors will begin next year . . .

If the three-student pilot program succeeds, it may be expanded to include more Humanities and Sciences graduate students from departments such as history . . . The Dean said some Freshman English lecturers may be cut if more graduate students are used. But she added that it is unlikely that all of the lecturers will be eliminated.

"We thought eliminating the lecturers would save us money at first," the Dean said. "However, the difference between a lecturer's salary and a graduate student's salary is not enough to merit creating the program for money-saving purposes alone", she said.

—campus newspaper, February 18, 1995

***

Freshman English budget: $800,000
Revenues from Freshman English tuition: $2.5 million

—source: English department chair

***

This year's discussions of possible effects of budget constraints on the Freshman English Program come at a time when many colleges and universities committed to excellent teaching are rethinking the substance and direction of their programs . . . Most relevant research findings for current changes has been the overwhelming evidence that having students practice writing academic essays and research papers in Freshman Writing programs bears almost no relationship to their writing needs across the span of their college life.

—senior English department faculty member in Freshman English newsletter article, Spring, 1995

***

I am in the midst of a frustrated rage. I have just been exposed to my first day of Freshman Writing, and basically all I see is a dysfunctional system . . . Maybe there are some people who would benefit from it, but they should know who they are, or maybe other teachers should recommend it for them. Says one friend of mine. "It's like cookie-cutter writing, very rigid." Says another, "It was my worst class so far." And another, "Pointless drivel."

—editorial in campus newspaper, April 2, 1996

***

Teachers must create the conditions that make good writing possible. There is no formula for setting up these conditions, but obviously the first requirement is to be fully competent—to be a good writer and good critic of writing. If you feel shaky on the fundamentals of, say, grammar, you should do a serious and thorough review without delay. . . .

Remember that the course is primarily one in composition. Don't overload your students with reading or with problems in logic. A good rule of thumb: not more than one-third of the out-of-class work for your course should be spent on anything other than the student's writing. . . .

Students must write at least 5,000 words each quarter. . . . At the beginning, assign at least one short paper (two-three pages) every week. As the quarter progresses, gradually expand to longer papers. . . . Ask your students to rewrite the equivalent of at least two essays. When totaling the number of pages per quarter, count rewritten pages as half. . . .

—*Freshman English Instructor's Manual, 1995–1996*

THE INSTITUTIONAL CONTEXT FOR FRESHMAN WRITING

From the documents quoted above, we can see some aspects of the context in which Tim took his mandatory writing courses. When Tim was a freshman, all students were required to take two quarters of freshman writing (EGL 101 and EGL 102) unless scores on AP English were high enough to place them in EGL 103, a one-quarter accelerated writing course. Though social conditions have changed for the better at the institution described here, the circumstances I have described—in particular, the curricular goals and staffing practices—will be familiar at many institutional sites for freshman writing today. The courses, staffed primarily by Ph.D. students in English literature or by writing lecturers with M.A. and M.F.A. degrees, were under the aegis of the English department. It is this social milieu, in part, that influences students' experiences in freshman writing.

One wonders, reviewing these documents, what freshman writing would have been if budgets and supporting graduate students at this university were not considerations. The outsider status of the enterprise in relation to the material and intellectual work of the rest of the university is reflected in the relatively low social status associated with teaching writing and in the overarching concern with budgets reflected in the institutional documents I have quoted. The fact that the writing program was overseen at that time by faculty who were not part of the professional community of composition and rhetoric scholars was also a contributing factor in the delivery of instruction. While many of the lecturers were hard-working and were acquainting themselves, as time permitted, with "best practices" in the field of composition studies, from what I saw it appeared that collective knowledge of the field among the writing faculty was limited.

There are other messages as well about the state of freshman writing from outsiders' perspectives in these documents: an ad hoc faculty committee on undergraduate programs feels the type and amount of writing does not prepare students well enough for the writing they will encounter in other courses. An angry student or two characterize the freshman writing course as "rigid" and "drivel." And a senior faculty member with expertise in English, in literacy studies, and in linguistic anthropology warns that the research in composition studies calls into serious question the benefits of freshman writing in increasing students' academic literacies. As others have said, there are numerous social dynamics in freshman writing, whether consciously acknowledged by teachers and students or not, that impact motivation, effort, and learning, often adversely (Bazerman 1997, Jolliffe 1995, Petraglia 1995).

The constraints at the institution where this study took place are fairly typical. Add to this the lack of consensus among teachers and scholars in composition studies on best ways of instructing college students to improve their writing and the fact that budget constraints prohibit hiring and retaining the most qualified teachers of writing. Some readers may proclaim there is limited hope for improvement in college writing instruction. Others may feel, given the multiple problems institutions in higher education face, the problem of students' less than adequate writing skills are overshadowed by more pressing educational and institutional issues. To either group I would say, let us look at Tim's experiences in freshman writing and beyond. While only a single student's experience at a single institution, I argue that his case will ring true to those experienced in the tricky business of teaching college students to write better. And more important, the theoretical framework that illuminates the data here, and its practical consequences for curricula and pedagogies, suggest this enterprise of college level writing instruction can be improved. I will examine the data gathered in this institutional site for freshman writing from several angles: the teacher's, the student's, those of other experts in higher education, and mine. In Chapter 3 I will set side by side Tim's experiences in his freshman year writing courses and his writing experiences in his history courses taken than same year (history was his declared major). That comparison will also bring to bear a valuable perspective on the problems of freshman writing.

Carla's Freshman Writing Courses

Tim was Carla's student for both courses in the freshman writing sequence. Carla, a poet with an M.F.A. in creative writing, had been first an adjunct and then a lecturer for three years in the English department's writing program at the time of this study. In spite of a two-hour commute one way to work and the low pay and low status, she loved her job, and as this book is written, remains at the same institution, happily, with a more secure and better-compensated position teaching writing.

At the time of this study, freshman writing faculty had a lot of room for interpreting the curriculum guidelines. Curriculum materials (in the form of mimeographed handouts and a Xeroxed instructor's manual) reflected a mix of current traditional and expressivist philosophies as well as pedagogy to teach the writing process. It was the norm for teachers to require multiple drafts and to hold peer review and individual conference sessions before students turned in final drafts. Curricular guidelines stated an expectation that teachers assign a personal essay and short papers in the first course, gradually increasing the length of essays assigned and incorporating instruction in the researched essay in the second course. Curricular guidelines also highlighted a variety of topics that could be addressed in the courses as well: the discourse modes (narration, description, argumentation, etc.), matters of unity, coherence, style, and proper documentation in academic writing. Instructors were free to choose a theme-based course or not; many chose literary or journalistic readings focusing on loosely defined themes.

Carla had been teaching literature-based courses in the department for four years prior to the time these data were gathered and was in the process of adding the theme of environmental issues and incorporating community service writing projects into her courses. I chose to work with Carla and her students (initially five of them) because of her openness to me, her enthusiasm for teaching writing, and her reputation as a fine teacher. While I will be critiquing some of Carla's approaches here and Carla and I do not see all teaching issues in the same ways (see our dialogue in the Epilogue), nonetheless my respect for her thoughtfulness about her teaching and for the smart and sophisticated ways in which she problematizes writing instruction is great. I do not consider myself to be an ultimate judge of good or bad teaching of writing. What I offer here, based on the work of others in this field and my understanding of these data and my own experiences teaching college writers, is a view that supports a different agenda for post-secondary writing instruction than will unfold here.[29]

I present now an overview of Carla's freshman writing courses (EGL 101 and EGL 102) drawn from these artifacts: the course syllabi, conversations with Carla and Tim about the course (recorded, transcribed, systematically coded for themes), other course documents, Tim's freshman writing work, his commentary on the work and Carla's feedback on the work as well as that of one outside reader Tim sought out, and field notes and transcriptions of selected class sessions.

First, it may be helpful to readers to get a sense of Carla's philosophy and goals for her students in freshman writing. Here is what she told me (emphasis in bold italics is mine.)

Anne: What is your philosophy of teaching writing? And how has it evolved?

Carla: The personal essay isn't just a warm-up exercise. The personal perspective is something I ask students to maintain regardless of the type of writing. That doesn't mean always writing in the first person, but reflecting constantly on how the writing relates. *I request that students stay involved, not get into that distracted academic mode.* I don't feel people who write on broader themes accomplish much without understanding on an intimate level. That's the reason for a liberal arts education—to start integrating where they fit into the larger pattern of things. Discourse at the broad level is very confusing. It's hard to know what it's about without establishing who we are first. So many courses take students and throw them into the big picture.

Anne: What are your learning objectives for students?

Carla: I have a lot of them. One, understanding what it feels like to have written something that works, that is honest, that moves the reader in some way, that has an appealing style. Two, the sense that writing is *part of an ongoing dialogue, giving a sense of participating in a huge discourse and understanding the dynamics of the conversation.*

These comments, part of an ongoing dialogue I had with Carla over the course of a year, begin to show some of her values in teaching academic writing: primary is that students be engaged with their work. She is well aware of the problems of motivating students in compulsory writing courses and the problems of newcomers to academic discourse feeling they are not fully engaged with the subject matter intellectually or emotionally. Her values regarding freshman writing tend towards the philosophical position of expressivism (writing for self-discovery and self-expression), although she is concerned as well about writing for civic action. She is one of several lecturers who work actively with the campus service learning center to build into her sections of freshman writing an assignment to write for a non-profit organization.

The sequence of assignments in Carla's EGL 101 class bear out Carla's view that writing from personal experience and for personal discovery are top priority in an introductory college writing course. Even though students were asked to imagine a variety of audiences for the various assignments, the primary material students were asked to draw from for the assignments was personal experience. In the first assignment, two journal entries or letters to different audiences, students were to address anything related to nature or nature writing (the course theme). The second assignment asked for a description of a process, place, or object in the environment the student had observed closely. The third essay asked students to draw some conclusions about the meaning of a personal experience in a larger context.

Tim had a high school English teacher who had required strict adherence to a formulaic five-paragraph essay. So Tim described Carla's EGL 101 course as an experience of "being set free." The "freedom" he was referring to was the opportunity to write in the genre of personal narrative or letter, or journal entries—not just in the five-paragraph essay format. There were no "formulas" given out for how to write in these genres either. He was an aspiring poet and songwriter and the expressive assignments suited him. He received high praise from Carla and A's on all his work. Repeatedly, in her end comments on his essays, she indicated she was entertained by his writing and said "You write beautifully" several times. Clearly, from her feedback to Tim on his work, Carla felt he wrote well, although it is not clear what her criteria were for this view.

Carla's EGL 102 class, in which students were expected to write a major research paper, makes a noticeable shift into more traditional academic work. There were two feeder assignments leading up to the major research project, a project which could become a hybrid form of the traditional term paper if students were doing community service writing as well. The first paper was to reflect on an interview conducted with an expert on a subject of interest. Although the course theme again was nature writing and environmental issues, Carla did not require students to focus their research on the course theme. So, for his first paper, Tim interviewed a religious studies professor on the effects of

Vatican II on the Catholic Church. In reflecting on what he wrote, Tim told me, "Vatican II seems more like something they find in one of these weekend news magazines, kind of short, focus on a person or using that person to actually discuss some other issues. You want to make it snappy and quick." He did not take the writing task to be academic in nature.

The second assignment was intended to build on the first—to look for a secondary source that would shed light on an unanswered question from the interview. Tim chose to go in a different direction, this time doing a report on an article on genetic engineering by an ethicist. For the major research project, Tim switched topics again, writing a white paper/report for the Sierra Club's environmental division on potential threats to a major lake in the Soviet Union.

Again, Tim received and high praise from Carla in her end comments on his EGL 102 papers and an "A" for the course. The only criticism from Carla came gently, in response to his report on the ethicist's article. She said, "The complexity of your ideas here . . . is handled with great finesse, but there are a few assumptions I question . . ."

With this broad overview of the structure and assignment sequences for Tim's two freshman writing courses now laid out, I turn to the five knowledge domains involved in accomplishing writing tasks in freshman writing in order to further illuminate what transpired for Tim.

DISCOURSE COMMUNITY ISSUES IN FRESHMAN WRITING

Carla frames her course and her assignments using rhetorical concepts. Matters of audience and purpose are raised in directions for every assignment and are reiterated frequently in class discussions. So, not surprisingly, four years after taking freshman writing Tim commented, "The biggest thing I guess from her that I learned, which I still hold onto, is that . . . audience is everything. That was her biggest and first point I think, for the whole year. Audience is everything and style is fun."

In the final assignment, the reflective essay concerning the community service project, Carla defines the audience as herself. But in the other assignments, she asks students to choose their own audience and purpose for the writing in order to encourage them to both think about these concerns and to try to help them get out of what she considers to be the too-narrow confines of academic writing. She told me a turning point in her own education was the opportunity one teacher gave her to link her love of poetry with academic writing, and Carla's desire to see students connect writing to their lives outside school was the primary reason for linking her classes with the community service program at the university. As Carla articulates in the directions for the community service writing project, "College writing seems pointless without the important goal of self-knowledge. But even so, college writing is disturbingly artificial because of its limited audience and limited academic purpose."

The concepts of audience and purpose can only take students part way toward understanding how social contexts influence writing and writers though. Researchers and theorists (Beaufort 1997, Bizzell 1982, Porter 1986, Rafoth1988, Swales 1992) have been using the concept of discourse communities—those loosely formed networks of writers/readers who communicate through written texts—since the early 1980s, and have uncovered multiple levels of social interaction associated with producing written texts that go beyond the limited view, in rhetoric, of an imagined audience and a writer's purpose. An imagined or real "addressee" for the text (i.e. the traditional Aristotelian concept of audience) is only one variable the writer must work with. I will show now the layers of social context beyond the stated addressee(s) for written pieces that were also affecting Tim's experiences in freshman writing.

First, there was the immediate discourse community of the course itself, made up of teacher, student, and peers. Tim writes in the required statements about audiences for his papers that he is addressing a friend in one, in another, a producer of ski films, or in other assignments, more vague audiences—"a youngish crowd of readers acquainted with adventurous recreation" or "newspaper or newsletter readers interested in the debate over ecology versus the economy" or "people not wholly unfamiliar with genetic engineering and traditional belief systems from the West and the East." But there are signs in the data that the primary audience Tim writes for is Carla and the institutional discourse community she represents. For example, while Carla praises his letter to a film director and wants to include it in her reader, in talking with me Tim refers to that piece of writing as "some dumb thing." It was not a piece of writing he took seriously in terms of his stated audience or his purpose. Rather, the task for Tim was, as others have stated, "doing school."

And Tim reckoned with the peer community in the course in an interesting way. The personal narrative on his experiences with land use in the US and Russia was a piece he liked, so rather than take the advice of peers in the course solely, through a dorm counselor who knew Richard Rodriguez, Tim elicited Rodriguez's feedback on his essay. Tim's seeking out feedback from a professional writer was, in part, a distrust of his peers' feedback, and in part, a desire to fuel his sense of himself as a writer. In my experience of students in compulsory writing courses, seeking out the advice of a professional writer is unusual. It is also telling of Tim's view of his immediate discourse community in the course. For most students, though, the primary purpose for writing in a compulsory writing course is completing the tasks necessary to get the needed grades, the credits toward graduation, etc.

This discourse community of peers and teacher (and the associated social pressures of meeting expectations of peers and teacher, the power hierarchies, etc.) is not a writing context/discourse community students would think about consciously or fully in its theoretical or practical manifestations unless there were an overt discussion of the ways the class itself functions as a temporary discourse community within a larger institutional discourse community. But nonetheless, standards for good writing, roles assigned to writers and readers, goals of the course—all of these social dynamics of a course as discourse communities affect writers' motivations, performances, and perceptions and extend the meaning of social context beyond that of a specific addressee for a writing project. Students will determine what to write, how much time to spend on the task, etc. based on their perceptions of the discourse community of the course and their personal motivations in relation to that discourse community.[30]

But Carla intended for the social context for Tim's freshman writing experience to extend beyond the community of the course itself. In one conversation with me, Carla mentions as a goal for the course getting students to understand they are writing . . . [as] part of an ongoing dialogue, giving a sense of participating in a huge discourse and understanding the dynamics of the conversation. But exactly whose conversation is being joined is not specifically stated by Carla, either to me or to her students.

Given the thematic content of Carla's course—environmentalism—it might have been possible that the target discourse community for students to study and dialogue with in their writing was that of environmentalists. What were the "ongoing conversations," the current issues, the new knowledge to be discovered in this field? What if writing tasks had been framed in these ways? But Carla did not conceptualize the students' work in this way, which inadvertently reinforced the predominant influence of the school context in spite of her best intentions to get students to connect in meaningful ways to the writing tasks.

Another possible discourse community Carla's students might have considered in their work for the course was that of literary journalism. She had broadened the scope of the course, so the composition reader she was developing included a few science writers (Stephen Jay Gould, Lewis Thomas), ethicists (Peter Singer, Jeremy Rifkin), and journalists (Sharman Russell, Cynthia Riggs). But the preponderance of readings students encountered were literary essays that would most likely be situated either in the discourse communities of belle lettres[31] or journalism. Carla's reader for the course included selections by John Muir, Peter Matthiessen, John McPhee, Annie Dillard, and Edward Abbey among others—nature writers whose work some would refer to as "literary journalism," or "creative non-fiction." Even the writings Carla used by Lewis Thomas and Stephen Jay Gould, for example, were aimed at general audiences interested in science and the environment, rather than epidemiologists or paleontologists.

What if students had considered the characteristics of the discourse community of these writers and those who read literary journalism? Would those considerations have enriched the focus, perhaps, even the motivation of these students? Some might argue this would push the course in the direction of a literature course and lose the focus on writing itself. But no text, no act of writing, occurs in a vacuum, and exploring the features of these discourse communities could have enriched writing activities in the course.

In addition to these two discourse communities external to academe, Carla's students could have dipped into several academic disciplines in their research for two of the assignments in the second course. For example, to do the single-source essay, Tim took off from the class's readings on genetic engineering (one reading by a philosopher, one by a journalist) and located an article published in an academic publication, *Perspectives on Science and Christian Faith.* The article, ten pages long, is scholarly in tone and content. It gives a medical ethicist's views on moral issues associated with gene-splicing and has the usual genre conventions of a scholarly journal article—extensive quoting of others' work, citations, etc. If Tim had considered what academic discourse community the writer was placing himself in and had taken even a cursory look at some of the journals medical ethicists publish in, his understanding of that text would have broadened.

Another way to come at the matter of the implicit discourse communities that were informing Carla's teaching decisions is to consider the genres she assigned, as genres are in a sense "owned" by discourse communities. The assignments for Carla's EGL 101 paralleled the genres of the readings: as we have seen, she assigned journaling and descriptive, reflective and narrative essays—all typical genres in literary journalism. Only the final assignment of Carla's EGL 102 moved the writing more squarely into academic discourse, and even that assignment, since it was also a service learning assignment, could have taken shape as a journalistic genre or an academic one. Carla also did not espouse students following the traditional academic essay's genre features. She referred to one essay assignment as "a rumination" and another as "a sortie"—both suggesting literary or journalistic essays with loose, open structures.

Besides dictating subject matter and genres for doing the work of the community, discourse communities also carry with them epistemological assumptions about what counts as truth, which in turn affects the types of arguments and proofs that are acceptable. So, for example, the way an ethicist such as Peter Singer will argue is different from the way a scientist or a poet would argue. "Truth," or proofs, are conceptualized differently depending on the discourse community's values and assumptions. When Carla and her students began discussing how to construct arguments and what types of evidence to use, the question was raised by a student: how are "facts" defined? Here is a portion of the class's discussion (emphasis mine):

C: But . . . remember this pattern about making a point or supporting or illustrating it in some way and then always attempting to draw a conclusion from it.

Student 4:   A personal example?

C: An illustration from experience? Your own or perhaps another person's. Then you have to consider what kind of conclusions you can draw from that.

C: Statistics, yes, absolutely. Facts and figures . . . everything from statistics to personal experience to reasoning. Statements of fact . . . What I'm getting at here is that there are differences between statements of fact, arguable statements, and opinions. What is a fact?

Student 3:   If it can be argued it's not a fact.

C: Is a fact necessarily true or accurate?

Student 3:   To our knowledge, as far as we know, it's supposed to be true.

C: uh huh. As far as we know . . . comes under the second part of the definition that we agree to measure them in a certain way. People argue about facts all the time, which is really a waste of time because rather than argue about a fact you go out and you find a reliable source and document it, right?

Student 3:   But to be a fact does it have to be universal or can something be a fact to one person but not to another?

C: Well that's a good question. Can something be a fact to one person and not another? (4 minutes later, after continued dialogue) I'm being a little tentative here . . . I don't want to go into this. There are claims of fact and claims of value and the way you support each of them is sometimes different.

—Excerpt from May 14 class session

If an understanding of discourse communities and epistemological values that inform standards of the discourse community had been part of the framework for the course, an alternative line of inquiry with the students at that point could have been what counts as "truth" in journalism, or in the fields of ecology and environmental science.

The dilemma of what discourse community freshman writing can legitimately attach itself to is a problem Carla was aware of, although she would have stated the dilemma in terms of the rhetorical concepts of audience and purpose. In her EGL101 syllabus for that term she stated:

> The problem with traditional academic writing is that it often feels artificial, an exercise bearing little resemblance either to writing as a real learning process or writing in the "real" world; academic writing tends to be not a dialogue but a one-way interaction, a report from the student to the instructor who wields the all-powerful grade. In this course, your readership will be expanded to include your peers as well as people outside the academic community.

Tim's comments to me, in retrospective interviews, demonstrate a perception of the possible discourse communities Carla espoused—at least tacitly. He talked about his goals for his freshman writing papers as "entertaining," and when pressed to name an audience or social context for his essays, he imagined the pieces perhaps as appropriate for The *New York Times Book Review* or another journalistic magazine. Tim was imagining, in other words, a discourse community of journalism and the general trade press for these types of writing. But I sensed this musing to me was an after-thought and not a real factor in Tim's process of doing the writing.

So, in doing the work of freshman writing with Carla, students encountered multiple discourse communities, including some academic discourse communities, but the discourse communities were un-named and their influence on writers was not probed. And because there was no meta-discussion in his writing class of discourse communities or the ways in which standards for writing change in different discourse communities, Tim told me he felt he had "sold out," from what Carla espoused when he wrote for history and later engineering. Tim assumed Carla's principles for what constitutes appropriate ways of writing to be universal norms for good writing. As we shall see in Chapters 4 and 5, he intuitively picked up some differences in writing for history teachers or engineers rather than for Carla, but the boundaries and differences between discourse communities were only hazily recognized through trial and error. Opportunities to give Tim a solid basis for transfer of learning from freshman writing to other contexts for writing were missed because the discourse communities which were informing what went on in the course were un-named.

Subject Matter Issues in Tim's Freshman Writing Classes

Carla's EGL101 and EGL102 courses were theme-based, unlike other writing courses that treat a wide range of topics from week to week. The specific subject matter of Carla's EGL 101 course was described in the syllabus as follows:

> It is impossible to explore the genre of American nature writing without exploring writing about broader social and environmental issues. Writers who write about nature do not always write exclusively about their personal relationship to the natural world; they write science, history, ethics and politics as well. American nature writing has always existed and continues to exist in a social context, and that is how we will approach both reading and writing in this course. However, despite its broader social implications, we will approach the theme of "writing nature" from a personal rather than an abstract perspective.

As the syllabus conveys, the subject matter of EGL 101 was very broad. Chapters in the reader were organized not in relation to course themes, but rather, in terms of rhetorical modes: Chapter 2—descriptions of places, Chapter 3—descriptions of processes in nature, Chapter 4 personal experiences of the natural world, Chapter 5 fictional accounts. Chapter 6 was the exception to a particular rhetorical mode: it focused on histories of the natural world within social contexts (for example, women's place in nature, the genocide of Native Americans, and environmental movements). Most reading selections were three to six pages in length, excerpts from longer works. Writing assignments were not specifically tied to the readings.

Carla had a number of competing goals to juggle in her course: introducing students to the subject matter of the course reader; introducing certain rhetorical problems for them to solve, and giving them freedom to move into personal interests that did not necessarily relate to the subject matter of the course theme. Carla specified that content of students' written work ideally should relate to the theme of nature, "or writing in general," but students also had the option to choose any subject matter that interested them, even if it was not related to the course theme. In fact, the overarching organization of both the readings and writing assignments suggests that rhetorical and personal interests were paramount in the way the course was organized, and pursuing a particular intellectual topic or field of inquiry for the duration of the course was of secondary importance.

In the second course, EGL 102, loosely centered on the theme of the environment, Carla chose two groups of readings to illustrate "how some writers have gone about investigating {controversial issues} and articulating their own views on the subjects at hand" (quoted from course syllabus). The first group of readings focused on issues of land use from the perspectives of environmentalists, ranchers, farmers, etc. and the second group, on the ethics of genetic engineering. The rest of the course was given over to the students' own research projects on topics of their choosing.

I was not present during the first course when readings were discussed, so I do not know in what ways the subject matter of the readings might have been taken up. In the second course, in which I observed several class sessions given over mostly to discussions of the readings, the primary thrust of conversation was around analysis of the writer's rhetorical moves in the selected texts, rather than any debate about the content of the essays. Here is a segment of a typical discussion in Carla's EGL 102 course, this one on the Peter Singer article on animal rights, which will illustrate the rhetorical focus of the discussion.

Student 2:   It wasn't really a statement, but a leap that he (Singer) made as he poses this question . . . He defends that question pretty well, but I just never got why that would be the question.

C: So it's not even a matter about that one statement it's about a series of statements. Did you notice how much he uses "if" or "since." "If this is the case then . . ." or "therefore this is the case." He's using a series of premises in order to draw conclusions from them and if you disagree with the premise then obviously you're going to disagree to some extent with the conclusion. And he does use a series of reasonings to arrive at the conclusions he does . . .

Student 3:   I think he's making a point about racism too. I think there was some mixed points . . . You're saying that here's an issue, racism, which is huge right now, look at this other issue, where underneath there are things combining the two and showing the similarities and that is very powerful . . . I really think that is a good technique.

C: Right! There's often a difference in an argument among what's effective, what has impact, and what really makes sense. What Michael is saying is that it is an effective strategy to compare speciesism with racism—because virtually nobody—nobody in their right mind wants to be associated with being a racist. So, you're right, it's very effective, but logically does it make sense to equate speciesism and racism the way he does?

Tim: If you use it the way he does—yeah, but it's a little incomplete.

Student 3:   I really don't see how he goes from with a single experiment that could save thousands of human infants. There's no connection whatsoever. He's just stringing it together.

C: Ok, just try to focus where he makes that leap and how he does it in language. Can you pin it down because all this is . . .

During this class session and subsequent ones, there was little discussion of the issue of animal rights, or mass production issues, or moral issues. Rather, the point of the discussion was to enable students to critically analyze the writer's logic and rhetorical moves.

A look at topics addressed in the rest of the course also confirms that an investigation into environmental issues took a back seat to issues of writing process and rhetorical strategies.

3/31	Class overview and discussion of first writing assignment (interview paper)
4/14	Discussion of two readings; evaluating sources, types of conclusions to draw from research
4/16	Community service (CSW) assignment explained
4/21	Discussion of two readings and the rhetorical strategies used; role of argument in academic work
4/23	Continued discussion of two readings and the rhetorical strategies used
4/30	Library tour
5/5	Writing process for research paper
5/7	Writing process for research paper
5/12	Bias in sources, taking notes on sources
5/14	Claims, warrants, evidence; types of evidence for arguments
5/19	Discussion of students' CSW research topics.
5/21	Feedback on research paper outlines; shaping thesis and conclusion

Closely tied to considerations of rhetorical strategies in the texts read were issues of what arguments are logical or conclusive. Here is another excerpt from a class discussion that highlights the ways in which analysis of others' arguments for their reasonableness was emphasized.

Student 2:   Well he says there is this hypothetical question and as long as it's hypothetical then let's play with it.

C: Yes . . .

Student 2:   And so logically it follows but I just can't agree. Something hard wired in us that won't do it to our own race but is more willing to do it to others.

Tim: Is there anything rational about that?

Student 3:   I don't think so it's just built in.

C: Well, let's see if there is anything rational about it . . . First there's a question if it is logically sound. What's he stating on the basis of a series of premises, assertions, evidence, reasoning. Second question is, "Is there a reasonable disagreement? A logical disagreement that you can think opposing that would not rely entirely on emotion . . . but could be siphoned through your reasoning abilities and stated in a way that would hold up logically.

—partial transcript, April 23 session of Carla's EGL 102 class discussing an excerpt from Peter Singer, *Animal Liberation: A New Ethic for Our Treatment of Animals*

***

Ten minutes later, in the same class session, Carla gives a mini-lecture on the Toulmin argument structure and the ways in which it approaches the logic of arguments.

As you think about how to use all this material you're unearthing from primary and secondary sources, this is one of these little pearls—if you manage to hold onto this concept then you'll be in better shape not only in this writing project but in others as well . . . if any of you have taken critical thinking courses, I know some of you have, I know Mike has. Has anybody else run across this whole concept of claim, evidence, and warrant? Quite simply, claim is the point you want to make, evidence is the support or illustration of the point. Then warrant is the conclusion drawn from it . . . . A lot of students, especially in argument writing or research writing tend to put a lot of emphasis on evidence. Right? They realize they have to put the evidence in some sort of context, right? They have to make a point. But very often they stop too soon, they forget to draw conclusions. They make a point, they support it, they make a point, they support it, they make another point and what you have then is an over-reliance on someone else's observations.

We can see in this excerpt from the class discussion that Carla is urging her students to interact with their subject matter not just at the level of comprehension, but also at the levels of analysis and synthesis. And yet in these discussions, the analysis of the writer's argument is done in a vacuum. The students must judge the work without the benefit of knowing the values, the goals, the ongoing conversations of the discourse community in which the writer was addressing his argument, and without the benefit of a knowledge base regarding the subject of the debate (animal rights). Some may feel this is a legitimate approach, but I argue that the fine points of an argument and the appropriateness of persuasive moves are best evaluated in the context of a specific subject matter as it is grounded within a particular discourse community.

As is often the case in freshman writing courses, in Carla's course other matters take higher priority than the topics read about and written about: managing the writing process, learning new genres or principles for making arguments. Even in a theme-based course such as this one, subject matter can become secondary to writerly concerns in part because the teacher has too many things in the curriculum to juggle and because the role of subject matter in a writer's success or failure at a writing task has been a neglected matter in the field.[32]

In Tim's case, there was an added problem in probing a subject matter in depth. Because Carla gave students freedom in choosing the topics for their essays, even beyond the course theme they could change topics for every writing assignment if they wished. Tim in fact chose to write on a variety of topics: a memorable ski trip, a river kayaking trip, personal experiences in connection with land use and conservation, issues of Vatican II's policies on theology, a Christian perspective on genetic engineering, and ecological issues associated with a lake in Russia. Given the range of subjects Tim wrote about and the length of the essays Tim wrote (in the 3–5 page range except for one longer paper, the CSW research project), he did not do much in-depth exploration of any subject over the course of his two quarters of freshman writing.

Some may argue this is not a shortcoming of a freshman writing course. But probing a particular subject matter also goes hand in hand with the development of critical thinking skills. If we look at Tim's papers through the lens of Bloom's taxonomy of critical thinking skills, we can begin to assess to what degree Tim was using higher order thinking skills beyond simple recall or restatement of others' work. In his journal entry and letter to the movie producer, in his descriptive essay, and in his personal narrative, Tim was in large part drawing from memory for his subject matter. The major tool for organizing memories into an essay was chronological. But in each essay, there was a point, stated or implied, so the recall and description of memories also entailed some critical thought or analysis. For example, he had to ask himself, "Where am I heading in this piece? What details will support my point?"

However, Tim's point in each of these essays, with one exception, was not particularly sophisticated: in the journal entry—to describe a good outing; in the letter, to state that global warming was inhibiting recreational snow skiing; in the descriptive essay, to show that a river kayaking trip was emotionally satisfying. Of the narrative and descriptive pieces he wrote, the personal narrative was the most complex piece of argument. His point—that eco-stewardship comes with a combination of owning property (unlike in communal states like Russia) and right attitudes—was carefully drawn from three or four personal experiences at different times and in different places. Even though on one level a simple chronology, there was a level of synthesis and analysis of personal experience beyond the level of recall or comprehension, unlike the simpler intellectual work or recall and reporting in the other pieces.

Three other essays were reports of information—a report of industrial uses of solar energy for a newsletter, a report of an interview with a professor of religion, and a summary of an academic journal article. For each of these pieces, the selection of information, putting it into a logical, coherent order would put the thinking at the level of "comprehension" or "synthesis" in Bloom's taxonomy. In fact, Tim was very skillful at synthesizing information. In the journal article on the ethics of genetic engineering, ten pages of fine print, Tim aptly summarized in less than 1200 words. Toward the end of his essay, most of which is summary, there is a paragraph of cogent deductive reasoning. Tim states:

> Dr. Bird's findings, however, seem to provide a universal basis for ethical decision-making. If one accepts these principles, the categorical denouncement of genetic technology is out of the question. The only alternative is fundamental rejection of all healing arts and reliance on spiritual healing alone.

In this essay Tim also raises the possibility that the author's optimism about ethical practices might not be warranted. But he only raises the issue. There is no in-depth analysis of the author's argument, nor his own. In both the genetic engineering essay and the Vatican II essay Tim raised large issues but did not go into them in any depth. Opportunities for more complex thinking or to consider source texts in greater depth were neither called for by Carla nor pursued by Tim.

It appears, then, that Tim's freshman writing experience was one of "writing to produce writing" (Dias 2000), rather than in-depth intellectual engagement with a subject matter through writing. And the writing itself, as a result, lacks sophistication in its exploration of the topics addressed.

Tim's Genre Knowledge Freshman Year

When I asked Carla if she thought about her curriculum in terms of teaching genres, she said, "Genres are synonymous with purpose." I suspect she was thinking of the selection of a genre for a given occasion for writing based on the writer's purpose. Genres are the ongoing, mechanism of communication for a variety of social purposes: for example, getting a grade or display of knowledge (most school genres), entertaining a reader, moving an audience to action, or the writer's catharsis.

But what Carla also meant by her reply was that she did not espouse teaching genres per se. Given the fact that genre theory became central in composition theory only in the last two decades and that writing texts and curricula have been dominated by earlier conceptions of types of writing in rhetoric, this is not surprising. Carla stands in a long tradition within freshman writing of giving students assignments to employ different rhetorical modes—description, narration, exposition, argument, etc. And yet Carla's assignments could be considered school genres—those genres that are explicitly for the purpose of teaching a particular skill or for evaluation purposes. Genre theorists argue that any text type, with forms, conventions, etc. that are used again and again over time, for specific social purposes, can be considered a genre.

In fact, some assignments married rhetorical mode and genre. In the first course, students were expected to write in the genres of the letter, the journal entry, and the literary essay. Or, as Carla put it in one of the assignment sheets, "Write about four pages in a descriptive, narrative and reflective style . . ." In the second course, the first two assignments were "essays." One was to be based on an interview, and the other, on a single source. Of the latter, she said, "This essay might be an analysis, an argument, or a report depending on the nature of the question you are trying to answer." And the final assignment was a researched report or researched argument. And as Table 1 shows, on the final drafts of seven assignments Tim gave me that included Carla's comments, Carla offered 35 comments on specific genre features of Tim's essays, of which three related to rhetorical purpose, 15 related to content, four to structure, and 13 to style/linguistic elements.

There is one detailed comment Tim received concerning the genre of literary journalism from Richard Rodriguez, who critiqued his essay on a river kayaking trip. Rodriguez wrote to Tim:

TABLE 1

Carla's Feedback on Tim's Freshman Writing Work

	Positive Comments	Suggestions
Genre Features (56 Total)		
Rhetorical Purpose (3 Total)	Effective quote Entertaining	Make point explicit
Content (36 Total)	Agreeing with analysis (2) Valuable content (3) Good synthesis (2) Good analysis (2)	Need more support (4) More analysis Question assumptions
Structure (4 Total)	Clear Paragraph organized better	Paragraph wanders Need transitions between paragraphs
Style/language (13 Total)	Literary qualities (5) Clarity (2) Good use of formatting	Inappropriate tone More vivid examples (2) Clarity (2)
General Comments (19 Total)	General comments, questions about subject matter (21) General praise (19)	

You sketch images well. The main problem is overwriting. Too much didactic over-stating, overuse of metaphors, clunky similes and symbolism. The third-person point of view also distances the reader from the narrator; I think the first-person voice would have been more powerful and intimate. If your aim is literary journalism, then you need to think everything through more deeply, beyond formulaic thought and hackneyed execution . . . In choosing this subject, you're weighing in with the finest writers of the language. This essay doesn't come close, but that's the challenge. The whole point is to come as close as you can to the mastery of the craft.

Here is a serious critique of Tim's approach to a literary essay. Rodriguez comments on several features of the genre—the use of an "intimate" voice, and understating, i.e. implying, the essay's meaning rather than taking a didactic rhetorical approach.

So genres had a role in this writing class, but an unacknowledged one.

Genres have many dimensions in addition to employing a particular discourse mode. In fact, several discourse modes could be employed in a single genre. And genres serve to regularize or coordinate a host of text features that both writers and readers use to achieve a communicative purpose: features such as choice of appropriate content, conventions regarding language usage in the genre, structural conventions, etc. Genre theory has added an extremely useful lens for teaching of writing that classical rhetorical theory does not offer. We will see later some of the problems Tim experienced in his writing because of the limitations of his understanding of text types.

There is an added problem with the "essay" genre. Essays are written in a variety of discourse communities, but in each, they take on a different set of linguistic and content-related features.[33] For example, a literary essay, in the tradition of E.B. White, is a loose collection of observations and ruminations. The overall point may be implied, or stated at the very end. An essay in philosophy takes a much different form, one dictated often by the basic format of a syllogism. Likewise, an essay in history or in literature has specific genre features that reflect the values and conventions of that particular discourse community. So to assign an essay in a writing class without identifying the discourse community that "owns" that particular essay form does not give students enough guidance on genre expectations. We will see, in the discussions of Tim's history essays, ways in which the implicit instruction in features of the literary essay led to negative transfer of learning.

In addition to what Tim was exposed to regarding genre knowledge in his freshman writing courses, I was able to get another window into his genre knowledge through a simple brainstorming and card sort task I asked Tim to do. At one of our meetings I asked him to name all the genres he could think of for me. Then, at a subsequent meeting, I asked him to perform a simple card sort task, placing the genres he'd named in whatever groupings made sense to him. Here then, is the list of genres he named to me:

> Poetry (including songs, free verse, graphic stuff, bard, rap), Annie Dillard, stream-of-consciousness, historical, scientific studies, textbooks, short essays, short stories, parables, technical writing, philosophical writing, speeches, personal writing.

Some of his names for genres—"Annie Dillard," "stream-of-consciousness," and "personal writing"—would not meet the criteria most scholars would use for defining genres. But the list suggests Tim has read widely and noticed differences in types of texts.

When asked to sort this list (each text type written on 3 x 5 cards) into whatever logical groupings he saw, he came up with this way of grouping the genres:

> one way you can sort these is by readers, people who are reading parables and autobiographies . . . have time. They're a captive audience . . . Biographies, these people have all the time in the world . . . Short stories . . . these end up being . . . I'm not going to say fuzzy, take your time, but more, um, cause they have just as much right to meaning as any other, but you do have a lot of time . . . Poetry, generally these people are pretty laid back.
>
> Other genres are information kings: just the facts versus process-oriented . . . the goal here is to walk the reader through to the conclusion in a less painful way that you've come to it yourself . . . scientific report—show how you arrived at the conclusion; journalism—just the facts . . . People would get upset if you don't stay coherent . . . whereas poetry, there's no real expectation of coherence . . . expectations are put upon you by your readers. Now parables, these people have quite a bit of patience because they're trying to figure out, they take a lot of the responsibility for understanding what it is you're writing, thinking about it and trying to draw conclusions from it themselves.
>
> research/technical report: here you would come out and give the framework right away so people would know where they were headed. And here [philosophical] you might be a little more laid back about telling people where they are headed . . . people in this kind of paper just take you one step at a time and don't show you the top of the stairs . . . they'll show you the other staircases you can take . . . and sometimes it's because they want you to arrive at the conclusion that they're taking you to and they don't want you to take any other staircases
>
> These two, scientific reports and research paper I'm having a little difficulty with, on which side they fall into . . . a report on research is often very structured, and they do tell you where they're going right from the start . . . in the research paper the process is really what is important . . . historical textbook—they break it up with excerpts from primary sources and time lines . . . that tend to add meaning, here the structure gives it meaning cause the structure is presented right up front. (Interview Transcript)

Clearly, Tim had internalized quite a bit about genre differences, being an avid reader on many subjects. His explanations for the differences among genres were frequently reader-based, for example, how would a reader approach reading this genre, and what structure will help the reader? Given Carla's emphasis in EGL 101/102 on audience awareness, it is not surprising that this infused his interpretation of genres. But the linkages he makes between audience needs and the structure, the length and the purposes of different genres extend beyond what was discussed in Carla's classes. Nonetheless, the question remains: what opportunities might there have been for deepening Tim's genre knowledge if this knowledge domain had been discussed more explicitly in the curriculum? Could it have enabled a more efficient and effective transition to understanding the shifts in genre expectations in the new discourse communities he would encounter?

Rhetorical Issues in Tim's Freshman Writing

Carla stated as one of her goals for freshman writing exposing students to a number of rhetorical issues. She said to me, for example, that the personal essay brings up rhetorical issues of "insincerity, dishonesty, or, on the one hand, writing so narrow that it's meaningless and on the other hand, generalizing inappropriately from personal experience." In more analytic, argumentative writing, she saw the rhetorical issues as "setting aside prejudices, the need to listen to others before judging, and learning how to coordinate viewpoints that are opposing." So for Carla, rhetorical issues were intimately tied to genre issues, and of course, to the matter of a particular audience for the piece of writing. Written instructions for the assignments did not spell out the rhetorical criteria for a successful piece, but theses points may have been covered in class discussion.

It appears from Carla's comments about Tim's writing that she was satisfied he had met the rhetorical goals of the expressive assignments. But she does question whether Tim's approach is rhetorically effective in the letters he writes for the first assignment, one to his best friend and one to a producer of ski movies. She says, "Do you feel the tone of your letter to Jim is right? Strikes me as fairly formal. But then again, I don't know Jim, do I? or you very well, yet." And of the letter to the movie producer, she says, "In addition to your lyric partnership with him, *perhaps* (emphasis mine) you need to put the point, the request to him more explicitly. You write beautifully and *perhaps*, if I were Warren Miller, this would be quite enough to do the trick." Because of her unfamiliarity with Tim's audiences, she qualifies her suggestions regarding rhetorical approach to the designated addressees. And there is no overt naming of rhetorical strategies as such; rather, Tim is being coached implicitly to consider how language may affect his reader, either hindering or helping to achieve the desired purpose with that particular audience.

There is one instance in the data that suggests a rhetorical challenge Tim faced: he was uncomfortable with the rhetorical approach he had to assume in writing a persuasive article for the non-profit organization. His reflective essay, a satiric commentary on the experience, refers to his "alienation" to "the conceptual distance between the publisher and me." He states, tongue-in-cheek:

> I decided, in my dismay, that the only possible way to bridge the distance between us was to unite with the publisher and become a genuine part of the newsletter . . . The rote, mechanical, letter-by-letter process of cranking out the article left me feeling compromised . . . The schism between my writing and my self stifled my interest. My goal was to get the facts down, plug the bottom line, and make it interesting and easy to read. My audience was not at all captive, so I had no "grace time" to develop style. The facts and the bottom line became my shackles.

It appears Tim did not like having to take a strictly factual approach to the piece. In the first three assignments of the course, Tim had been able to write (or over-write) in a lyric, almost poetic style. He had an appreciative audience in his instructor. For the community service assignment, he was being asked to write an informational, rather than reflective or expressive piece and this felt too limiting to him as a writer.

It is ironic that the assignment Carla conceptualized as the most authentic in terms of "real world" writing, Tim felt the most artificial because he was required to assume the perspective of an organization he felt no particular affinity to. This irony—that the assignment that was to create the most overt sense of audience in fact only fostered rebellion—points to the difficult challenge of students' perceiving writing tasks in school contexts as authentic in any other context and making the appropriate shifts in rhetorical stance. Tim's reaction to this assignment (and to other assignments given by later teachers) was perhaps, in part, because of the contrast with Carla's assignments, which were very open-ended and gave the writer lots of choices for subject matter, genre, and rhetorical purpose. Tim was able to write most of his freshman writing essays in an expressive style, designed to achieve the rhetorical aim of entertaining the reader, which he enjoyed.

Feedback on Tim's major research project in the second course (a study of the ecology of a lake in Siberia) was not available, so it is not clear if Carla felt he achieved rhetorical skills in academic writing. But it is evident from Tim's reflections at the end of college that Carla was very successful in bringing to his awareness the need to consider audience, even though the concept of audience, divorced from an understanding of a given discourse community, has limited usefulness in achieving rhetorically effective writing.

Writing Process Knowledge and Practices in Freshman Writing

Carla's syllabus stated:

> Everyone is expected to revise Writing 2, 3 and 4 following peer review and discussion of drafts in conference . . . You will have three scheduled conferences with me during the quarter. . . . Everyone will be asked to share one revision with peers in a class workshop . . . You will have the opportunity to revise further following the workshop session . . .

I was not able to see sequential drafts of Tim's essays for Carla's classes, but her comments on his final drafts indicate that she saw evidence of revision. She noted on the final draft of his Vatican II essay, for example, "You were right to overburden this paper with abstractions. And I think you've been quite successful in avoiding this, substantiating, illustrating, articulating, explaining quite adequately in the revision." It can be inferred that the revision offered a fuller development of ideas than the earlier draft.

Here is an excerpt of the transcript from a class session in the second course, in which Carla is discussing the process of doing researched writing. Her detailed description of the writing process confirms her attention to the matter in her instruction.

Student 1:   How long to do you think it (the outline) should be if you're going to write a 10 page paper?

C: It's hard to tell. People's outline styles are different. I don't care.

Student 2:   Put down everything we think we're going to use?

C: It (the outline) will continue to evolve because writing is a thinking process and the outline, if it's any consolation, although it seems to be a big pain in the neck and outlining is utterly useless for sure for short essays and personal essays. But in a paper like this where you have a lot of complex detail to deal with and you have to be thinking on so many different levels like how to use your source material, how to support your statements, different kinds of course material and what context to put this in and what is my thesis anyway it really helps to have a kind of trial run at this. And then when you sit down to compose the draft, you'll experience the freedom of being able to follow a tangent and say, "Oh well, that didn't work, so now where was I?"

—May 14 Class Session

Carla's concept of the writing process, we can see here, is organic—moving from questioning, to searching, to formulating, to questioning and searching some more, and trying then to arrive at a reasoned position. It is also clear there is no "right" way to handle the writing task, but rather, a set of guideposts for reflection at each stage in the process.

At the end of college, as will be shown later, Tim could articulate a process for getting writing done that had become, by that time, routine. Whether this was the case already for him in freshman writing or is something he learned there is not clear. At the least, in his writing courses he was expected to produce multiple drafts in order for a piece of writing to improve. Carla also preached the value of one's journal as a place for testing ideas, for writing to think, and outlining as a tool that would be useful for longer essays. She also had the students, during one session, freewrite on their research topics after some preliminary research, with computer screens turned off, to stimulate "thinking on both sides of the brain." Carla was clearly knowledgeable about writing process pedagogy and made that a central part of her courses. Later, we will see what Tim's version of the writing process became in the context of writing for history.

SUMMING UP: FRESHMAN WRITING

His senior year of college, Tim summed up his freshman writing experience with Carla this way:

> She basically came down on the five-paragraph essay and just said, 'That's not what we're about here.' That plucked a chord with me. I was like, I know this is right and I'm glad I'm finally hearing it and now I can begin to learn. Because I felt very frustrated with . . . the arbitrary kind of you have to have five sentences in every paragraph and five paragraphs in every essay. The only thing I did learn in that class in high school was the transition because you do have to transition from paragraph to paragraph.

Tim felt "liberated" by Carla: he gained permission from an authority to write in multiple voices and different genres, letting subject matter and rhetorical choices dictate form.

In terms of freshman writing serving students within the broader context of their university educations, the critiques of freshman writing by various committees and individuals at Carla's institution seem to have some validity, if Carla's class was typical for the program. The emphasis in Carla's first course was on narrative writing or on journalistic projects (the community service writing) rather than on more conventional academic writing. In the second course, there was more emphasis on academic writing, but requirements for academic writing in some of Tim's other courses were more rigorous. The amount of reading and writing in freshman English, as we will see in the next chapter, was not large compared to expectations in other courses. The seven essays I saw for the two courses totaled 24 pages. This does not count the 10- to 15-page research assignment; if that were added, then Tim probably wrote 34–39 pages of polished writing in the two courses, combined.

On the essays Tim gave me from freshman writing, Carla gave 40 positive comments on Tim's writing, and 14 comments offering ways of improving. Her summary of his work in the first course included these comments:

- Journal work: consistently productive

- Participation in class: active, insightful, leadership role

- Willingness to revise: open to constructive criticisms, balanced with own solid judgment, tenacious reviser

- "I hope you will be willing to offer one essay for inclusion in my anthology. Problem is to decide which one"

- Final grade: A+

She felt Tim had met her standards and her department's standards for what a freshman writer should do.

But unresolved are the questions I raised in Chapter 1 about freshman writing's role in helping students to advance as academic writers. How well did freshman writing prepare Tim for the writing he would do in history, in other general education courses, and even, in engineering? There is also the question of developmental progress: if Tim was an A+ writer in his second quarter of college according to Carla's standards, what motivation did he have to increase his writing skills in the three and a half years to follow? And not to be ignored is Carla's assessment of his skills with the literary essay: Carla gave high praise but Richard Rodriguez set a higher bar for Tim on that essay.

Of course, Carla could not train Tim in the fine points of writing in history or writing in engineering. But what if Tim had been introduced to the concept of discourse community and genre and had been invited to view the readings and assignments in freshman writing through those conceptual lenses? What if he had had to analyze the genres he was reading and writing for freshman writing? What if the intellectual content of the course had been more challenging—would his abilities in logic and reasoning have been challenged and strengthened? And can a teacher of writing teach one to write for a discourse community the teacher is not a part of? These are the tough questions I will continue to explore as I present the rest of Tim's story.

In the next chapter, I will look at the differences between the writing Tim was required to do in his freshman writing courses and in his first year history courses in order to offer yet another perspective on the freshman writing experience. In addition, in the Epilogue, Carla offers her perspective on her teaching when these data were gathered compared to her teaching now. She also talks candidly about her experience being a research subject and reading this report.

3

FRESHMAN WRITING AND FIRST YEAR HISTORY COURSES

In history courses students acquire skills that should be of value in many occupations and endeavors: how to think critically, evaluate evidence, and write with force and clarity.

—History department web page

Write an essay of 1,000 words. Discuss the film in light of the readings and discussion to date. . . . The point of this exercise is to demonstrate that you have read the materials and can apply them to thinking about the film.

—History course syllabus

The details of Tim's writing experiences as he progressed through the coursework for a major in history will be given in the next chapter, but here I hold up for the reader's view the parallel ("parallel" in the sense of being "simultaneous") experiences Tim was having in his first year in his writing courses and in his entry level history courses—History 101 *Western Civilization,* and History 185 *History of Islam.*

READING-TO-WRITE DIFFERENCES

I begin with several charts that juxtapose freshman writing and Tim's experiences in his entry-level history courses.

As Table 2 (next page) shows, in freshman writing Tim was asked to read short essays or excerpts from books—in all about 20 pages a week. This amount of reading resonates with what the instructor guide for freshman writing said:

> Remember that the course is primarily one in composition. Don't overload your students with reading . . . A good rule of thumb: not more than one-third of the out-of-class work for your course should be spent on anything other than the student's writing.

In history, weekly reading assignments included roughly 50 pages a week in course texts and readers in addition to reading book-length works. Four books were assigned for the first essay assignment in the

TABLE 2

Comparison of Reading-to-Write Freshman Writing and First Year History

Reading Assignments in Freshman Writing	Reading Assignments in 100 Level History Classes
EGL 101	**HIS 101**
journals & letters—Lewis, Muir, Matthieson, etc. descriptive essays—Thoreau, Momaday, Thomas, Dillard personal narratives—Mairs, Walker, Hubbell, etc. short fiction—Huxley, Lopez, Eisley, etc. histories—Bible, Stegner, Perrin, Silko, etc.	Augustine's *Confessions* Benedict's *Rule* Benz, *The Eastern Orthodox Church: Its Thought and Life* (portions) *Western Thought* (textbook—including primary source materials: treatises, letters, diaries, historical records)
EGL 102	HIS 185
essays: Abbey, Singer, Quammen, Rifkin, Gould, etc. individual research—journal articles, interviews	4 single-author texts on Islam novel—*A Palace Walk*, by Mafouz books on Islamic law & course packet

Islamic history course. In the Western Civilization course, Tim read two texts—Augustine's *Confessions* and Benedict's *Rule*—and skimmed another text on Eastern Orthodoxy for his first essay.

In addition to a greater quantity of reading in history than in freshman writing, the purposes for reading and the relationship of texts read to texts composed also differed between the two discourse communities. As we saw in Chapter 2, in the first freshman writing course texts were used to instruct in rhetorical strategies and to serve as models for writing. Actual subject matter of the texts was of secondary importance in the first course. In the second course, EGL 102, all three writing assignments required summarizing of sources but in-depth analysis of sources was not required. Students were instructed to consider how reliable their sources were, although criteria for establishing reliability were not clearly spelled out. Subject matter of the texts in EGL 102 became sources for writing, but the more important object of study was the student's own writing, not the texts being read.

In history, texts were read to build subject matter knowledge and to provide opportunities for historical interpretation of texts and issues. In all four essays Tim wrote his freshman year in history, he was reconstructing events by synthesizing information from multiple texts, he was comparing authors' interpretations of events, and he was attempting to

TABLE 3

A Comparison of Writing Tasks in Freshman Writing and First Year History

Writing Assignments in Freshman Writing	Writing Assignments in 100 Level History Courses
EGL 101 journal entry (1,200 words) process description (1,400 words) personal narrative (1,148 words) newsletter article (726 words) reflective essay (825 words) *Total word count = 5,299*	**HIS 101** comparative analysis of texts (1,976 words) argumentative essay (2,304 words) *Total word count = 4,280*
EGL 102 essay based on 1 interview (1,300 words) single-source essay (1,200 words) researched essay / position paper (2,500 words) *Total word count = 5,000*	**HIS 185** textual analysis / event reconstruction (2,184 words) summary / event reconstruction (2,529 words) comparative analysis of texts (2,259 words) *Total word count = 6,972*

account for the differences in textual accounts of events. In history, texts were the object of study.

DIFFERENCES IN WRITING TASKS

Besides differences in reading-to-write tasks, there were differences between the writing tasks required in Tim's writing courses and his entry-level courses in history. Writing itself was an overt and primary topic of discussion in freshman writing but not in history; multiple drafts were expected in the writing courses and not in history; and students were required in the freshman writing courses to supplement class sessions with 1:1 or small group tutorials on writing with the writing instructor, whereas in history there was little support for writers. Tim told me that he might run an idea for an essay by his history TA and that he talked to the history TA after he had received feedback on his essay (for the purpose of disputing the TA's evaluation of his work) but as far as I could see, there was no instruction in writing in his history classes.

But beyond the predictable difference in attention to writing process, there were some other differences between the writing tasks in freshman writing and in entry-level history courses that might not have been expected, as Table 3 begins to reveal. In HIS 185, Tim produced three essays of seven to eight pages each, compared to the requirement for EGL 102—two short essays and one 12– to 15–page researched report. Length by itself is not automatically an indication of complexity of task (an essay could be short and highly analytic, or longer and primarily summary), but a requirement of greater length usually demands more complex analysis and more complex organizational strategies than in a three- to four-page essay.

The types of assignments were also different: in EGL101, the journalistic or expressivist emphasis (writing from personal experience writing or to report news or entertain) was markedly different than the emphasis in HIS 101 on textual analysis and argument. Moreover, Carla's flexibility, letting students choose the purpose of the assignment, resulted in Tim's writing descriptive or summary reports rather than in-depth analyses or arguments. In EGL 102, Carla was stepping the students up to a research project gradually, beginning with single-source essays, whereas in the history courses, Tim had to work with multiple sources for each essay.

The writing assignments in history required not only more reading, but also, more in-depth exploration and argument. Tim did not always succeed at the writing tasks in history, as we will see, but the challenges in terms of handling reading-to-write tasks, subject matter, critical thinking tasks, and rhetorical tasks were greater than those placed on him in freshman writing, as two sample essays will demonstrate (see Appendix B for full text of these essays).

DISCOURSE COMMUNITY AND GENRE DIFFERENCES

I offer now a collage of comments on Tim's history writing in his first year: first, his professor's (or TA's) feedback on an essay, which reveals more of the expectations for writing history, and then Tim's commentary on the task and his professors' feedback, which will further highlight some of the difficulties Tim experienced in writing for his first history courses.

Augustine and Benedict Essay (full text in Appendix B)

Professor's Feedback
"I think you've got a good argument, very imaginative and certainly based on a lot of thought. What the paper lacks is clarity and focus; you frustrate the reader by meandering hither and yon and not moving in logical fashion with your thesis . . ."

Tim's Comment (one year later)

"I could have presented my point better, but he just disagreed with my conclusion . . . in order to get the grade on the paper you had to say what you'd been told in class about the book. Maybe in a new way, maybe in more depth, but basically say the same thing."

Tolerance and Talents Essay

Professor's Comment

"Your hypothesis is interesting and sophisticated. The logic with which you apply it to the readings is sometimes faulty . . . Strive for a better balance between the logic of your hypothesis and the content of the readings. Your writing has improved, but is still somewhat turgid."

(Tim did not comment on this essay to me.)

Islam Essay

Professor's Comment

"This is very fine. You show a high level of ability to integrate and analyze the material."

Tim's Comment

"It was an exercise in regurgitation. What we could tell we had learned or know. So it wasn't a real paper. I got my A or whatever, which I thought was ridiculous."

These comments from Tim's history professors begin to reveal that the epistemological expectations of the discourse communities of history and norms for genres and those of freshman writing differed greatly. In freshman writing, genres that were "loose" and "open," such as the reflective essay, were encouraged. As Carla said, "My own bias: one of the things that's so beautiful about the essay form {is that} you don't have to come full circle. . . . The reason I teach writing is to promote a spirit of free inquiry and to write according to one's conscience." So, for example, when instructing her students on the choices for types of conclusions one might reach in exploring a topic, Carla posed the possibility of saying, "I don't know," or "I'm not sure." But when Tim turned in essays for his first two history courses that did not proceed in a linear, deductive fashion, with a clear argument and adequate support of each point, professors (or TAs) told Tim his writing lacked focus and "meandered."

Underlying epistemologies drive the norms for communications in a given discourse community. In Carla's course, where inquiry was valued above "answers," truth was something to quest after but with an open mind, looking at many possibilities. The more open, meandering form of the literary essay and the use of metaphorical and lyrical language fit the epistemological stance of literary or journalistic discourse communities. One senses from the history professors' comment that they desired a greater certitude in students' writing and a more formal essay structure as a result, with the writer placed more in the background, at a distance from the audience. To be credible, in the history classes Tim was taking, it appeared one needed to make a clear-cut argument.

SUBJECT MATTER AND CRITICAL THINKING ISSUES

In the Augustine and Benedict essay (see Appendix B for text), which I explicate further in Chapter 4, there is a complex argument being attempted. First, Tim is trying to argue a cause–effect relationship between political conditions and the development of religious thought. Second, he is trying to make a comparison of the theological views of two theologians. As his professor indicated, he did not control his argument successfully, but the attempt involved more complexities in terms of critical thinking than he engaged for the analysis of an article on genetic engineering essay written about the same time for his freshman writing course. In the essay on Augustine and Benedict, Tim had to understand, analyze, and synthesize two primary source texts and two secondary source texts and then decide what focus to take in his essay. He was also applying his general background knowledge about the political climate at the time these texts were written. The task for the Augustine and Benedict essay required a grasp of some complex subject matter and an analysis of multiple texts, a more difficult task than an analysis of a ten-page journal article on genetic engineering.

Surface features of the literary and the history essays Tim wrote also differ. In the genetic engineering essay, there are no citations, whereas in "Augustine to Benedict," there are 37 citations. There are no syntax problems in the genetics essay, whereas in "Augustine to Benedict," there are a number of dangling modifiers, which the teacher points out. The syntactic errors in the more complex essay could be due to cognitive overload: in handling the complexities of his subject matter, Tim quite possibly gave less attention to surface features of his writing. Or, his reading of the professor's expectations may have been that there would be room for errors, and therefore, less caution and time was spent on proofreading.

But more important are the ways in which the writing and history professors are reading Tim's work, as evidenced in their written comments on the texts. In exchange for giving students maximum freedom of choice about topics they researched and wrote on for freshman writing, Carla limited her ability to give students feedback from an "insider's" perspective on the subject matter. Carla did not have Tim's source text for the genetic engineering essay, nor could she be considered an expert or insider in the discourse community of medical ethicists, which was the audience for the article Tim was analyzing. Her feedback was primarily regarding the degree of clarity in the writing. Her one comment on subject matter was that Tim raised interesting questions. She said "I wonder about your critical role in this?" The question suggests she wanted him to be able to analyze the writer's ideas further, but she does not suggest how he might go about this, no doubt because her responses were more as a general reader than as a subject matter expert.

For example, she wanted Tim to state more specifically what he meant in general statements such as "Dr. Bird . . . responds to these solutions with a different framework." Carla wrote in the margin, "Different from what? Characterized by what?" She was seeking specificity. In her end comment she stated:

> An intriguing perspective, which you've related very well. I wonder about your critical role in this . . . You leave your speculation for the last page. And here I have some problems with clarity. The complexity of the questions you are posing and attempting some response to might call for a bit more analysis?

She then returned to praise: "This is intelligent and articulate writing though, driven and illuminated by highly pertinent questions."

In contrast, the history TA who is commenting on Tim's essay on Augustine and Benedict indicated in his margin comments that he knew the texts Tim was critiquing. For example, to a point Tim makes on Augustine, the TA said, "But what about Augustine's strong doctrine of . . ." and to a point Tim makes on Benedict, the TA said, "But isn't Benedict reacting to . . ." This reader was an insider in the discourse community of historians. His evaluation of Tim's essay focused a great deal on the subject matter of the essay. It is of course logical that the reader who stands inside the discourse community being addressed can provide a more accurate read on the potential success or failure of the text within the discourse community.

GENRE ISSUES

As mentioned already, Tim was criticized by his history TA for an essay that meandered, that had no clear-cut argument. Yet in Carla's class students were encouraged to let form evolve from the content; they were invited to explore questions and issues, and they could write a report, a thesis-driven essay, or a more loose, literary essay that explores a topic in associative fashion.

This poses a problem: features of an essay as a genre vary depending on the discourse community that is being invoked to respond to the genre. In one discourse community—creative non-fiction or journalism—the essay form is loose; in history, there is a need for an essay to take a position, to argue against an interpretation of texts in a clear, logical manner, with a great deal of evidence from sources to support the argument. These genre differences, and the larger goals of these genres in relation to the discourse communities they were coming from, were not clear to Tim as he moved from freshman writing to history. His interpretation of his history reader's feedback was that the reader wanted "regurgitation" of ideas. What he did not see was the norms for genres that the history TA was implicitly holding up as a standard by which to evaluate Tim's writing differed from the standards Carla was using.

For example, the TA who read Tim's "Augustine and Benedict" essay also pushed Tim to be clearer. He said in response to the opening paragraph, "Poor start. You have not stated clearly what the paper is about. Too many pieces; not focused." And the TA's final comment on Tim's essay summarized the most critical issues with the essay: that the essay "meandered" and didn't proceed in logical fashion.

The TA was asking for an essay that not only fulfilled the subject matter requirements of a history essay, but also one that followed conventions for structure of historical essays. Tim did not understand the TA's feedback in terms of the differing genre expectations for the "essay" within different discourse communities. He interpreted the TA's feedback without understanding of what was behind the comment—the genre expectations in history that the TA was using to evaluate Tim's work.

RHETORICAL ISSUES

In one respect, rhetorical issues were similar in freshman writing and history: in both cases writing for the teacher was the paramount consideration. The social context of school superceded any disciplinary concerns. Nonetheless, disciplinary differences also played a role in the rhetorical effectiveness of Tim's writing in both fields. In freshman writing, Tim sensed his professor's enjoyment of his papers. He reported that he wrote "to have fun" with language and play with ideas. And since topics for papers were wide open, Carla could read as an interested "lay" reader, but not as subject matter expert. The majority of her comments on his essays were ones of an interested reader trying to engage with Tim's thinking; or, she expressed enjoyment of his vivid images, metaphors, and other stylistic features.

In history, from all apparent signs, Tim approached the assignments diligently but was disappointed with the feedback. Among the five essays I saw from his first year history courses, readers' comments focused almost exclusively on content—matters of interpretation of historical texts—and on rhetorical effectiveness, i.e. how well Tim fulfilled the genre expectations in history. But Tim concluded that writing in history was just about giving back to the teacher what s/he had lectured on in class. He said of the paper he wrote for his Islam class, for example, "It was an exercise in regurgitation. What we could tell we had learned or know. " The instructions for one assignment were: " The point of this exercise is to demonstrate that you have read the materials and can apply them . . ." It is not surprising that Tim felt it was "an exercise in regurgitation." Tim interpreted the history TA's comment on his Augustine to Benedict essay this way:

> He would say you came to the wrong [conclusion] . . . I could have presented my point better, but he just disagreed with my conclusion . . . in order to get the grade on the paper . . . you had to say what you'd been told in class about the book. Maybe in a new way, maybe in more depth, but basically say the same thing.

From all appearances, the primary rhetorical situation (with the exception of Tim's community service project in freshman writing) in both classes was writing for the teacher and the grade. In freshman writing, Tim had a sense of an appreciative, interested audience in his teacher. In history, he felt quite removed from the teacher as audience for his writing. He disliked the writing he did in his first two history courses.

SUMMING UP: FRESHMAN WRITING AND FIRST YEAR HISTORY WRITING

In sum, there were some similarities in writing in freshman writing and writing in introductory history courses. Tim needed to read and summarize what he was reading; he needed to generate topics for writing; he needed to consider the occasions for writing. In both situations, Tim was consciously interpreting the writing assignments through the lens of being successful in school, i.e. he was writing for his teachers.

What was different though was the relationship of reading to writing and the level of difficulty of both the reading and writing tasks between freshman writing and introductory courses in history. And there were different norms for written texts that stemmed from the different discourse communities each represented.

Tim was somewhat aware of other aspects of the social milieu in each course: he understood the freedom to play with ideas and forms in Carla's freshman writing course and that a teacher's interpretation of history was what one should espouse when writing for that teacher. What Tim missed was the differences in genre requirements and critical thinking stances required in the discourse communities represented in these courses. Though intelligent, Tim was not primed by teachers in either discourse community to understand different values and community purposes as they would affect writing goals, content, structure, language choice, rhetorical situation, etc. Tim's view that his history professors were trying to get him to agree with their points of view was probably caused by Tim's not understanding the requirements for supporting arguments in the discourse community of historians. And from his freshman writing courses, Tim could have taken away the impression that his personal views carried weight when making academic arguments, as one of Carla's goals was to make academic writing more personal for students.

The difference between the two contexts for writing raises the question of transfer of learning and what role a required, entry-level writing course can play in preparing a student for the rest of his/her college education. These matters I will return to in the final chapter of the book. In the next chapter, I look at Tim's experiences writing in history in upper level seminars.

4

LEARNING TO WRITE HISTORY

You get good at taking a situation that's extremely diffuse and . . . infinitely variable. With so many variables you would have to write a huge linear equation to describe [it]. It's not even linear. You get good at saying okay, really casting out what's not relevant . . . reduce it to one or two or three variables so you can kind of see what's going on . . . if I had to I could always say something cogent about the material . . . although I flapped a lot, I could always kind of reduce these big things to, you know, something.

—Tim, senior year

This comment, about history writing, was made after Tim had completed the requirements for a major in history and had started his second major in engineering. So in part, it is a reflection of his understanding of writing in history, and in part a reflection of the differences he perceived between writing in history and writing in engineering. The comment was made "off the cuff." It is glib and cursory. And yet, there is truth to the comment as well: it represents the limited knowledge and skill Tim gained in history writing as an undergraduate and suggests the road to expertise in writing in a discipline is a long one. This chapter will reveal, in part, what the beginnings of such a process were for this writer.

A brief look at the literature on the nature of history writing and writers' developmental processes in history will provide a backdrop for examining this particular case of one history major. To date, there have been no comprehensive studies of writing expertise in history, though some have identified key elements entailed in expert history writing performance. The analysis here adds to that goal of a comprehensive view of the development of history writing skills, beginning with my interpolations from the literature on history writing of the ways in which the five knowledge domains for writing expertise are particularized in history. I summarize these discipline-specific features briefly here.

The *discourse community* of historians is multifaceted and loosely constructed around a set of underlying values and methodologies for asserting historical truths. There are debates as to whether history is primarily a humanities-oriented field or a hybrid field that borrows many tools of the social sciences in order to establish historical trends, etc. MacDonald

(1987), a rhetorician, sees historians as conflicted between the goals of rendering the past ("what" questions) and finding generalizable patterns, i.e. interpreting the past ("why" questions). Others have traced the influence of master narratives (or meta-discourse) dominant in intellectual circles at a given time period, such as nationalism, progressivism, or relativism, in shaping the specific interpretations historians make in their writings—or shaping the meta-discourse of the discipline. In other words, historians themselves are situated in time, influenced by their times as they interpret the past (Appleby et al.1994). The norms for acceptable texts within the discourse community of historians change accordingly. And, as those who have worked with discourse community theory know, discourse communities in general are not fixed entities. They change and vary as all human enterprises do, and yet can be stable enough, "for the moment," to be recognizable and influential.

Leinhardt (1993) gets to the "what," or the *subject matter* of history, as follows: 1) events (relatively delimited episodes such as wars and biographies), 2) structures (large systems or institutions such as governments), 3) themes (interpretive patterns present across events or structures) and 4) meta-systems (disciplinary methods of inquiry, interpretation, and argument). Another way of thinking about subject matter in history is in terms of specific critical thinking tasks: 1) event reconstruction (Britt et al. 1994, Wineberg 1991, Wineburg 1994) 2) event interpretation (Bohan and Davis 1998, Greene 1993, Wineburg 1994) and 3) generalizing broad social/historical patterns and concepts (Hallden 1994, MacDonald 1994). But, the indeterminacy of "truth" in history makes acquisition of subject matter expertise challenging. Wineburg (1991) states, "Historical inquiry differs considerably from problem solving in well-structured domains . . . in history goals remain vague and indefinite, open to a great deal of personal interpretation" (pp. 73–74).

As for *genre knowledge* and *rhetorical knowledge,* in the historical essay the historian must manage the tension between storytelling and analysis, between rendering the past and claiming generalizable patterns (MacDonald 1994). But the interrelationship between narrative and argument in history is complex. Stockton (1995) has explored the way in which argument can be embedded within the narrative structure, rather than in explicit expository fashion. She states, "Writing history is not a matter of simple argument: it is not even a matter of simple narrative. It is, rather, a complex interweaving of several genres that work together for specific effects" (p. 71).

The difficulty in distinguishing the features of historical genres is compounded by the problem we have seen already in the discussion of discourse community norms of determining what "counts" as historical proof, i.e. what precise types of warrants and claims constitute the rhetorical features of an argument in history. The most common rhetorical frame employed in historical genres is a causal one: "x because of y." And the author's ethos is extremely important in establishing the validity of an historical argument. Stockton (1995) states that the way in which historians establish the credibility of their interpretations is through "the establishment of an autonomous subject of meaning who is always speaking from outside history about a distant and objectified past" (p. 47). Other genre norms—for example, whether the central argument is stated explicitly or not, and if so, at what point in the essay it is stated—seem to be at the writer's discretion. And, the immediate rhetorical occasion for writing in history might include demonstrating the correctness of a particular interpretation or its usefulness and importance, particularly in relation to previous work.

As for *writing processes* specific to historians, other than the literature on expertise in reading-to-write (Wineburg 1991, Young and Leinhardt 1998), I could find no studies of historians' writing process knowledge. But in all, these studies begin to fill in a model of the key areas of knowledge and skill necessary for expertise in writing history.

DEVELOPMENT OF HISTORY WRITING EXPERTISE

Although to my knowledge there are no other studies documenting multiple aspects of a history student's development of writing skills, a number of studies have focused on development of specific skills such as historical thinking or approaches to reading historical texts (Bohan and Davis 1998, Britt et al. 1994, Hallden 1994, Jacott et al.1998, Stahl et al.1996). As in general studies of writers' developmental progress, researchers have found similar developmental problems among history students: retelling the story of an event instead of explicating causal relationships (Greene 1993, Halden 1994, Wineburg 1994); understanding historical events as the result only of human agency and not seeing broader, more complex causes for historical events (Hallden 1994, Jacott et al. 1998); and seeing only a two-sided polemic regarding explanations of historical events (Bohan and Davis 1998). This could lead to students in history needing significant developmental work in order to write effective historical arguments (Greene 1995, Greene

1993, Langer 1984, Newell and Winograd 1995, Stockton 1995, Young and Leinhardt 1998).

In addition to studies that have analyzed the content and critical thinking aspects of novice history writers' texts, researchers have earmarked the following genre features as signifying competencies of more advanced writers in the discipline: the use of *multiple source texts* to support a point (Stahl et al. 1996, Young and Leinhardt 1998); the *use of source texts in multiple ways*—to supply content, to locate a faulty interpretation of events, or to support the writer's own line of argument (Greene 2001); *citation language that contextualizes and analyzes the source*, and use of organizing structures and causal connecting words that result in *causal arguments* (Young and Leinhardt 1998).

In this study, Tim's progress will be compared, where applicable, to existing research into developmental gains in history so that a fuller understanding can be had both of the nature of writing expertise in history, and of developmental processes of history students.

***

Here I describe Tim's experiences writing for history over a span of three years and twelve history courses taken during that time. As will be revealed, Tim began from a strong base, receiving a lot of praise in early courses from professors for his critical thinking and general writing skills. But the multiple lenses of analysis will show only a few gains during his undergraduate education in some knowledge domains important to composing historical essays.

TWIN DISCOURSE COMMUNITIES: DOING SCHOOL AND DOING HISTORY

Two things stand out in the content analysis of early interviews with Tim about his writing experiences at the beginning of his work in history with regard to discourse community knowledge: (1) as others have reported (Bazeman 1997, Greene 2001, Young and Leinhardt 1998), the classroom discourse community takes precedent, in fact is the only social context Tim is aware of, rather than any sense of the larger disciplinary discourse community. And (2) his second priority is creative self-expression rather than communicating to support overarching discourse community goals.

An example of his *not* understanding the broader picture of discourse community goals shows up in his early essays. In History I, an overview of ancient and medieval history, Tim's essay on the differences in the theology of Augustine and Benedict, which is reproduced in Appendix B, met with this criticism from the TA who graded his paper:

> I think you've got a good argument, very imaginative and certainly based on a lot of thought. What the paper lacks is clarity and focus; you frustrate the reader by meandering hither and yon and not moving in logical fashion with your thesis . . .

I read this comment as laying out the underlying standards of the discourse community for focused, cogent arguments. But Tim interpreted the teacher's comments (both written and oral) as the constraints of the classroom discourse community. Tim told me:

> He would say you came to the wrong [conclusion] . . . I could have presented my point better, but he just disagreed with my conclusion . . . in order to get the grade on the paper . . . you had to say what you'd been told in class about the book . . .

An analysis of the essay itself bears out the teacher's concerns. Here is the opening paragraph of Tim's essay:

> One of the recurrent questions of religion is the explanation of change in religious belief. Christianity has repeatedly altered its character according to the needs, desires, and outlooks of believers, taking on widely varying forms through the centuries. In St. Augustine's *Confessions* and the *Rule* of St. Benedict, fundamental differences appear in concepts of good, evil, God, man, Christ, a Christian's purpose, lifestyle, the secular and spiritual worlds, and finally the writers' approaches to spirituality. These variations pose the question: What were the causes and effects of these changes? Viewed in the context of history, we see in *Confessions* and the *Rule* how the destabilizing effects and moral crisis of the fall of Rome widened the gulf between Eastern and Western Christianity.

On the one hand, Tim has set himself a task appropriate to the discourse community—analyzing two religious texts in light of their historical/social contexts. But on the other hand, Tim has set himself the tasks of analyzing and comparing nine facets of the two source texts (concepts of good, evil, God, man, Christ, a Christian's purpose, lifestyle, the secular and spiritual worlds, etc.), as well as making links between the texts and the social/political forces influencing the two writers. The task he gave himself was more than he could handle in a relatively short essay (five pages) and leads, as his professor points out, to a lack of clarity and focus. In addition, as we will see later, he made some assumptions about the two texts that led to misinterpretations. Had Tim grasped more deeply how historians work with texts, he would have taken a different approach to the assignment.

In his Islamic history class his freshman year, again, Tim felt constrained by the writing tasks. The first was to compare the points of view of four authors on the rise of Islam. Tim felt "there was no real focus to the paper . . . it reads like a textbook." He said to me a year later, looking back at the paper, "It was an exercise in regurgitation. What we could tell him that we had learned or know. So it wasn't a real paper. I got my A or whatever, which I thought was ridiculous." The grade consciousness, the lack of articulation of any purposes of assignments that would align with the discourse community's goals, and the desire to be independent of any social constraints on his writing are all indicative of Tim's outsider status in the discourse community of history at this stage. And, it is certainly possible that the assignment itself was not "authentic" in the sense of allowing Tim to do a piece of work that historians would undertake.

There is a notable difference in the writing tasks assigned in his history courses in his sophomore and junior years: the tasks required attention to primary source documents, tasks that more closely match the work of professional historians.[34] In his Muscovite Russia course, he analyzed the letters of an English priest who served as ambassador to Russia. For his colonial American history course, he read an account from 1909 of the small Seventh Day Baptist denomination and analyzed a letter written from a tiny congregation in New Jersey to another congregation in Rhode Island. In his technology and society course, he worked with *Scientific American* editorials from 1860 through 1861 and a 1917 report of the American Railway Engineering Association.

It is perhaps because of the change in assignments that Tim made a few comments to me at the end of the sophomore year that reflected a beginning articulation of some of the discourse community norms in history. He said, for example, comparing his writing from freshman writing with his history writing, "In history they're not going to pay as much attention to your writing. More to your conclusions and your chain of thought . . . You know, the style will just kinda slip away . . . " At this same time Tim said to me, ". . . in fact, I saw one historian calling himself a futurist once, so he would use a little bit of history and just common sense to make predictive [statements]." But then he contrasted this historian's view with another whom he read, saying (his paraphrase) "I'm a historian and I believe in the unpredictability of history." These comments reflect some knowledge of the meta-discourse among historians. Also, in a recent phone conversation with Tim, I learned that he chose the course on Puritanism because he felt the other options in American history were focused on "the race/gender theme" and that this theme "was all-consuming. [It] didn't offer room . . . the line of thought or analysis was set . . . it felt stifling." An awareness of a paradigm dominating historical interpretations was another piece of discourse community knowledge Tim had picked up by this point in his undergraduate education.

As Tim moved through his sophomore and junior history classes, the issue of discourse community norms surfaced in another way. Because of Tim's strong church affiliation, he often chose religious topics for his papers in a variety of courses—for example, the Augustine/Benedict comparison, two essays on Puritanism, an essay comparing views of the industrialists of the 19th century with the views of Protestant clergy, and an essay on the views of an English clergyman/ambassador to Russia. When I talked with him in his senior year, noting this theme in the selection of topics for his papers, he said,

> I'm a Christian, so that's kind of interesting to see my own kind of heritage and kind of how . . . I guess it helps me personally understand what can go wrong in a church. You see a lot of examples, you know, the good and the bad in history . . . I don't want to just ignore it, but as a historian I want to understand it.

He was aware of differences between religious and historical discourse communities in terms of what topics and what arguments would be deemed acceptable, counting as "truth" in each. Of one of his papers that includes a discussion of religious issues he said:

> In some respects I still feel like it's outside the realm of history. You know, we look at history . . . Well, we don't look at the supernatural. We don't deal with that here, okay? Go next door . . . it might be a lot easier to write if it were being written for a Christian historical magazine let's say. You don't have to justify what you're doing as much.

He was aware of how religious content is shaped, depending on whether it is written for a discourse community of academics or a religious discourse community, and he was aware that certain assumptions can be made within the one discourse community that are not possible within the other. Although he may not have been able to articulate fully discourse community goals and values for each, he at least sensed some of those differences.

In sum, by the time I interviewed Tim in his senior year, he demonstrated an understanding, not articulated in his freshman year, that discourse community norms do indeed place certain expectations on a writer. Content analysis of interviews with him, over the four years, revealed some understanding of the "meta-discourses" prevalent in history at the time, a sense of how one topic, religion, must be treated differently in history writing than in religious discourse communities, and some sense of the overall purposes of history writing (". . . really casting out what's not relevant . . . reduce it to one or two or three variables so you can kind of see what's going on . . ."). But he still did not have the ability to choose topics and shape arguments that would be considered part of the "ongoing conversations" of the discourse community, as will be evident in the analysis of his treatment of historical subject matter in his essays. Writing for a grade was also his paramount purpose, as evidenced in his comment about "regurgitation," and "I got my A or whatever." But the solo creative writer had been displaced to some degree by a more social self as writer, a writer at least attempting to write within and against the discourse community of historians.

Subject Matter Challenges: Understanding the Interpretation of History

The requirements for the history major at Tim's university included a breadth requirement of six to eight courses in three geographic areas (the Middle East, the Americas, and Europe/Russia) and four courses in a field of concentration (in Tim's case, Russian history).

The writing tasks assigned in Tim's 100 level history courses were generally ones of event interpretation (Wineburg 1994). In Tim's Islamic history class in his freshman year, he received a B+ on a paper—his lowest grade on the three essays he wrote in that class. He said to me in an interview in his sophomore year:

> I missed some historical points . . . [that] inevitably happens when you don't study one thing deep enough. We're studying a lot of things and then you're asked to write a paper on one thing. So you kinda jump in; you're gonna miss a few things unless you really spend a lot of time researching it.

What prompted this comment is, no doubt, the end comment the professor wrote on his paper: "Your comparison is imaginative but you push it beyond the range of utility. As your last paragraph suggests, the decline of Maliki thought in Medina is far more complex than you assert." In fact, the course covered the rise of Islam, several branches of Islamic law that developed, and the relation of Islam to the rise of nationalism in Egypt. For his first paper in the course, on the rise of Islam, he read at least parts of four different commentaries on the roots of Islam. For the second paper, he drew on a novel, a film viewed in class, and the secondary source text. This was a huge amount of material for a newcomer to the field to grasp.

More significant is not the volume of factual knowledge of a given historical period Tim did or did not possess, but rather, whether he had at his command an appropriate interpretive framework—a sort of meta-knowledge of issues, trends, etc. that historians would deem the fitting means of interpreting given texts. Without such a framework, Tim would not know how to select the materials most relevant for making an argument.

In his ancient history class, Tim's written work demonstrates the effect of not having these interpretive tools at hand. A medievalist whom I asked to examine Tim's comparison of Augustine's *Confession* and Benedict's *Rule* said, "His analysis is missing one crucial factor—the genres of the writings. A confession is self-reflective: Benedict is writing a 'rule' for his monks. Of course it is going to focus on works." In other words, in spite of reading these texts carefully, Tim was not employing an appropriate interpretive framework for analysis of the texts. Regarding Tim's second essay for that course, the medievalist pointed out a similar lack of ability to use an appropriate interpretive frame. The historian explained, "Unfortunately, the argument is for a point that really isn't worth making . . . the point that tolerance is connected to economic interdependence is simplistic, and thus his attempt to prove it by analyzing the sources is artificial." This professor's critique of Tim's early attempt at interpreting history exemplifies the first stage of intellectual development that Alexander (2003) terms "acclimation:"

> students in acclimation have characteristically limited and fragmented knowledge. This piecemeal knowledge comes with little personal investment in the domain and strong reliance on surface-level strategies. Together these attributes mean that students in acclimation require guidance in determining

what content is central and what is peripheral . . . these students also need explicit instruction on how to be strategic within a domain

Even in Tim's chosen concentration, Russian history, lack of background knowledge sometimes caused him to make a faulty interpretation of source documents. In his Muscovite history course, the essay on the relationship between Ivan IV and Prince Kurbskii evoked this comment from his professor:

> You can extrapolate all those issues of concern from the texts . . . but I'd be leery of counting too much on such an extrapolation technique, because it imposes concerns on them that are not quite in the same spirit of their discourse. They think they are arguing about piety, virtue, and sin; you, from afar, pragmatically and with modern eyes, say they are arguing about power, and maybe you are right. But you should also think about the idiom of their discourse and what that means about their worldviews.

In contrast to this evidence of deficiencies in Tim's interpretive skills, Tim was able to draw effectively from his knowledge of Protestant church history and theology whenever he wrote on a topic that entailed the church's role in history. In his rhetorical analysis of the 1750 Shrewsbury letter from one church congregation to another, Tim made an appropriate comparison to one of the Pauline letters in the Bible. His analysis of Fletcher's condemnation of Russian Orthodoxy also drew on knowledge of the Protestant reformation. He spoke with authority in the essay: "These comments remind us that the Reformation had turned the traditional concept of laity and priesthood completely on its head." In another passage he said, "[Fletcher] broadly refers to all objects of veneration as 'idols,' in clear keeping with Protestant values." In all these instances, his professors accepted his analyses of the religious issues at hand as appropriate.

There were a few signs of increased subject matter knowledge in history outside of the religious arena: in several essays written his junior year Tim referred to larger historical concepts beyond the texts he was analyzing. In an analysis of editorials in the *Scientific American* in 1861 Tim drew directly from a required text in his colonial American history class from the previous year for an explanation of why the strong voice of scientific progress in the editorials is not balanced by the voice of mainstream Protestantism. And in his analysis of the committee report of the American Railway Engineering Association in 1917, Tim referenced a number of historical concepts or themes—social Darwinism, the rise of corporations in US industry, the move from an agrarian to industrial society, and Thomas Jefferson's view of "the common man"—all matters not directly addressed in the source document, but now part of his accumulated knowledge in history.

In sum, content analysis of Tim's essays in his junior year, compared to his freshman essays, showed some knowledge of central historical concepts of the 18th, 19th, and 20th centuries that he was able to employ in more than one essay, and he chose to focus increasingly on religious topics, for which he had more background knowledge. But his interpretive frameworks were sometimes inappropriate to the subject matter at hand, even in his chosen specialty, Russian history. This problem can be seen from another vantage point as well—the critical thinking work Tim was doing.

Critical Thinking Challenges in History: Shaping Arguments

An integral aspect of subject matter expertise is the ability to do critical thinking appropriate to the discipline—specifically, in history, to see similarities and differences across source documents and to apply a critical framework to a particular text, seeing connections or disjunctures. Subject matter knowledge as I have described it so far might be considered declarative knowledge—knowing "what." But procedural knowledge (knowing "how") is equally important—the ability to apply, manipulate, and draw from declarative knowledge. Critical thinking skills can also be viewed as the "procedural" aspect of subject matter knowledge.

At least one teacher, Tim's Islamic history professor in one of his freshman survey courses, praised his ability to synthesize information. At the end of Tim's essay on Egyptian nationalism the professor wrote: "You show a high level of ability to integrate and analyze the material you've read." Another professor in Tim's freshman year was more critical of Tim's analytical skills, saying he was ". . . not moving in logical fashion with [his] thesis." (Augustine paper), freshman year) On the "Tolerance and Talents" essay for the same class the professor commented, "Your hypothesis is interesting and sophisticated. The logic with which you apply it to the readings is sometimes faulty."

In addition to noting the few comments on Tim's essays by his professors that directly spoke of critical thinking issues, I looked at two aspects of his essays that would be indicative of critical thinking: the super-ordinate structure of the essay i.e. the overarching thesis and the relation of paragraphs to each other and to the thesis (Kuhn 1999), and indications from both his use of source materials and content of the essays of types of reasoning used to generate the content (Gilbert 1992). While there is evidence of critical thinking in his essays rather than simple regurgitation of facts, the content and structure of his essays reveal a lack of ability to sustain a clear focus.

In his first college history paper, "Augustine to Benedict," as we have seen, Tim tackled several challenging questions that demonstrate both his historical curiosity and his desire to understand cause–effect relationships between political forces and religious thinking. But his teacher commented in the margin: "Poor start. You have not stated clearly what the paper is about—too many pieces; not focused."

Tim had done a considerable amount of reading in preparation for writing the essay: Augustine's *Confessions,* Benedict's *Rule,* parts of his textbook (*Western Heritage*) and parts of a secondary source he sought out on his own, (Benz, *The Eastern Orthodox Church: Its Thought and Life.* Also of note is the fact that he set himself a difficult task—as it turned out, too difficult for either his skill level or for the amount of time available to write an essay of this scope. But the essay demonstrates Tim's attempt at going beyond the level of mere comprehension in Bloom's hierarchy of critical thinking skills (which, in writing, manifests as summarizing a text)—a hurdle some students have difficulty with in their developmental process.

Tim's attempted comparisons in this essay can be mapped in a matrix structure (Calfee and Chambliss 1987). The matrix he used to structure the essay reveals he had a clear plan for how to think through and articulate the issues he wanted to examine. But as the Table 4 (next page) shows, there are gaps in the matrix where he failed to fully articulate the comparison he set out to make. Also, the enormity of each subtopic in comparison with the amount of text Tim devotes to each (two paragraphs at most) is indicative of claims being made without in-depth marshalling of evidence to support those claims (Toulmin 1958).

To further complicate the writing task, Tim also attempted cause-effect reasoning along the lines that x historical/political event caused y change in theological interpretation. An analysis of his cause-effect reasoning and the relationship of claims to evidence reveals more precisely why the essay ultimately fails as an attempt at sustained critical thinking. Tim documented in the third and fourth paragraphs the increasing role

TABLE 4

Structural Analysis of "Augustine to Benedict"

	Eastern Orthodoxy	Augustine	Benedict
Nature of God	¶ 5	¶ 5	¶ 6
Nature of evil		¶ 7	¶ 8
Means of salvation	¶ 9	¶ 9	¶13
State & church relationship		¶ 13	¶ 13
Christ's role	¶ 14	¶ 14	¶ 14
Individual vs. Community		¶ 15	¶ 15

of clergy in political affairs as a result of weak secular rulers in the fifth century in Rome and Constantinople. But at the beginning of the fifth paragraph, he jumped to the issue of the nature of God and argued that by Benedict's time, God had become more vindictive, more the parent, the lawgiver because of ". . . the people's need for justice and stability in such times." There is no poof given that this is the reason for a theological shift. In paragraph eight Tim made the claim that Benedict saw man's nature as more evil than good. The reason, he stated, was ". . . the contemporary fear of new evils facing Roman society." Again, there are no examples to support the claim with textual evidence.

In the next to last paragraph of the essay, Tim turned to more global comparisons of the two primary sources. He noted a number of other points of comparison that were not in his original proposal for the scope of the paper. For example, he stated, "Augustine's thoughts and writings are intellectually complex whereas Benedict strives to simplify. Augustine values the individual search and choice whereas Benedict promotes stability through community supremacy. " These comparisons, sweeping and unsupported, are nevertheless remarkable for their attempts to digest these major primary sources and offer even a rudimentary analysis. The question is, where do these initial attempts lead him in his developmental process as a critical thinker? The instructor's end comment on the paper—"Work on communication; then the substance of your argument will shine through"—does not provide a clear directive for Tim.

An analysis of four other history essays Tim wrote in his freshman year shows a similar set of issues: he raised interesting questions when a writing assignment was open enough to allow him to do so and he worked with a number of primary and secondary texts for his papers, tasks that demanded analysis and synthesis (Bloom 1971). However, in all five essays from his freshman history courses, each of which averaged about five pages in length, he was unable to sustain a line of critical thinking with ample support from beginning to end of the essays.

In his sophomore year, Tim's essays were narrower in scope, as the classes themselves became more narrowly focused and his analyses became more sustained and focused as well. The writing task for all four of the essays from this period was to determine through what lenses were the authors of these texts interpreting their worlds—clearly a task at the more advanced stages of Bloom's hierarchy of thinking skills.

One such essay was written in his seminar on Muscovite Russia at the end of his sophomore year. The professor's comment is indicative of Tim's accomplishment: "You do a good job of enumerating [Fletcher's] many condemnations of the church and linking them with a Protestant's preoccupations. It's tightly written, with well chosen examples." Indeed, the essay is tightly organized: the thesis is stated clearly, simply, at the end of the second paragraph. He transitioned to the next paragraph with the phrase, "In the first place. . . ." Each paragraph has a transition from the previous one, and a clear topic sentence. The paragraphs give examples all supporting the proposition in his thesis.

Although Tim presented his points mostly in the same sequence as the chapters of the source text (he draws on Chapters 11, 12, 11, and 13 in that order), he was interpreting the chapters using an analytical framework (Protestant theology) he superimposed on the text. He also found ways to link the topics of each chapter/section of his paper in a logical chain of reasoning. For example, the lead-in for the fourth paragraph is, "Beyond word choice itself, Fletcher takes on the intellectual sphere." Tim made another appropriate logical transition between paragraphs five and six. In paragraph five, he discussed rituals Fletcher considers "superstitious." His transition into talking about institutional abuses in paragraph six was a causal link: "The resemblance of Orthodox rituals to Europe's wayward past leads him to look for the institutional abuses and sinfulness once experienced in the West." Here he was in fact moving from Chapter 12 in Fletcher's document back to Chapter 11, but the logic of his transition works. He made a similar logical connection between his summary of key points in Chapter 11 when he moved to Chapter 13, stating ". . . the disturbing traditions and institutional abuses lead Fletcher on to investigate the substance of Orthodox belief." Fletcher's report is a lengthy, descriptive document. Tim excerpted what was relevant to make his point and created a causal chain between the chapters that in fact Fletcher does not.

This essay, written late in his sophomore year, is Tim's most accomplished in the entire data set. The thinking is original and within a framework appropriate to the discourse community, the argument is clearly articulated, and all paragraphs relate to the central argument. One might hope this essay was a turning point, evidence of a breakthrough in Tim's reasoning abilities and writing skills, but the last three papers produced after "Fletcher's Mirror" are less successful. One essay fails because of an inappropriate interpretive framework and the other two lack a clear super-ordinate structure.

For example, Tim's essay, "American Railroading," written in his junior year, lacks focus and a clear super-ordinate structure. The essay was an attempt to gloss a lengthy news report from the American Railway Engineering Association in 1917, a disparate collection of technical reports on various facets of the railroad's operations. What Tim saw as a unifying theme was the profit motive. It is a plausible one, as mention of "profits" is interwoven throughout the report. However, Tim's essay is a loosely structured list of topics covered in the source document. Here is the second paragraph of the essay, in which the thesis appears:

> The American Railway Engineering Association's Bulletin provides a record of the changing meaning of technology in the period of the railway's prime. A report published in January 1917, the "Report of Committee XIX – On Conservation of Natural Resources," reflects the railroading community's view of technology, resources, and humanity. Committee XIX's work clearly reveals industry probing at the edges of its resources—a thought strange to early 19th-century America. More subtly, however, the report rests on science and money in a new way. The profit motive stands out as the linchpin, the justifier of every human activity, in this report. Money, therefore, provided the "why" of industry, and science (loosely defined as the systematic study of any process) provided the "how." Whether this view is shared by other segments of society is a question not under the scope of this paper; it is sufficient to note outside sources the report draws on, the report's lack of drive to defend assumptions of these values, and the fact that the railroad had played the

starring role in American industry. These points suggest that the acceptance of science as the legitimate method and money as the measuring stick was at least commonly held.

"The report rests on science and money in a new way." What is the meaning Tim intends here? Two sentences later, he clarifies: "Money . . . provided the 'why' of industry, and science . . . provided the 'how.'" But the following two sentences do not offer any further development of this idea. It is not clear what the scientific method is being employed for and how science and money are interrelated in relation to the railroading industry. Nor does the rest of the essay illuminate this murky idea.

Whole paragraphs are irrelevant to his thesis. In paragraphs that do mention the profit motive, there is no explicit connection drawn between the claim and the evidence, i.e. no explanation of how the evidence supports the claim. For example, Tim noted the breadth of industries the railroad committee is concerned with. He described those industries, noted the shift from an agrarian economy, and then concluded, "The railroad indeed was forced into creating new industries in order to pursue the profit." He assumed the motive was profit, but gave no logic or textual evidence to support the interpretation. And the next paragraph jumps to the topic of how railroad companies "fully defined the nature of the corporation in America," an issue unrelated to the profit motive.

In another essay in his junior year Tim analyzes editorials in three issues of the *Scientific American* in 1861. His commentary on this essay in an interview with me indicates a degree of complexity in his thinking not present in the essay he actually produced. He explained:

What I think I was trying to do is . . . What was the spiritual climate [then]? People think . . . now we're liberated, boy, but back then we were kind of under the yolk of religion or whatever. I think it goes much more like this: their revivals are there like ebbs and tides . . . there are always segments of society that are kind of outside . . . I was just trying to get at that a little bit and so what kind of affect was this technology having on society, were the values of society, particularly Christian communities, shaping it at all, were they kind of at odds with each other, were they kind of not even communicating . . . That's what I was talking about . . . to take this diffuse situation and say, what kind of plane or three-dimensional space or line do I want to look at . . .

TABLE 5

Organizing Structures in Tim's History Essays

Essay	Year	Genre	# of sources and type	Word count	Organizing Structure
Augustine to Benedict	1st	argument re. historical theme	3 primary 2 secondary	1,976 approx	Matrix: topical comparison sub-structure: cause / effect
Tolerance & Talents (Middle Ages)	1st	argument re. historical theme	1 secondary 1 primary	2,304 approx	chronological by source date sub-structure: cause / effect
Rise of Islam	1st	descriptive analysis: event reconstruction	4 secondary 1 primary (film)	2,184	matrix: topical comparison
Rise of Egyptian Nationalism	1st	descriptive analysis: event reconstruction	1 secondary 2 primary (novel and film)	2,259 approx	list substructure: loose comparison novel vs. events
Islamic Law	1st	summary: event reconstruction	2 secondary	1,866 approx	chronological substructure: cause/ effect
Puritans and Witchery	2nd	argument: event interpretation	3 secondary	1,830 approx	proposition & examples
Shrewsbury Letter	2nd	descriptive textual analysis	1 primary 1 secondary	2,475 approx	topical net
Fletcher's Mirror	2nd	argument: textual analysis	1 primary	1,034 approx	propsition & examples
Muscovite Russia	2nd	descriptive analysis: event interpretation	1 primary	1,344 approx	matrix: topical comparison sub-structure: cause / effect
Response to Stalinism	3rd	descriptive analysis: event interpretation & textual analysis	4 primary (3 novels, 1 film) personal experience	3,404	summary sub-structure: specified list
Scientific American	3rd	argument re. historical theme	1 primary	1,736	propositon & examples
American Railroading	3rd	descriptive textual analysis	1 primary	1,852	list sub-structure: proposition & examples

Unfortunately, the line of argument in the actual essay is much less complex.

Looking across the 12 essays, it is evident that Tim used critical thinking in a variety of ways as he worked with the subject matter of his essays: to draw comparisons across readings, to apply an analytical framework to a single text, to interpret motives and cause–effect relationships from the evidence, to interpret the sub-texts of sources—i.e. authors' biases and purposes for writing. And he used several types of structures in his essays to attempt to think through and order his materials: comparison of rhetorical purposes of texts, cause–effect relationships among events, analysis by analogy, analysis of characteristics of historical movements, a chronology of events or sequence of written records, and listing or chunking of information either with no connecting structure or in a loose associative structure.

As the Table 5 (next page) shows, the most frequent method of structuring his thinking and his writing was a matrix for comparative analysis, which he used in five papers. Four of the essays ("Puritans and Witchery," "Fletcher's Mirror," "Response to Stalinism," and *Scientific American*) showed the most coherent arguments: the line of reasoning continued from start to finish of the essay with little extraneous material inserted and there was some effort to support claims with textual evidence. The other eight essays employed no super-ordinate unifying structure, but rather, were organized like a list or topical net or were a straight chronology. Also, a clear super-ordinate structure for an essay did not necessarily coincide with a strong use of evidence to support claims.

In sum, by using a combination of the taxonomies of critical thinking and expository text structures developed by Bloom (1971), Calfee (1987), and Kuhn (1991), I was able to ascertain that critical thinking skills appeared strong even in Tim's freshman essays: he was able to generate original ideas and in some cases, the scope of what he undertook to argue was ambitious. There is much critical analysis of complex source documents and synthesis across texts evidenced even in the early essays. What was not consistent or in greater evidence over time was his ability to give a unifying super-ordinate structure to his essays or to sustain a focused argument. But in part this may have been a result of a lack of time spent on the writing task or in part a result of a set of assumptions Tim held about genre requirements in historical writing.

Genre Challenges: the Historical Essay

The ill-defined qualities of genres of historical writing complicate analysis of Tim's development of genre skills in history writing. As Tosh (1984) explains:

> Historical writing is characterized by a wide range of literary forms. The three basic techniques of description, narrative, and analysis can be combined in many different ways, and every project poses afresh the problem of how they should be deployed. This lack of clear guidelines is partly a reflection of the great diversity of the historian's subject matter: there could not possibly be one literary form suited to the presentation of every aspect of the human past. But it is much more the result of the different and sometimes contradictory purposes (pp. 94–95).

A historian can write for different purposes and hence, in different genres, but in Tim's case, the assignments given—the purpose for each occasion for writing in Tim's history classes—were not clear. Directions for assignments were given orally in Tim's classes. When I asked what the task in a given writing assignment was, Tim could only name writing tasks that invited either "regurgitation" of subject matter presented in the class or, at the opposite extreme, ill-defined explorations of a broad range of subject matter. It seems, in most instances, the genre choice was not altogether clear to Tim. Hence, as I will demonstrate, his texts approximate features of several genres with differing purposes often within the same document.

Although Tim did not talk in terms a historian would use to describe the genres of the discipline, at the end of his sophomore year he articulated some awareness of genres, based on the different types of writing tasks his professors assigned. He said:

> There's so many different kinds of historical writing . . . there's the textbook, there's the Shrewsbury-type paper which just focuses on one little document and squeezes as much blood as it can out of that . . . there's the kind of typical history assignment which would be something like one of the Islamic [papers] . . . take one of these writers or these books and discuss it in a certain context. . . .

Boiled down, Tim is articulating two sub-genres of the historical essay—a textual analysis and a thematic argument. The text analysis he sees as an expository essay with a loose structure and the thematic essay as thesis-driven. He articulated to me in greater detail in his senior year the purpose and resulting form of a textual analysis:

> None of us had ever done it before so it felt a little strange, and basically, he was just reassuring us that yeah, you take this single piece, and you really just get very, soak it. . . . I always talked about these different cutting planes . . . take as many as you can and umm, try to provide transition between them as you kind of switch. Go from one to the next . . . And just say, you know, I'm going to talk about this or whatever. And just try to get as many different angles on the piece as you can. So that's different because it's not argumentation. It's just kind of description, but it's analytical.

Five of his essays—the analysis of the letter from the Shrewsberry congregation to another congregation, the analysis of Fletcher's commentary on the Russian Orthodox church, the analysis of the correspondence between the Czar and his count, the analysis of editorials in the Scientific American, and the analysis of the Railway Association report—were textual analyses. Each essay offers an interpretation of the source—usually, a rhetorical analysis, i.e. an attempt to understand the text's biases, its subtexts, its particular historical framework. But the form of the five essays varies: in three (Fletcher, the Czar/count correspondences, and the Scientific American editorials) there is an attempt at a focused argument throughout the essay. But in two others there is a thesis in the introduction (reiterated in the conclusion) that sets up the expectation for a sustained argument, yet the body of the text presents a loose exploration of the source documents for themes, patterns, and influences that do not pertain to the thesis or even contradict the claim made in the thesis.

In all cases of writing thematic arguments, the other genre Tim was working with (essays on the rise of Islam, the rise of a legal tradition within Islam, the rise of Egyptian nationalism, the conflict between church and state in Roman times, the West meets East theme in the Middle Ages, the rise and fall of witchcraft in New England), Tim attempted a focused argument. The introduction presents the reader with a thesis statement that takes a debatable position. But as with the textual analyses, the results were mixed: sometimes the essay sustained a focused argument, and sometimes the body of the text became a loose exploration of the topic without any relation to the thesis.

When I asked Tim if he felt making an argument was essential to the success of a history essay, he hesitated:

TABLE 6

Use of Citations in Tim's History Essays

Essay Title	Year	Sources	Citations	Word count
Augustine to Benedict	1st	3 primary 2 secondary	37	1,976 approx.
Tolerance & Talents (Middle Ages)	1st	1 secondary 1 primary	23	2,304 approx.
Mohammed in History	1st	4 secondary 1 primary (film)	3	2,184
Voices of Cairo (Egyptian Nationalism)	1st	1 secondary 2 primary (novel and film)	16	2,259 approx.
Malik's Religious Reactions (Islamic Law)	1st	2 secondary	6	1,866 approx.
Puritans & Witchery	2nd	3 secondary	15	1,830 approx.
Shrewsbury Letter	2nd	1 primary 1 secondary	35	2,475 approx.
Fletcher's Mirror	2nd	1 primary	0	1,034 approx.
Muscovite Russia	2nd	1 primary	0	1,344 approx.
Response to Stalinism	3rd	4 primary (3 novels, 1 film) fieldwork	0	3,404 approx.
Scientific American	3rd	1 primary	12	1,736
American Railroading	3rd	1 primary	6	1,852

Yeah. Maybe not in those, umm, I guess I did here, but this is a little different. This is a more synthetic approach. This one doesn't seem to be very argumentative. Here I say, "There lies a stark contrast." Okay well, so what? I guess you're kind of trying to make the point that your analysis is valid.

Tim's words, "kind of trying" suggest a writer not 100% sure of his purpose. He thought through the issue further as he talked with me:

I don't think I necessarily always do a great job of saying, you know, this is the proper cutting plane. Or *a* proper cutting plane . . . Maybe I should make a point to say . . . there are other ways of looking at it, but this is the way we're looking at it today . . . So establish that this is the way we're going to look at it . . . and sometimes . . . you have to make assumptions. I might play it fast and loose sometimes with that just to keep people tracking with me . . .

When I asked what he meant by playing it "fast and loose," he said:

> I think sometimes I value the flow in the writing over the step-by-step kind of point-by-point analysis. So people will be able to say, yeah, well, what about this? Then I'd have an answer for that, but I don't want to bring it up myself because it gets in my way . . . valuing the rhetoric, you know, over the substance.

It is interesting to see Tim characterize what in fact were rather loosely structured essays as "playing it fast and loose."

These comments were made at the end of Tim's senior year, after he had completed his double major in history and engineering. Writing in engineering required that Tim did not ignore assumptions. Rather, he had to learn to anticipate every possible objection to a particular engineering design and inform the reader that he had thought through all the options. It is from this vantage point, I suspect, that he was reflecting back on his history papers. I question whether these fine points of the history genres he was writing in were apparent to him at the time he was writing the essays.

In addition to mixed purposes in some of his essays and the content issues previously discussed (using faulty interpretive frames, lack of focus, or lack of evidence to support claims), Tim's essays do not exhibit any systematic use of citations from source materials to support his claims—an important rhetorical feature in history writing. Greene (1993) and Young and Leinhardt (1998) have demonstrated history students' uses of citations for three purposes—to create content, to locate a faulty interpretation of events, or to support the writer's own line of argument. But in Tim's case, there is no discernible pattern either for frequency of citation or the purpose for a citation when there is one. Three essays written in his sophomore and junior years have no citations and the two essays with the highest number of citations (see Table 6 next page) each show different patterns of citation.

In the early essay on Augustine and Benedict, an essay of approximately 2000 words with 37 citations from five sources, Tim's citations follow either a paraphrase of the source text or directly quote a brief phrase—cases of what Greene (1993) would call building content. The quotations in this essay lend a surface validity to the essay: one can go to the source to corroborate Tim's information. But the peppering of every other sentence with a quotation suggests a writer not in command of ways to draw others' texts appropriately into his own either for documentation purposes or for rhetorical purposes. There is no introductory phrase or follow-up statement after the citation to support a point Tim wants to make. And at the other extreme, in the same essay there are whole paragraphs of summary of historical events or interpretation of those events with no citations. In the other essay with numerous citations, a rhetorical analysis of the Shrewsbury Letter, a 2500–word essay (approximate) with 35 citations drawn from two texts, the citations are brief quotes that either build content or illustrate Tim's points about the language of the letter itself. The frequency of these citations makes sense, given his topic and purpose—a close explication of the text. In other essays, citations are used mostly to credit an excerpt (if a direct quote)—for example, in his explication of Mahfouz's *A Palace Walk* and his explication of the editorials in three issues of *Scientific American.* In the "Puritans and Witchery" essay, approximately 1800 words in length, with 15 citations, there is again an inconsistent pattern. In some paragraphs, citations credit the source of Tim's analysis; in other paragraphs of analysis, there are no citations. In sum, the inconsistent use of citations in this corpus of essays suggests Tim is not certain when and how to use citations to serve the rhetorical purpose of building the argument or creating credibility in the historical essay.

Because of the subjective nature of historical interpretation, another important genre feature worthy of consideration is the writer's manipulation of the voice addressing the reader, which can also affect the essay's credibility. At several points in our conversations, Tim in fact discussed authorial stance as manifest in several different linguistic features of history writing. One way in which he tried for a voice of authority was in the choice of linguistic register. He said to me at the end of his sophomore year:

> This really kind of official very strict kinda language . . . you kinda tend to slide into it . . . because everything you read is written in this style in history classes . . . so you just kind of get into this mode of sitting down to write a paper, you need to shift gears completely [from writing for freshman composition]. I wouldn't say it's a requirement, although it wouldn't surprise me if I wrote a paper that's much more readable, accessible, colloquial perhaps and I would get docked for something. Cause perhaps subconsciously . . . the grader is reading as a history paper and the reader's also in this mode and it's scripted for stilted language.

However, a comparison of a sample essay written for Tim's freshman composition course and three of his history essays (one written when he

TABLE 7

Analysis of Linguistic Complexity

	Mean T-unit length (number of words)	% of words five syllables or more in random sample
Freshman composition essay, "Vatican II"	18	3%
Freshman history essay, "Tolerance & Talents"	23.3	.08%
Sophomore history essay, "Puritans & Witchery"	21	1%
Junior history essay, "Technology, Purpose and the American Church"	19	.05%

was taking freshman composition, one written in his sophomore year, and one in his junior year) reveals very little difference in linguistic register and only a small increase in syntactic complexity in the history essays (Table 7).

In addition to word length and sentence structure, specialized vocabulary can also be an indicator of the typical linguistic register of a given genre. In three sample history papers I found only a few words with particular "saturated meaning"(Flower 1979) for historians: for example, "multiculturalism," "americana," "bipolar world," and "secular humanism." The one slight difference in register in his history essays compared to his freshman composition essays was the use of more metaphors in the freshman composition essays. He wrote in one freshman composition essay of the "halls of the Western mind," ideas "echoing" and "resounding," a "resonance" of ideas, "under the magnifying glass" and "throw out the window." In the three history essays I analyzed, fewer metaphors appear. The metaphor "under the magnifying glass" appeared once, an idea "rings out" appeared once, and he referred to a "black, damning picture" in describing a historical event.

Tim did enjoy word play—he wrote song lyrics in his spare time—and a few more metaphors in later history essays also demonstrate this propensity. I sensed Tim's unique register—his attempts at word play within an academic essay—were evidence of a writer quite intentionally asserting himself against the norms for academic genres. He wrote of "the linchpin of each article" in the Scientific American analysis. He referred to Enlightenment humanism "dressed in the latest emerging ideas of social Darwinism" and "the heavy footprint of materialism" and "the movement of industrialism [continuing] on the rails of progress and the steam of the modernist ethic of progress." In the American Railroading paper he played with an engineering concept in the sentence "Technology occupies an indisputably *plastic* role in the story of American culture." He commented in an interview in his senior year about the use of "plastic": "It's totally using the engineering lingo . . . You know, because they have their . . . technical meanings in engineering, but people outside understand them and they're really striking when you use [them]." He referred in the same essay to the timber industry as "woodworking." In the Puritan and witchcraft essay, he referred to "well-heeled witches." Most likely, these types of metaphors would not be used by expert history writers.

Another aspect of the writer's stance in relation to readers is the linguistic choice of what person to write in. In most cases, Tim used the third person. In a few cases, he used the first person plural. For example, in the "Technology, Purpose, and the American Church" essay he wrote: "The spirit which seized the land has fascinated historians . . . An examination of technical literature can demonstrate that the manufacturing culture was not Christian or post-Christian. . . ." But in the next sentence, he switched to first person plural: "The literature bequeathed *us* by the Industrial Revolution is rich with varied genres." In his essay, "Fletcher's Historical Mirror" he wrote, "Although only complete knowledge of Fletcher's character and values can explain his impressions conclusively, *we* can suggest a simple reason by keeping Europe's religious and ideological experience in mind." When I asked why he used "we," he replied:

> I have no idea. Everybody else does . . . Well, actually, some . . . Partly because saying "I" felt like, then they are going to investigate my credentials [laughs] I'd rather just hide behind the ideas and let them present themselves and you know, saying "I" would be like, well who is this guy anyway. Well, he's a student. I mean come on, what does he know . . . So "we" is a little vague. You can hide behind it I guess. But also, I think I've seen myself, actually when I read this, like "we" with the reader. You know, so "we would like to do this so wouldn't we" It's kind of like Mr. Rogers. Won't you be my neighbor.

The use of "we" was perhaps not conscious when he wrote the essay, as suggested by his first response to my question—"I have no idea." But there was a tacit knowledge of audience, the reader, and his need to be persuasive that he could articulate upon further reflection. In his essay on Ivan and Kurbskii he tried another approach to addressing the reader: "An analysis on the points the authors differ on *leads the investigator to the conclusion that . . .*" Later, he wrote, ". . . and from both writers' perspectives the reader sees that . . ." These are linguistic moves of a novice historian trying on different voices in these essays—some more intimate, some more distant, and none used consistently. According to Stockton (1995), the norm in history writing is for an "autonomous voice capable of telling time . . . not subject to history, not entangled in self-doubt, self-reference, or the webs of discourse" (p. 69). Tim's voice varied essay to essay. He appeared to be still experimenting with finding the appropriate authorial stance for writing about history even in his junior level essays.

In sum, with the help of Slevin's (1988) framework for analyzing genre knowledge, I was able to document some beginning genre knowledge in history by the time Tim had completed his courses for this major. He wrote in two major sub-genres of the historical essay—the textual analysis and the thematic essay. He understood the need for analysis, not just summary. He tried to raise questions of interest to the reader, indicating some awareness of the larger purposes of the genre within the discourse community. He sensed that there is a formal register that enables one to sound like a professional historian. But there remain many signs of a novice not in full command of all features of the genres he is using: the inconsistent use of citations, mixed or unfulfilled purposes in some essays, and lack of control of the essay structure, as well as the content issues previously discussed.

Rhetorical Conflicts in Novice History Writing

In addition to the standard rhetorical moves of a given genre, the writer must contend with the immediate rhetorical context of a specific text. There is much research documenting students' acts of writing focusing solely on the business of getting a grade, getting through school (Greene 2001, McCarthy 1987, Nelson 1995). However, in Tim's case, while this school-driven purpose was certainly a strong one, there is evidence in his writing of several layers of rhetorical purpose and audience in addition to this one—perhaps because Tim was a self-motivated learner (he genuinely liked history and liked writing), perhaps because his freshman English teacher emphasized and created opportunities for her students to practice writing for more than one imagined audience.

A statement Tim made about his writing for history classes in his freshman year suggests two rhetorical purposes and audiences for writing that he perceived as being at cross-purposes. He talked about the assignments in History 1 as being exercises in "regurgitation," i.e. writing to the teacher, to display knowledge, to acquiesce to the teacher's authority. He characterized writing for history courses as limiting the "fun" he could have with the task. This suggests that a second audience/purpose Tim wanted to hold for his writing was himself—to satisfy his own creative urges. Further evidence of his need to write for personal reasons is suggested by the pattern in his choice of subject matter for his essays in all six history courses. As noted earlier, Tim had an active religious life during college and spoke to me of his need to "see my own heritage and . . . personally understand what can go wrong in a church . . . as a historian I want to understand it." Five of the 12 essays dealt with issues of faith informing the views of historical figures he chose to study or issues of institutional religion's role in social issues of a given age.

Tim also had a strong interest in Russia: he spent one year after high school studying in Russia and worked summers in college for an international youth organization that took him to Russia again before the end of college. He chose Russian history as his area of concentration and on numerous occasions spoke highly of one of his Russian history professors. He also told me in his interview at the end of his senior year that his favorite paper in college was "Response to Stalinism." The essay is structured as two parallel stories: in the one, the drama of Tim's encounters with bureaucrats in charge of an orphanage in Russia unfolds; in the other, an interpretation of the writings of Milosz, Witkiewicz, Konwicki, and Baranczak on Stalinism is developed. Each of the parallel stories helps to interpret the other. He said to me, "Dang, I love this. Yeah, oh man, this is cool. I like this one because umm, it very much merged like real life and a piece of writing . . . to analyze whatever." Not only was a strong personal interest a part of the purpose for this occasion for writing, but also, Tim imagined an audience beyond his professor. He said, " . . . it kind of is in some ways populous. It's aiming at a popular audience like you know an intellectual audience I guess . . . when I was writing it, I was thinking of a *New York Times Book Review*." But the two purposes— Tim's own, and his professor's in assigning the writing—apparently did not align. Tim commented, ". . . it ticks me off because, umm, because I love this piece and because I got a B+ in that class."

On another occasion Tim told me he wrote one introduction using an analogy between a young child's behavior and historical processes because he knew his professor had young children. He explained, "The first paragraph is the direct benefit of English . . . the emphasis she [the English teacher] put on . . . audience." The history professor did not comment on the introduction, nor does it serve to illuminate the subject of the essay. The other introduction in which he tried an analogy—the Islamic law paper—was not aimed specifically at the professor, but at an audience Tim imagined in his head who would be aware of the present-day situation he was referencing. The professor commented that the analogy did not fit the subject matter at hand. But nonetheless, these moves indicate Tim at least tacitly made choices about the specific rhetorical situation of a given writing assignment, whether just for a grade or for additional social and personal aims.

It is hard to measure Tim's rhetorical expertise or to assess growth in rhetorical skill. If the predominant rhetorical purpose was to get a good grade, to earn units, to graduate, Tim was very successful. Of the graded essays he showed me (nine out of 12) two-thirds received A's and one-third B's. The B+ in the junior level course angered Tim, so it is reasonable to assume he generally received A's after the initial B's in his History I course. He was able to "read" the rhetorical situation of the classroom. Furthermore, from content analysis of the interview data it is evident that Tim was an individualist: he wanted to write for his own purposes, not just the teacher's. He could imagine different audiences and somewhat adapt his tone, his content, and even the structure of his writing (in the case of the Stalinism essay), to suit the particular rhetorical task he gave himself beyond the teacher's rhetorical demands.

Tim was not a mature rhetor at the end of his undergraduate education if one is considering as the target contributing to the discourse among historians. Tim's primary purpose throughout college was to write for a grade. And, his compelling need for personal creativity as well prevented him from combining these aims with the larger aims of the discourse community of his professors. In none of his essays did he attempt to link his ideas to those of others who had written on the topics he chose: each rhetorical act was self-contained, rather than part of any "ongoing conversation" (Bruffee 1984). Rhetorical skills go hand in hand with knowledge in the other areas though—discourse community knowledge, subject matter knowledge, and genre knowledge—so it is not surprising that these rhetorical limitations existed in Tim's writing as an undergraduate history major.

Honing a Process for Writing in History

Writing process knowledge that is specific to a given discipline involves knowing the specific tasks in reading-to-write and in drafting and revising involved in that discipline. In history, reading is a core aspect of the pre-writing process. A historian is either reading one text over and over, to unearth its nuances, or s/he is reading lots of texts to get a range of viewpoints, to compare, synthesize, analyze multiple perspectives on a single event or issue. Others' texts were the "stuff" of Tim's essays—both in the sense of straightforward "borrowing" from others' texts and in the sense of using others' ideas for generating new thinking of his own. Here's how Tim described the reading-to-write transaction:

> I underline. I take notes on eight and a half by eleven sheets of paper. Write down the thought and the page . . . this might be before or after I've come up with my idea. So let's say it's before. I don't have my idea. So now we got all this stuff. So I get my fifteen sources on the table and go through them. I've already read through them let's say. So I know that they're okay sources. They're relevant. Then I go through, and I'll underline and make notes as I go . . . Then I look at them and say, okay, what are the themes that are going on here . . . then I'll start to code these different comments on the paper. So they're all coded then, and some of them I cross out because they don't apply or can't develop a point, and then I try . . . I guess I look and well what can I say about each of these things based on these data.

Fifteen sources is probably an exaggeration. In the 12 essays he gave me, there were no more than four or five sources used in one essay. Nonetheless, even in first-year history courses, several of Tim's writing tasks involved coming to terms with two or three book-length works in critical ways. The critical thinking task, in this pre-writing stage, was an inductive synthesizing process: he sought to find points of similarity and contrast, to find what one could say about others' texts, hopefully in a new and interesting way. He said, for example:

> I have four themes. Then is what I am saying about each theme coherent among the different themes or you know, am I contradicting myself in a serious way? Can I work that out? How do I work out the contradictions? Do I just

nod to them? Maybe I'll change my line. Maybe I'll drop a theme . . . and that kind of narrows down what my thesis statement is pretty much.

Another comment Tim made on his writing process makes clear the generative nature of the writing process itself for him. He writes in order to think, in order to get an idea. He said, ". . . the first paragraph was always the toughest. What am I writing about anyway? Once I got that out, then it would start to come together." He also discovers a structure for the essay as he writes: "I pretty much go into the first theme and um, decide once I'm in it, like, what order I want to deal with the different points."

The question of what drove the decisions he made as he was writing is not one that can be fully answered from content analysis of interview data. But there is a suggestion of his overall problem-solving process in this comment: ". . . I kind of have an idea of exactly what my point is, and who I need to nod to, and who I need to wipe off the slate or work with on my way there. And then I pretty much start writing. . . ." At another point in the conversation he said:

> Let's assume that I read some stuff and I'm supposed to write a paper about it. It's like 'cause that's my job, or like that's my assignment. It's not like there's a pressing need, but I need to generate an idea about what I've learned or studied or read and um, one that's hopefully interesting and important to somebody. Figure out who that is or alternately, I could say, who's important to me, and then say, so out of this stuff I read, what issues umm, might actually happen more.

The rhetorical context, i.e. completing an assignment, or trying to reach interested readers, or satisfying his personal interests helped Tim define the task. Particular attention was given to satisfying the imagined audience of the professor—his/her need to see that the student understood the material, knew the important sources to quote, etc. And the text created so far also influenced Tim's writing process: he worked out inconsistencies in his thinking or in his sources and sequencing issues as he wrote.

When I asked about the time it took him to write his essays and if he revised his essays at all, Tim said:

> Well it all depends on how big it is obviously. But . . . I'd definitely start the reading a few days ahead, and I'd usually start the writing like a day ahead and then, hopefully I would always have the evening before or the morning

of or something like that to kind of look it over. Never enough to kind of let it sit for a while, which is ideal.

When I asked how much he tended to revise, he said, "I kind of get it all out there, and then I decide well, this just doesn't flow well and then maybe I should move things around and so they build on each other and kind of transitions more . . . active verbs. Clarity. Getting out the verbosity." He did not give me drafts except in one case. In that essay, there were only word changes in the revised version. Either his revision process happened as he wrote, rather than in successive drafts, or his "ideal" revision process did not happen in this instance.

These comments on his writing process came at the end of Tim's senior year. When I asked if his writing process had changed much over the four years of college, he said,

> It definitely improved as far as the academics . . . Like I could pretty much count on, this last year, putting in an hour per page to get something done, and then kind of work on it from there. Okay, now I've got an idea. . . . Once I had the idea, then going from there to starting to write was definitely lubricated a lot just by practice.

Unfortunately, there was not an opportunity to triangulate his self-reports of his writing process. But I have no reason to suspect that he was consciously manipulating his comments. Tim may not have been fully conscious of his writing process as he was writing, but he could articulate, in hindsight, a pattern to the process. He knew some of the steps to take leading up to drafting; he understood at least in principle the value of revisiting a piece of writing later; he saw that a piece of writing could take shape as he wrote it. And his sense was that his process became more "regularized" and more efficient as a result of the sheer quantity of writing tasks assigned.

GAINS IN WRITING FOR HISTORY

What then, were the developmental changes in Tim's history writing from freshman through junior years? This case confirms the complex interweaving of multiple factors that are simultaneously interacting in a writer's growth in context-specific writing expertise. Overall, there were small gains in discourse community knowledge, in subject matter knowledge, and in efficiency in accomplishing writing tasks. Critical thinking skills, genre knowledge, and rhetorical knowledge showed the least growth. There were spurts of moving to more expert performance in these areas, but the spurts were not sustained in repeated performances.

Adopting the identity of one who writes history, which is a part of the developmental process for gaining discourse community knowledge, is not an easy process. Except for one essay (Stalinism), writing for the professor or grade rather than connecting to a larger community of historians was Tim's main reason for writing. By the end of college I suspect Tim would have felt he had gained only slight insider status in the discourse community of historians. Those historians who read his essays considered him a novice in the field. And according to Alexander's (2003) model of the stages of moving toward expertise, Tim would still be in the preliminary stage, acclimation. As James Gee says, "If you have no access to the social practice, you don't get in the discourse, you don't have it" (*Social Linguistics and Literacies* in Smit, p. 181).

And yet, there were clear signs that Tim was at least beginning to understand what historians do when they write and he was trying on that identity rather than writing solely for self-expression, as was the case for the most part in his freshman writing classes. He was beginning to understand how historians take on the rhetorical analysis of historical texts, and through textual analysis, broader social analysis, although he wanted to avoid the "race, gender, class" themes prevalent in much of the discourse in history at the time. Given the overwhelming influence of "school" on students' writing (Bazerman 1997), that Tim made any progress toward legitimate participation in the discourse community of historians is of note.

The relatively small gains in subject matter knowledge over the three-year period suggest the enormity of this aspect of the developmental process. As Alexander (2003) has noted, subject matter knowledge includes both "domain knowledge," referring to "the breadth of knowledge within a field," (p. 11) and topic knowledge, which has to do more with depth of knowledge on a single topic (such as Stalinism). No doubt the breadth requirement of the major (typical for most academic majors in undergraduate education) in some ways delayed gaining topic-specific knowledge and at the same time could not facilitate but a cursory overview of history as a field. Whether Tim's subject matter knowledge grew to a level that educators would find reasonable for undergraduate education cannot be assessed here. It does appear, though, that it may be unreasonable to expect "competence" or "proficiency" (Alexander

2003) in the subject matter in a given discipline even at the end of undergraduate education. Subject matter issues have a direct bearing on overall writing proficiency as well, as the data here demonstrate.

Related to topic knowledge is the strategic knowledge needed to work with a given subject matter, i.e. knowledge of central concepts and appropriate frames of analysis for subject matter. Others have articulated this type of expertise primarily in terms of critical thinking and rhetorical skills: Leinhardt (1994) points to the important critical thinking task of building a "case" in history; Britt (1994) refers to the critical thinking in history similarly as knowing how to construct an argument model. Tim understood and was interested in critical analysis of historical issues even in his freshman year, unlike some undergraduates who opt for simple summaries of materials (Greene 2001). But as Alexander points out, novices often lack the ability to sort out what information is strategic within a domain when they do not yet possess a well-structured grasp of the subject area. This could account for the inappropriateness of some of Tim's attempted arguments in his essays (Augustine and Benedict, and Muscovite Russia, for example). According to Alexander, at the stage of acclimation, learners need explicit guidance from experts in being able to select and structure important subject knowledge. This appears not to have happened in Tim's case, as there was lack of noticeable progress in being able to apply appropriate frames of analysis for his essays even in his upper division courses.

Tim did exhibit some of the behaviors associated with general types of more developed critical thinking skills: there were a few instances of considering opposing points of view in his essays, i.e. generating rival hypotheses (Flower et al. 2000) and his ability to cast light on his writing in hindsight, through retrospective, discourse-based interviews, suggests some ability at least, when prompted, to think meta-cognitively about history and history writing. But without sufficient depth of subject matter knowledge or knowledge of the "ongoing conversations" of the discourse community and the appropriate interpretive frameworks to apply to texts, Tim's ability to write "authentic" historical analyses was hampered.

In addition, there were no discernible signs of sustained progress in building genre knowledge: one essay in which key elements of a genre were demonstrated was followed by an essay in which several key genre features were absent. Features of historical essays that were evidenced in Tim's work and that he could discuss were mostly surface features of the genres—certain stylistic features, and general knowledge of rhetorical and content issues. Other studies confirm that these surface aspects of genre knowledge are acquired first, before acquisition of highly context-specific knowledge of the complex web of interdependent features of a given genre (Beaufort 1999, Eller 1989, Greene 2001, Himley 1986). In fact, Tim did not exhibit by the conclusion of this study some of the specific genre skills others have documented as critical in history writing—use of multiple source texts to support a point (Stahl et al. 1996, Young and Leinhardt 1998), use of source texts in multiple ways (Greene 2001), or use of organizing structures to support causal arguments (Young and Leinhardt 1998). And without understanding the formal features of history genres, it was unlikely that the social purposes of those genres would have been evident to Tim either. Tim was caught, too, in the murky distinctions Tosh points to between the need to explicate and describe versus the need to argue in history writing.

Rhetorical knowledge was demonstrated only in the most rudimentary aspects (writing for the teacher, writing to make an argument) and there was not enough data to document developmental progress (or not) with writing process knowledge. Tim indicated he had a method for accomplishing writing tasks in history by the end of his junior year, but whether or how that method, and the meta-knowledge to use the method, changed over three years the data do not show.

Alexander (2003) has noted that progress in gaining expertise in any domain is complicated by the fact that different areas of mastery are interdependent; hence, progress toward expertise may proceed slowly. This appears to be confirmed by the data in this study. The five knowledge domains each begged for greater mastery in order for expert historical essays to be produced.

It is possible that Tim's limited progress in history writing was unusual for several reasons: he started in his freshman year already strong in general reading-to-write skills and in general critical thinking skills. Was Tim considered "exceptional" by the standards of his teachers from the outset, and hence, not pushed to develop his skills? He was also consciously resisting the discourse community norms in some cases. So individual resistance to discourse norms must also be considered as a possible factor impeding progress toward acclimation.

Furthermore, there is much about the context of Tim's writing in history that remains unknown: how class time was spent for example. Was there any explicit instruction in how to approach writing tasks? Tim

TABLE 8
Analysis of History Teacher Feedback

	Praise	Criticism
Rhetorical purpose		
Content	Good argument (x2) Good synthesis Good analysis (x3) Creative approach (x4) Well-chosen examples	Faulty logic (x2) Faulty interpretive frame (x2) Too speculative Not defining terms
Structure	Best point comes last	Lack of focus
Style	Tightly written	Turgid prose, not clear

reported only one such instance: in his colonial American history class the professor gave some guidance on how to do an in-depth rhetorical analysis of a primary source. Nine of the papers I received do have the teachers' comments. Analysis of those comments reveals the genre feature the professors focused on the most was subject matter, and in a few instances, organization. As Table 8 shows, praise and criticism were fairly equal.

Without more contextual information, what can be concluded about how the context in which Tim was writing might have factored in his limited progress? There was minimal feedback on writing, with one exception, Tim's seminar on Muscovite Russia,[35] and the feedback professors did give was largely focused on content. Another major contributing factor to Tim's lack of progress in history writing is that assignments in lower division courses were roughly equal in difficulty to assignments in upper division seminars in terms of types of rhetorical task, length requirement, and types of reading and analysis expected, so the assignments were not pushing Tim to continue to grow as a writer. And Tim was unclear as to the purpose or genre expected in the tasks assigned. All of these factors could at least in part explain the lack of significant growth in Tim's disciplinary writing skills. The uneven nature of Tim's growth as a writer also suggests that even at advanced levels of literacy, certain "emergent" features of expertise can be within the writer's grasp sometimes but not all the time. Repeated practice and feedback on performance is essential to foster competence (Lajoie 2003). A writing curriculum that consistently, logically fosters developmental growth in writers is also essential.

INSTANCES OF NEGATIVE TRANSFER FROM FRESHMAN WRITING

Cognitive psychologists define "negative transfer" as the situation where knowledge or learning from one context is inappropriately applied in another context. There were some notable instances of negative transfer between writing for Carla's two freshman writing classes and writing in the history classes Tim took that should also be noted:

- The genre of the "essay" in freshman writing was characterized largely as a loose exploration of a topic, whereas in history, for the most part, Tim's professors wanted focused, linear arguments in "essays." Tim did not perceive this difference and received criticisms for failing to writing focused arguments in history. He misinterpreted these criticisms as the teacher's limitations rather than the conventions of the discourse community.

- The focus of essays in history was on textual analysis or comparisons of sources from "objective" points of view, whereas in Carla's freshman writing classes the emphasis was on self-exploration and connecting personal interest to wider social issues. So in two instances where Tim tried personalizing the historical issue—either to a situation in his life, or to a situation he knew of in his professor's personal life, he was rebuffed.

- It was acceptable to state personal opinion without substantial backing from the work of others in Tim's freshman writing essays. Most of Tim's arguments in history were poorly supported and conventions regarding in-text citations were not observed.

- The concept of audience that Tim appropriated from freshman writing was that of a particular individual to be addressed, or group of readers, rather than a discourse community of, say, historians. So he wrote analogies for historical situations, for example, that related to childrearing, because one of his professors he knew had young children, or another, to a political crisis in the news at the time. The professor responded that the analogy was inappropriate to the historical issue under discussion.

Specific skills Tim needed to write effective history essays—ways of incorporating others' ideas, including use of in-text citations as rhetorical tools for supporting one's argument—were not emphasized in freshman writing.

What was gained from freshman writing that could serve Tim as he encountered writing situations requiring different sorts of knowledge and skill? The question remains elusive and troubling. And as we shall see in the next chapter, when Tim had to move into an entirely different discourse community, that of engineering writing, the issue of transfer of learning and benefits from a general skills course in writing become more thorny.

5

SWITCHING GEARS
From History Writing to Engineering

I never used to have patience with techies who would turn up their noses at fuzzy classes but I'm starting to sense why they do. I'm starting to get impatient with people for going on and on about nothing.
　　　　　　　　　　　　　—Tim, two years after college

The first few classes that I took, they were "weeder" classes, so they just cleaned my clock. In response, I just kind of lowered my standard and also kind of held on to history as my, "I don't need that while I have history." Kind of as an excuse. Something to hide behind. . . . Even the individually designed major was something I was hiding behind so I wouldn't have to take classes that I was afraid of.
　　　　　　　　　　　　　—Tim, senior year of college

During autumn quarter, my passion and determination united to bring me out of a slump that had roots in a three-year hiatus from technical studies. At mid-quarter, I was brought to a crisis by my growing desire to pursue advanced smart product design and by my slipping grades. After testing my passion to be certain it was genuine, I dug in my heels and got busy relearning how to learn. By the end of the quarter I turned two failing midterm grades into final exam and project grades of B+, A– and A. That quarter marked a sea change in my approach to studies that will serve me the rest of my engineering career.
　　　　　　　　　　　　　—Tim, graduate school statement of purpose

Junior year of college did in fact bring a "sea change" for Tim as a student and emerging professional engineer. While completing the last few requirements for his history major, he resumed math and science studies and began core courses for a major in mechanical engineering. Spurred by practical concerns—what his livelihood after college would be—he admitted to trepidation when faced with switching from history to the more exact, technical courses in math and science which he had not taken since high school. But he pulled the transition off successfully, in part because of his awareness that what he needed to do was "relearn how to learn." He sought help from classmates, from TAs, from professors during office hours, and ultimately, garnered self-confidence, good grades, and after graduation, a job with a small engineering firm that produces biomedical products for cardiac patients.

But along with the psychological adjustments required for this transition from one academic discipline to another came new varieties of critical thinking and writing: there were new genres to learn and the discourse community's values had to be discerned, as well as the demands of different rhetorical occasions, a vast new subject matter, and the constraints and rewards of collaborative writing processes. But before describing Tim's learning process, I will briefly summarize others' analyses of the particulars of engineering writing, which begins to demonstrate the "sea change" entailed when transitioning from writing in history.

WRITING IN ENGINEERING

More than any other researcher, Dorothy Winsor has pursued issues of learning to write in engineering over the past decade and a half. Winsor's research and the work of others in technical communications have been aimed at the pursuit of theoretical questions of concern to compositionists and rhetoricians—particularly, issues of composing processes used in workplace settings, and rhetorical and social issues associated with text production. Here, I parse this small body of research from the standpoint of the knowledge domains I have identified already: discourse community knowledge, subject matter knowledge, genre knowledge, rhetorical knowledge, and writing process knowledge.

The *discourse community* of engineers has a set of interesting characteristics. Engineers are stereotypically considered to be skilled in math and science and less skilled as communicators. And yet, researchers have found that texts play significant roles in the professional world of engineers—in fact, Winsor (1990) argues that engineers' writing is what signifies their membership in the professional community of engineers. As an engineering colleague told me, "Writing is used to enhance the defining, implementing, and assessing of engineering projects." (Ferguson, personal communication, 2005). Another sign of the significant role of written and oral communications to this discourse community is the fact that these skills are one of the performance measures the Accreditation Board for Engineering and Technology (ABET) requires. Engineering programs teach and assess their students in these areas as a result. And Hagge (1995) notes that the beginning of the 20th century marked increasing professionalization of engineering, which included textbooks that outlined standards for written communications in engineering. One engineering faculty member told me that those on the industry board for his department say they hire engineers first for ability to work well with others, and second, for communications skills. Industry members say that they can train new engineers in technical skills; the other two skills they need to have when they finish school. Another board member told the engineering faculty member, "If a graduate of your school wrote incorrect sentences, I'd fire him and not hire another graduate from your school for a long time."

In spite of these factors, texts (and writing) are viewed ambiguously by inexperienced engineers. On the one hand, the emphasis in engineering is on producing "things," i.e. objects. As Winsor (1990) explains, textual mediation of knowledge is difficult for engineers to accept because they see themselves as working directly on physical objects. And yet, much as in the discourse community of a science lab, there is much interplay between physical objects and texts in engineering. Texts used in the discourse community of engineers also signify social hierarchies. Work orders, written by managers for shop floor technicians, are one such example (Winsor 2000). Winsor says, "The written script of a work order is a kind of fiction describing a simple, logical sequence of actions that the engineer chooses and the technician follows" (p. 176). And yet Winsor and Witte and Haas (2001) found that social hierarchies could also be bridged by collaborative writing projects, in which members of different work groups, with differing levels of social status, shared situated knowledge that no one individual could possess in entirety.

Discourse community goals and values appear to center on texts demonstrating the empirical validity of hard data and the decisions that logically ensue from such data. A chilling analysis of the rhetorical situation of the Challenger space mission points to the fine line between valuing "facts" and valuing persuasion in the engineering discourse community. Engineers rightly advised against the launch of the Challenger space mission because they felt there was an engineering flaw in the spaceship, but their warnings were unheeded by upper management decision-makers. Possibly if they had presented their evidence more persuasively, within a framework that considered the expectations, pressures, and accountability issues upper-level managers faced, the outcome might have been different

(Herndl et al. 1991; Ferguson, personal communication). And Winsor's longitudinal study of four engineers working at one company also confirms, in the words of one of her subjects, that "Engineers tend to prefer saying that they are being convincing rather than persuasive. Persuasion has associations that are not applicable to the relationship between engineers and their readers (1996)." But, Winsor argues, reality may be different than what is publicly acknowledged in the engineering discourse community. She noted from her observation on several engineering firms that documents were frequently written after decisions had already been made, based on partial data, intuition, and tacit knowledge.

Writers' roles in the engineering discourse community are also of note: Texts in engineering are frequently co-authored and collaboratively written, so "originality," or a single author's words are not proprietary. Rather, as Winsor (1989) reports from a case study of an engineer's work in one engineering firm, "Words generated by employees were viewed as reflecting the company's shared insight, not the individual's" (p. 277) and a writer was free to use them and adapt them to his/her own needs. Selzer (1983) found that over half of a proposal one engineer drafted came from other documents. What is valued, from a communications standpoint, is the action that results from the text, rather than the text itself.

Subject matter knowledge in engineering is an interdisciplinary, composite body of knowledge, always changing. Math, physics, and chemistry all inform the multiple branches of engineering (aeronautical, mechanical, electrical, to name a few). Because of the commercial nature of the field as well, engineers also must become cognizant of legal and regulatory statutes that dictate safety standards, protection of patents, and marketplace forces. Even within one branch of engineering, mechanical engineering for example, the range of topics students study is broad: "elements of energy science and technology, propulsion, sensing and control, nano- and micro-mechanics, design, mechatronics, computational simulation, solid and fluid dynamics, micro-electromechanical systems, and biomechanical engineering" (department website at Tim's university). Educational objectives in Tim's engineering program included:

- Understand basic principles, mathematics, science, and mechanical systems, with an ability to analyze, model, synthesize, ideate, iterate, prototype, and implement engineering solutions in a broad range of fields.

- Understand product development and manufacturing and acquire the capability to work effectively in multidisciplinary teams, provide leadership and technical expertise, and serve as effective communicators.

As in history, the amount of subject matter to be grasped in engineering was immense.

Genres in engineering are those both of business (memos, complaint letters, orders, reports, etc.) and technical fields: the technical documentation manual, the project proposal, the logbook. As in architecture (Medway 2000), "text" in engineering also entails an integration of visual diagrams, charts, and narrative. In fact, engineering students take courses in drafting and visual thinking along with their math and science courses. Even the formats of typical engineering documents suggest a different handling of texts from both reader's and writer's vantage points: documents are visually organized so as to be reference tools and to allow non-linear reading (Miller 1998). Miller also points to the need for some repetition of information in sections of reports, in order for sections to "stand alone" and make sense to readers who are not reading the entire document. Information in technical genres is also layered, again, to facilitate different readers' needs and non-linear reading. For example, a great deal of detailed information will be put in separate appendices rather than in the body of the text so as to not bog down the reader who does not need those details.

What is *not* common in engineering genres is the long prose passage typical of essays in the humanities (including history). "It is bashed into their heads," an engineering colleague told me, "to be short and to the point. They are writing up the chain and executives do not want to read past the first page" (Kincaid, personal communication). Presentation graphics (PowerPoint) is now another important communication skill engineers need.

It is also of interest to note that an analysis of the standards for engineering discourse set forth in early style manuals for engineering writing emphasized norms that are still held today: technical vocabulary that is impersonal and objective, accurate and unambiguous, and maximally efficient; headings and sub-heads that aid the reader in quickly grasping the material, and yet, on the other hand, for letters and informal reports to audiences other than engineers, a more natural, speech-based register (Hagge 1995).

As for *rhetorical issues* in engineering writing, composition specialists have been able to identify several typical rhetorical occasions for writing: writing to coordinate work activities among differing groups, writing to describe future actions for others to take, writing to "fix an account of {one's} past actions" (i.e. writing for self-protection) (Winsor 1999). And as for rhetorical strategies valued or accepted in the discourse community, in spite of some in engineering perceiving their written communications as arhetorical, Winsor found that cost and marketability were the two common persuasive strategies used (1996). She also notes the purposes behind one of the predominant stylistic choices—use of passive voice:

> Passive voice slows down reading, lessens comprehension, and . . . may make assigning responsibility for actions difficult because it removes the actor from the scene. So why do engineers, who are great believers in efficiency, use it? One reason might be that removing the actor or knower is a rhetorical move by which an engineer removes himself from sight and thus increases the believability of his or her findings (1992).

As we have seen, the issue of the O-ring seals on the Challenger space shuttle was at least in part a rhetorical issue. Herndl et al. (1991) report, "The warrants of each set of interests, or social groups, were insufficient to the other" (p. 302). Rhetorical issues in engineering discourse can have a major impact not just on manufacturing and economic outcomes, but on the safety of human lives as well.

As for *writing processes* of engineers, several studies have documented that there is no single model of the ways in which engineers produced texts. Selzer (1983) observed that one engineer composed a routine progress report in linear fashion, with little revision or recursive drafting. In most cases, the format of documents are fixed by the company, which influences the ways in which engineers approach writing tasks. Winsor (1989) observed documents being drafted and then revised by committees through several iterations. Sometimes the composing process is a single engineer's responsibility, but often, projects are jointly written, with different individuals or departments contributing to the final document. Also of note: several studies of the pre-writing stages of drafting have documented the use of lists, notes, post-its, diagrams (Winsor 1994), and even hand gestures in face-to-face meetings (Witte and Haas 2001) as tools for generating thinking that led to the final written product. Writing was a tool in these instances for thinking and creating solutions to problems, not just a tool for reporting.

DEVELOPMENT PROCESSES OF NOVICE WRITERS IN ENGINEERING

A few studies have documented engineering students' issues with learning to write in ways appropriate to the discourse community. Herrington (1985) observed and described the social contexts for writing in two chemical engineering classes as having two very different purposes for writing and differing roles for writers as a result. In the lab courses, purposes for writing included learning the basics of the discipline and displaying knowledge. In the design course, the purpose of writing was to discover solutions to unresolved problems in the "real world." Lines of reasoning in the lab and design reports produced for these two classes differed as well, and students and faculty did not share common perceptions of standards for effective writing.

Winsor (1996) conducted a longitudinal study of four engineering students during school and in their cooperative education assignments in an engineering firm. All but one of the students felt engineering writing was arhetorical from the beginning to end of their studies, although two did mention audience more frequently in interviews at the end of their studies. But the students primarily felt that their purposes in writing were "simply" to analyze data, leaving persuasive tasks to their managers (in the workplace internships). Also of note: as Freedman found in business classes (Freedman et al. 1994), Winsor (1994) found that even in an internship situation or in an assignment for a "real client," engineering students wrote their final reports primarily for teachers. Winsor found that students mimicked the language of the models for reports, without understanding the rhetorical import of that language. In a follow-up study (Winsor 1999), when the students were now employees of the engineering firm, Winsor found that their understanding of purposes for writing (for example, to document actions and protect themselves from possible recriminations) increased. The students-now-employees also experienced the conflicting needs of different discourse communities or activity networks—for example, the discourse communities of labor relations (internal), of the company at large, and of the national union employees were members of.

I turn now to the data from Tim's engineering classes his junior and senior years of college, as well as data from a follow-up interview conducted when Tim had the added perspective of two years of work experience in a small engineering firm. Because of the dramatic shifts from his perceptions while in school and afterwards, on-the-job, I will contrast these two settings throughout the report.

A NOVICE IN THE *DISCOURSE COMMUNITY* OF ENGINEERS

Because "discourse community" is a concept that encompasses all of the other categories of expert knowledge I explicate here, what I choose to isolate as discourse community knowledge is not meant to limit the multiple dynamics of what is going on, but rather to parse the complexities of the communicative situation in useful ways. As in the previous chapter, it seems most valuable to focus on the underlying values and goals of the discourse community and how those goals are typically realized through and influence communicative processes and the social roles of writers.

More empirical than philosophical, engineering requires exactness, specificity, and "hard" data of its community members both in their thinking and writing. The importance of these characteristics will become evident in Tim's experiences with writing for engineering.

Then: The Discourse Community In School

The writing tasks Tim showed me from his engineering course work were all based on "real-world" instances of unresolved technical problems. Here are the projects he shared:

- A review of literature on modulating reflecting systems and recommendation for design of a "close-proximity communications system"

- A proposed design of a soil moisture sensor system/automated irrigation system

- Design of a "planetary rover" for space explorations

- Design of a "down-converter" to convert high-frequency signals transmitted from cellular phones into lower frequencies

In the case of the "down-converter" design, the professor had elicited the engineering request from a local manufacturing company. The company was anticipating greatly expanding its business and needed a more streamlined, cost-effective way to manufacture greater quantities of this item. For the report on this project, collaboratively produced as four team members, Tim wrote the introduction (seven pages, double-spaced) and four pages of detailed discussion of the design. In the discourse community of engineers then, purposes for writing pertain to documenting solutions to physical, material problems.

But enroute to these outcomes, for Tim, there had to be a shift in epistemology and development of different types of critical thinking in order to fulfill the discourse community's expectations. Here is how he explained this shift:

T: I was having a real academic crisis, and this [engineering] profes-
      sor, he was helping me with the classes I was in with him, and umm,
      at one point, he just kind of turned around, and he said, you know
      what your problem is, you believe yourself too easily. [laughing]

A: He said that to you?

T: [laughing] Yeah, it was great. I was like, wow, I like hearing this kind
      of feedback. And I was like, what do you mean? . . . He told me . . .
      And so, that taught me, that felt like kind of an assault, not on his
      part, but in general, like an assault for the whole crisis upon my
      style of thinking because it seemed to be demanding of me that I be
      detailed, a master of details, which I freely admit I'm not. I haven't
      become that, *but I have learned to value the thing over my opinion. In his-
      tory pretty much, you know, you can make any point you want as long as you
      make it well.* And you get an A, you know . . . In engineering, well, you
      can make your point as well as you want, but if you're wrong, you're
      wrong ([laughs] . . . And I think, actually, that's true in history too,
      but, or should be perhaps, but you can kind of play fast and loose
      with the details and kind of keep the customer tracking with you so
      that they end with your conclusion. If they sat down and thought
      about it, they might have come up with something else they like bet-
      ter. But you don't have to satisfy them as completely as because there's
      this kind of subjectivism, kind of relativism . . .

A: So is engineering more exact?

T: Yeah. I mean, at least . . . when you need to be exact, you need to be
      exact, and when you don't, you don't . . . There's certain things that
      you have to be exact about like will it break, and you have to consider
      all the different ways it might break . . . But as far when you get into
      kind of the design, well, there's different ways of making it so it won't
      break.

                                   — Tim, interview senior year of college

Given the work in recent years in the philosophy and rhetoric of science (Bazerman 1982, Bazerman 1988, Latour and Woolgar 1979), we know that scientific work is not solely a matter of creating factual evidence. Even Tim can begin to discern when the "truth" in engineering is absolute (will this break?) versus subjective (is this the best design?). But he recognizes that his thinking and decision-making and rhetoric need to be grounded in precise, empirically based data. There is less room for subjectivity of interpretation in engineering than in history and detailed analysis is a necessary path to informed and believable proposals. This was his first insight into the discourse community he was entering.

The need for precision in his thinking process was echoed in the norms for written texts in engineering. When his professor gave out an outline for the sections the design report must contain, Tim was chagrined. There was not much room for creativity in form or in style. But at least, in talking to me his senior year, he could rationalize the standards, as he explains in the following comments:

> You don't have a need, since you're talking about, I don't know, particle physics, you don't have a need to really beef it up and make it sound a little, any smarter. It's already going to. You want to keep it simple because you already have enough tough stuff in there.
>
> Style would be clarity in this context. It would be like, if it's clear, it's understandable. You can easily find your way through the report and understand what it's doing, then that's good.
>
> —Tim, interview senior year of college

I will parse the genre knowledge Tim accrued as he began his work in engineering in a later section, but here, note the norms for writing that are embodiments of the community's values: keep it simple; be clear; be concise; follow standard formats. Easy, quick reading of texts, as well as accuracy of information were the paramount concerns that shaped the genres in engineering, and professors assigned those forms that would help novices such as Tim communicate with credibility in the community.

Tim began, then, to pick up the norms of the discourse community in engineering, perhaps because of his professor's feedback, and perhaps because the differences from history writing were so striking. But as in freshman writing and in history, there was the added social context of school which influenced Tim's approaches to writing tasks for professors—in spite of the real-world purposes for writing, in spite of actual "clients" for at least one of the projects ("down converter" project). Tim told me, "We kind of joke about it and say that the thicker {the report} is, you know, the better. . . . We were joking about let's just add a bunch of stuff. Another time he told me, "{The professors} enjoy it if one of their students wins the competition. . . . We were like, you know, it's a lid" (laughing). Two years after college Tim told me:

> You have to kind of manufacture this stuff. They have that all-important grade you know. In the introduction class for chemical engineering they make you do your logbook and they grade you heavily on how much you put in . . . not the quality, how great the ideas are, not how many different methods you use or how interesting it is to read . . . Some people do it all the night before, they stack up ten different colors of pens to try to make it look like they did it {over time}.

As I will show in the next section, Tim's view of written discourse in engineering, particularly its larger social purposes, changed considerably when he was out of school and in his first engineering job. And, as my engineering colleague pointed out to me, professors cannot fire their students. Students are told what industry standards are for written communications, but remain skeptical. Even though the writing tasks assigned in engineering courses were aimed to simulate real-word practices of the discourse community, the immediate social purpose of the task was getting a good grade rather than continued employment and good standing with one's colleagues. But nonetheless, the forms of discourse that Tim would encounter in the workplace would look familiar.

Then: The Discourse Community In the Workplace

> One of my professors said, you know what your problem is, you believe yourself too easily . . . I would make a quick cut and decide that's the way I'm gonna look at it and just race, and let assumptions sneak in and not question them and end up with an answer . . . It's only recently that I've begun to see exactly what the difference is and how I can use . . . I'm not sure I'm even to the point of knowing how to foster both and knowing how to turn one on and turn one off but I think I see the difference.
>
> —Tim, two years after college

Like the students Winsor followed from school (and co-op work experiences) into their first jobs as engineers, Tim found himself deepening his understandings of the reasons for practices his teachers had introduced students to. The company Tim went to work for designed mechanical devices that would be inserted into human bodies. Lives were clearly at stake when engineers designed, tested, and manufactured these devices. Tim could see, instantly, that the work must be accomplished with precision or there would be serious legal ramifications for the company.

In addition to the care he was required to take with his work, his writing, too, had to conform to the same standards of thoroughness and precision. A number of comments in this follow-up interview after he had been in an engineering job for two years suggested his increasing awareness of the "whys" for the means of communication of the discourse community and the social purposes for texts. Here are some comments from Tim that signal the reality of the discourse community norms in the workplace that couldn't have been replicated in a school environment:

> [Writing is] very frustrating. It's very detailed. There's many more drafts than I've ever done before, much more exhaustive peer review and the peers are not very stable so you have to show the thing to them once and they'll have their comments, if you show the same thing to them the next day they'd have different comments. So when you incorporate the comments and send it back to them it's still not done . . . it's a good opportunity for me to consider whether it's just that I'm not writing it in the right way that'd just wow them . . . I think it's mostly I'm convinced it's the nature of the industry, um, the medical industry is heavily regulated . . . you have to be so sure about everything, never assume anything, and this job taught me even more *not* to believe myself . . . it's not a screwdriver, it breaks you throw it away, get another one you know . . .
>
> The peer review seemed kind of artificial in class, you know . . . how much do they know what good writing is . . . in what I'm doing now, that's the way it is. You don't want to be done with it until other people have read it . . . protect yourself for one thing . . . you wanna make sure you're understood. You're too involved in it to read it the way someone else would. Legal and also if you're trying to convince people this is the direction we should go, you wanna make sure you sound, you answered the questions. Often if you make one change in one document it might affect all the other documents for the entire product, which would be six documents possibly so it's a lot of work initiating an engineering change notice, . . . something we've come to groan at.
>
> —Tim, two years after college

Through the gradual understanding of norms for writing and purposes for written documents in the workplace and immersion in writing processes required by the organization, Tim became aware, at least tacitly, of discourse community goals, values, and norms. Writing not only got work done; it had legal ramifications as well. The writing is high stakes—it becomes a necessary "by-product" of the actual material objects being manufactured to keep the company financially solvent, and out of the courts. As he says, "You have to be so sure about everything, never assume anything." Peer review is now meaningful. And the fact of "controlled documents" means five or six individuals who have contributed to the text sign their names on the last page, signifying that they stand behind the accuracy of what is written. Tim's comment about having to make changes in five or six documents if a change is made in one document is an example of what Devitt (1991) identified as "sets of genres" that function synergistically within the discourse community.

And there were social ramifications for the writer as well: he talks about negotiating ideals orally "because you might be off base and you don't wanna have your name on it. You wanna kind of check with some people." He only wants his name on a document if he knows his ideas are sound. There is communal negotiation of ideas and of what ultimately gets signed off. In addition, the writing must be accomplished quickly: there is not a lot of time to attend to the writing, nor will readers want to spend lengthy amounts of time "consuming" the documents produced. Tim estimated that he spent approximately an hour a day writing—or one full day every two weeks. Tim is also learning what needs to be communicated orally versus what needs to get put in writing, and what process helps the aims be accomplished efficiently.

In sum, though Tim's professors gave him the genres of the discourse community in course assignments, they could not replicate the social dynamics of the discourse community of "real-world" engineering: the critical role of texts in assuring the smooth operation of production, the importance of accuracy and detail in the writing as much as in the physical processes of manufacturing the products, the communal negotiations of what would become "best practices" through written documentation. Much of Tim's understanding of the practices of the discourse community in engineering could only come in his first job.

LEARNING THE *SUBJECT MATTER* OF ENGINEERING

Specifications are pretty tight . . . there were all these problems. The biggest engineering problem was that we could never make anything . . . We had to do everything on paper . . . complicated geometry.

—Tim's description of a class project

Even engineers need pictures . . . drawings, photocopies of material properties from handbooks, from the manufacturers, calculations . . . Often when you start talking about an idea, often people are like I can't see that, draw it, let's do draw . . . it's kind of a fun way of thinking. . . . they [professors] taught us a whole bunch of brainstorming techniques . . . one would be use letters of the alphabet, so use C, everything that starts with C . . . write it down, see where it takes you . . . ME 101: it's called Visual Thinking, Then the next one is ambidextrous thinking, which is a graduate version of the same thing . . . different drawing techniques, like how to express your ideas effectively in drawing like some had never drawn before.

—Tim, two years after college

Then: Subject Matter in School

Tim told me he started with a handicap in learning the subject matter of engineering. He had not taken calculus or physics in high school. And the subjects that must be mastered in engineering are numerous: Introduction to Electronics, Programming Methodology, Applied Mechanics, Thermodynamics, Introductory Fluids Engineering, Fluid Mechanics, Dynamic Systems, Heat Transfer, Mechanical Systems, Engineering Design, and Manufacturing and Design is just a partial list of required courses. Tim's first midterms and projects in engineering his junior year earned failing grades.

But Tim's steep learning curve to acquire the subject matter of engineering was not just because of a lack of the knowledge of these subjects. He also needed to change his habits of thinking. As we have heard, Tim quickly found that the subject matter of engineering—and the type of thinking required—was more detail-oriented than in history. The latter Tim characterized as "playing fast and loose" with ideas. But in engineering, thoroughness, precision, thinking through all possible solutions to a problem before choosing one, and then being able to explain the logic of the chosen solution—these were the habits of mind Tim had to acquire.

For example, when explaining the write-up of the design project, Tim noted that while the main part of the report included only the proposed solution to the manufacturing problem, the appendices included all of the other options they had considered, and the reasons those options had been rejected. Whereas history allowed for several plausible interpretations of events and there were no serious consequences if one's interpretation were less well accepted, in engineering a "best" alternative was a part of the discourse community's norms for action.

But Tim's comment that one of the assignments in the course Visual Thinking was to "think of everything that begins with C" suggests another of the properties of critical thinking essential to engineering: being able to look at problems from multiple angles in a brainstorming mode. Also, as Tim's comments above show, engineering combined computational skills, logic, and visual thinking. Tim talked about "Visual Thinking," a required course, enthusiastically. He saw the immediate application in solving the design problems required in his course work. Looking at diagrams, creating diagrams, even, if circumstances allowed, creating three-dimensional mock-ups of designs was an aid to thinking that could not be accomplished simply verbally. He found it exciting to learn how to represent three-dimensional objects, how to quickly represent people, etc. Tim's reports of the visual element of engineering thinking echo what Medway (2000) found with architects: verbal descriptions can only go so far. Then, the visual record—the architectural sketch, the engineering diagram—must be added in order to accurately record the fine details and aid communication in these fields.

I do not know how stellar Tim's record was with his engineering courses. But the design project he and three others collaborated on (which, I surmise, Tim took a lead role in accomplishing) did garner the professor's praise and his prompting them to enter a nationally sponsored engineering design competition for students.

Now: Subject Matter in the Workplace

> It's typically the content that people are concerned about. Sometimes words that I'll use will have a meaning that I don't intend that would be troublesome down the road . . . 'validate' versus 'qualify.' Those are very different things . . . there's a whole kind of school on how to validate stuff and then qualify would be part of validation.
>
> —Tim, two years after school

The medical industry is heavily regulated . . . you have to be so sure about everything, never assume anything, and this job taught me even more not to believe myself. Even if I learned that once in school then . . . I learned it again at another level.

—Tim, two years after school

The question is how do you know that machine works and they say we've used five different machines and they all give us basically the same result. And that would convince most people but like after this experience I would say yeah but have those machines been calibrated, what's the actual data you got from those machines, and how do you know what the data means, does it mean a rivet, have you ever tested this machine under similar conditions with and without rivets.

—Tim, two years after school

So let's say you've proven it, you prove everything which is a lot of work but under the circumstances it's worth it, it's a medical device and it's staying in people's bodies so you wanna be sure it's not gonna be the source of a problem . . . it's not a screwdriver, it breaks you throw it away, get another one you know.

—Tim, two years after school

Of course, subject matter learning did not stop after school. I have only traces of what Tim was learning in his first job after engineering school, but enough to confirm that he was indeed building engineering knowledge. Sometimes, it was the wrong word chosen—"validate" instead of "qualify"—that triggered learning. The other example, his hypothetical questioning of someone's rationale for a course of action, "Yeah, but has it been calibrated?" suggests his deepening understanding both of the importance of "hard data" and of doing thinking that includes brainstorming and testing out of all possible options before committing resources and certainty to a plan of action. As he says about working with medical equipment that will be surgically implanted in individuals' bodies, ". . . it's not just a screwdriver." He has learned at another level what it means to be thorough, precise, and analytic in the process of doing the work of engineering. The importance of knowing his subject well has been driven home. And, again, a small comment in reference to his engineering log, "I'm in over my head . . . if I don't write it down it's gonna get lost, I'll have to do it again . . ." suggests the learning demands of the job and the usefulness of writing as a tool to aid his thinking and learning on-the-job.

Also, he's still trying after two years to understand what the differences are between engineering and the type of thinking he associates with historical studies—the one more precise and empirical, the other less data-driven, and more in the realm of "pure ideas." He senses a place for both, although he cannot yet articulate how or when to use these different styles of thinking he has learned in history and engineering. And visual diagrams, as in school, prove essential to getting the work of engineering done on the shop floor.

It is clear that acquisition of subject matter knowledge doesn't stop at the end of school; in fact, probably learning never stops if one is geared to continual learning and increasing of skills. School set Tim on a path of thinking like an engineer and understanding the broad principles in a number of subject areas; in the workplace, that knowledge became more specialized and attached to authentic tasks.

GAINING *GENRE KNOWLEDGE* IN ENGINEERING

The complex social dynamics of writing in engineering and subject matter complexities already demonstrate a different discourse community than that Tim experienced in freshman writing or in his history courses. It is in the examination of the text themselves—the genres of engineering—that we can see the differences most tangibly.

Then: Genres Knowledge in School

> Here it was a series of questions that the TA gave us. So the structure was kind of given to us boom, boom, boom, boom investigate all these issues. We just basically went one to ten or eleven and just addressed all those things. And within those sections there was organization but not of the whole paper.
>
> —Tim, junior year (referring to soil moisture project)

Project proposals and reports of design projects were the two genres Tim was expected to learn in school. He was also introduced to the logbook, which could be "manufactured" the night before due, or, if the student chose, could be used as a real tool for writing to think through engineering problems. Unlike Tim's history professors, his engineering professors gave their students a definitive structure for the writing they would be expected to do. Tim's comments suggest, though, that just being handed a list of questions to guide one's thinking or writing, or a list of the sections in a design proposal was not enough. He went down the list of questions the professor gave him and answered them without any particular understanding of an overall purpose behind the questions, or how to create a connection between sections of a proposal, or a sense of how form and function might be connected in the genre of the engineering product design proposal.

What did appear to be very clear to Tim from the start in engineering was that a very different set of stylistic or sentence-level features was expected. Clarity and conciseness were all important, and what Tim referred to as "aesthetics" were not. These comments are consistent with the small amount of research suggesting that sentence-level genre features are acquired first (Beaufort 1999, Himley 1986). Tim also equated the need for clarity and conciseness with the density of the subject matter, and sensed, rightly, that one did not need to "put on airs" so to speak in engineering: just getting the complexities of the subject matter across clearly was a worthy-enough stylistic goal.

Tim's comments about writing in engineering at the end of his senior year suggest some progress in learning the discourse community's genres during his two years of engineering coursework. Here is a sampling of comments that suggest increasing understanding of the genres of engineering, and in particular, the social purposes of the particular formal features of the genres:

> They basically give us an outline which is standard in the industry . . . these reports all have their kind of standard formats otherwise people would just be, 'cause you could write forever. . . . There is not a whole lot of creativity in deciding on how to organize it, but I guess working with your information and the given outline, how to get it across . . . What I didn't like about the previous report [I did] was that it wasn't clearly delineated . . . By looking at it you couldn't tell what was introduction, what was objectives, what was background. It was all kind of mish-mashed in there together. So for me, making it clear meant sticking to the purpose of each section.
>
> —Tim, senior year

> The other thing is that because you also know so much, it can be difficult to decide where you're going to put information. I mean realistically, a lot of the stuff could go in different parts, so how do you decide what goes where? We didn't want a lot of redundancy. We had a fair amount in the previous report . . . That's okay because there's a certain benefit to reviewing the material for the reader, but it also seems kind of sloppy
>
> —Tim, senior year

It was a tough job [laughs] to kind of integrate everything and make sure it all agrees.

—Tim, senior year

The biggest thing I learned regarding writing for engineering—the bullet. It's option eight on the Mac keyboard. . . . basically not because they were so great in themselves, but they were a tool to kind of break it down and make it simple and make it easy to follow . . . So you don't have to follow the five sentence paragraph format 'cause one sentence is clear . . . and headings . . . This is broken up to introduction one page, project objectives one page, background one page. A lot of open space. Headings so you can kind of get a feel for what's being talked about without actually reading . . . So you can read it on different levels.

—Tim, senior year

Aesthetics are not a primary concern, but "lines must be clean and the surface must be printable"—"Lines must be clean" is like, that sounds cool. It's not poetic, but it sounds cool.

—Tim, senior year

By the end of his senior year, Tim saw the advantages of the preset structure his professors had given for engineering proposals and reports. One of his earlier reports he was now critiquing for its lack of clearly delineated sections.[36] He spoke of the formal features of the genre in terms of the readers' needs—headings to allow the reader to skim, and content that indicated a thorough analysis of possible solutions had been done, but that highlighted clearly the proposed solution. He found the bullet point approach to conveying information (rather than in paragraphs) a useful tool for thinking as well as a way to accomplish coverage of information more concisely. And again, he was clear that "aesthetics are not a primary concern," referring to imaginative or clever turns of phrase or word choice. And yet, on the other hand, he felt information could go in one of several sections of a design report, which is indicative of not yet fully understanding the deep structure of the genre in relation to rhetorical moves and reader needs.

An examination of Tim's engineering reports produced in his junior and senior years corroborates the growth in genre knowledge conveyed in his interviews with me. The earliest writing sample I received, "Soil Moisture Sensor and Automated Irrigation System," shows a number of signs of going through the instructor's list of points that needed to be covered without a sense of how to integrate the information into a coherent text. The report begins with a page and a half overview, followed by these sections: customer profile and desired specifications, related technologies under patent, a list of "other citations," and finally, "the preferred design." Except for the overview section, the rest of the proposal is written exclusively using underlined headings, and bulleted lists (often in the form of sentence fragments). There are no transitions between sections. And, at the end of the report, in the "preferred design" section, there is a curious rhetorical move. I quote:

> The latter option will be incorporated into this sensor for two reasons:
> (1) I understand it, and
> (2) I thought of it.
> If it doesn't work well, I can always just wire up the capacitance-to-frequency converter.

This passage is indicative of Tim's novice status in the discourse community of engineering, and, as well, his sense of audience (the professor, not the client).

And the introduction to the report has the ring of one of his history essays: "The problem of knowing when and how much to water the crops has accompanied nearly all of human agricultural civilizations. Through the centuries, learned wisdom has been passed down to direct the cultivation of foodstuffs. The European heritage is not rich in this respect however . . . "And even at the sentence level, there is an awkwardness to the phrasing that is uncharacteristic of Tim's writing in freshman writing or in history. For example, he writes: "The small volume reduces the trustworthiness of the data and requiring a number of sensors." And yet, on the other hand, there is considerable technical information conveyed in order to propose the appropriate automated sensor system that would trigger irrigation of farmland: ways of measuring soil moisture, the specific electronics entailed in a soil sensor device (infrared thermometry, neutron probes, capacitance, etc.), and mathematical equations to justify the design of the sensor recommended. After looking over Tim's school writing, my engineering colleague said, "I've seen this before," implying that this level of work was typical for engineering students.

In his senior year, Tim collaborated with three other students on the design of a down converter for transforming high frequency signals at cellular base stations to lower frequencies. This project was undertaken for a local manufacturing company, at the company's request. The design the company was currently using was too costly and time-consuming to produce in mass quantities, and a burgeoning cellular phone market prompted the need for mass production of this unit. Tim wrote eleven and a half pages of the final report on the proposed product design: the introduction (including project objectives, background, design specifications and method of approach), a functional description of the recommended design, manufacturing issues, and a more detailed discussion of the product design.

Unlike the soil sensor proposal Tim wrote in his junior year, this senior project proposal has more of the genre features of a professional engineer's writing: prose paragraphs are used to introduce sections followed by more detailed, bulleted information; sections of the report fit together logically in a sequence that allows the reader to follow easily, the recommended solution is given right after the introduction, followed by more detail and rationale, rather than coming at the end of the report as was the case in the soil sensor proposal. The register is formal—"To shield against electromagnetic interference, the cover will be chemically metallized . . ."—and there is no awkward syntax. Perhaps "metalllized" is not the way an engineer would express the idea of giving a device a metal covering, but for the most part, Tim is using appropriate nomenclature and is showing greater mastery of the form, styles, and rhetorical moves necessary in the engineering proposal genre. The gains in genre knowledge in two years' time are notable. He is understanding more fully the genres' intended social functions and the ways in which content, structure, and style of the genre were intended to support the genres' purposes.

Now: Learning Genres in the Workplace

What Tim talked about most when I asked about his workplace writing were the purposes and conventions of the genres he routinely wrote. Here are a few of his comments about the genre activity in his workplace setting that suggest what he's learned:

> There's a published format for every kind of document and at first when I heard that I was like that's terrible how bureaucratic is that, but if it weren't there, it would just be impossible to read anything anybody wrote. Everyone would look different, you wouldn't know what it was you're looking at until

the end . . . I'm in an engineering world, everyone will understand what I write, but they don't . . . a lot of them are from different disciplines . . . so you do have to explain a lot . . . you find someone who's responsible for regulatory affairs, and that person is basically concerned with OK, when an auditor comes.

***

I wouldn't have known that your typical manufacturing company would have standard forms for these five different documents . . . I used to be asked, "Do you have a protocol for this?" I used to look at them and say, "Well, I'm doing it. . . . what do you mean protocol?" And they'd say "procedure, we have a way of doing things." They mean a written, officially signed off, something you put your John Henry, Hancock to . . . it makes your product easier to move from R&D to manufacturing . . . So you spend a little extra time in your logbook explaining what you're doing and drawing. I've pulled up way more logbooks than I've ever before at this place.

***

These [procedures] are controlled documents signed off by five or six people and they can't change . . . so that's procedures and then the other would be studies, that would be protocols, which would be how we are going to do this study and the report from what we found . . . and those again would be signed off by those people so that you know they've seen it, they agree with how you went about it and know what your results are.

***

Procedures don't have bullets. They would have numbers . . . everything is point by point . . . you don't do more than one thing on a line . . . paragraphs boy that would kill no that doesn't always hold like in a report or a study you'll end up with paragraphs and they usually make people's eyes roll back into their heads and they fall asleep and fall over.

***

I write memos, email, and some of those require some thought and preparation and peer review. Some are quick, dirty, disorganized, get the main points out there, let people organize them. Then there's the procedure, which is basically authoring how we make a product and all the directions for making a product . . . that's written typically with an operator in mind.

—Tim, two years after collage

Perhaps most striking about Tim's expanded genre knowledge in engineering at this point are: 1) the expanded repertoire of genres he's now writing (operating protocols, emails, quick memos as well as proposals and reports), 2) the very concrete sense of audience needs, and 3) a sense of expediency—genres are means to an end, rather than ends in themselves. All during school, even through his engineering coursework, Tim wanted to feel a sense of individual authorship, a sense of creativity and "artistic expression" in his work. But it is clear from his accounts of workplace writing that even if he did not particularly think a document was well-written, he would sacrifice his own sense of good writing for the sake of getting the action he wanted. This was a huge step for one who prized aesthetics and creativity so strongly: he had acceded his personal need for self-expression for the sake of participating effectively in the discourse community of his workplace.

Since the audiences for Tim's workplace writing were all internal to his company, he could learn and respond to their needs as readers in an immediate way. He appeared to understand the role and mindset of the production line workers, as well as the mindset of the legal and regulatory experts in the company who would need to sign off on the documents. And he had to juggle their competing needs as he crafted documents. The standardizing of formats for technical documents also made more sense to him now that he saw that there were multiple readers who needed to be able to read the documents at multiple levels of understanding and processing. He also articulated what he thought were genres' relative importance within the discourse community— which genres required careful attention (those that were "controlled documents") and those that could be dashed off and not even well organized (emails, quick memos).

And even the logbook, which Tim was introduced to in school, became a more meaningful tool both for accomplishing work and for personal reflection. Tim was able to write more informally in his logbook, he explained, even though it was technically a legal document "owned" by the company, because he was not working on projects that entailed new patents. Pages from his logbook that were relevant to particular projects could be signed and copied to be included as appendices in reports. Here is his explanation of the genre of the engineering logbook:

Tim: . . . now I was pretty good at logbooks in R&D but here I'm much better now, like everything goes in a logbook . . .

Anne: What makes it better?

Tim: Probably not having a desk, and also being in over my head and knowing that if I don't write it down, it's gonna get lost, I'll have to do it again, and also you just get comfortable with it and it becomes a pleasant place to be, like, I do stuff that's not even work related in here . . . write songs . . . what am I gonna do today . . . in school I learned that they thought it was important . . . often when you start talking about an idea, often people are like I can't see that, draw it, let's draw . . . it's kind of a fun way of thinking . . . It's a bound book so you can't take anything out of it and if you paste something in you have to sign across the edge and date it, and down at the bottom you want to put your John Hancock and have somebody witness it . . . if I do a study and I have data that I've collected then I'll have everything witnessed and signed so we can just photocopy that and throw it in a report as backup, I mean, you have to prove everything you know.

Here we see form and function complementing each other and a writer who understands not only the genre's form, but also the social purposes that the form serves. This is a huge leap forward from the school practice of creating a logbook the night before it was due—i.e. responding to the writing of a logbook as school genre (". . . some people do it all the night before, they stack up ten different colors of pens to try to make it look like they did it at different times.")

Because of the confidential (i.e. competitive) nature of Tim's work, he felt comfortable sharing only a few documents with me: two technical reports of inspections of new manufacturing equipment, one protocol for ongoing inspections of the same equipment, and a memo to eight colleagues arguing for refined procedures and standards for cosmetic inspections of equipment. But from these documents I can begin to corroborate the genre knowledge conveyed in his conversations with me and assess where he might still need some deeper understanding of the genres' functions and standards.

Standard formats are used for the two technical reports. They are assigned document numbers and the visual formatting is identical: lots of white space, a numbering system for sections of the report, boldfaced headings for each section, underlined headings for sub-sections, and charts incorporated into the body of the documents. Also, both technical reports begin with these sections: purpose, tools and equipment, personnel, procedures; both include a "conclusions" section. In the body of each report, there are different sections that reflect the variations in content of the two reports. But both reports are similar in register: language is formal, technical, even obscure. ("This validation demonstrates that the operator performing visual inspection and taking necessary measurements can determine to a high degree of accuracy whether or not the strut is within tolerance.") Passive voice is predominant, suggesting a lack of human agency, with the exception of a few phrases that stand out for their irregularities. For example, this phrase—"Our own calculation coincides with theirs; we accept their calibration certificate at face value" —is in marked contrast to sentences like this one: "This figure is arrived at by taking measurements of gradations on an extremely consistent, generally two-dimensional glass scale." Or, "In conclusion, the equipment and operators are found to have met the requirements of TR-0074."

Another syntactic feature that removes any traces of human agency is the personification of inanimate objects, as in this sentence that begins: "This test demonstrates with confidence that . . ." In sum, these technical reports appear to follow standardized formats and the content is technical and specific to the particular work site. And yes, bullets are used heavily to get as much information across as succinctly as possible and in a manner that allows the reader to skim key points. It is also notable that logbooks are referenced for evidence to support claims, and pages from logbooks are copied and included in appendices.

The operating procedures memo has the same visual features as the technical reports: the use of numbers and bold-faced titles for each section, use of charts, and ample white space. The only differences are the use of imperative verb forms to indicate actions to be taken, and the break down of the steps for the inspection procedure into a separate section, with a separate number (4.1.1, 4.1.2, etc.).

The internal memo is addressed to eight individuals in Tim's work group, including the operations manager, the manufacturing/quality manager, the manufacturing engineer, the technical manager, and the quality assurance-regulatory affairs manager. The purpose of the memo is to persuade Tim's colleagues that another protocol needs to be established for cosmetic appearance of the equipment being manufactured other than the protocol that has been proposed. There is ample white space, sections of the memo are introduced with underlined headings, and bulleted points are used in addition to very short paragraphs (in some cases, one sentence long). But unlike the technical reports and the operating procedures document, this memo uses a much more informal register. There is agency: "I have reviewed . . ." "I agree substantially . . ." "I disagree heartily . . ." "I would label these photos . . ." "I am heartened by . . . " There are also slang expressions and clichés peppering the prose: "Familiarity breeds contempt," ". . . labeling these stents as rejects now is burning bridges . . .", "other companies have shot themselves in the foot this way . . ." " . . . a reasonable basis for establishing a criterion that we could engrave in stone . . ." and "we need information instead of simply drawing a line in the sand . . ." One anomaly in the memo genre stands out in Tim's sample: in spite of using a standard memo heading (Date, To, etc.) Tim adds after that heading, "Ladies and Gentlemen:" and closes the memo with "All the best, Tim." An engineering colleague, reading this memo, said to me, "We'd yell at students if they wrote a memo this way. A good writer can be friendly without clichés."

In sum, while it is not possible to assess whether the texts Tim shared with me achieved their desired purposes, it is clear that Tim had at least been able by this point to mimic the surface features of technical engineering genres. And perhaps most important, he could also articulate the rationale for the various genres' features in relation to the social purposes of those genres within the discourse community of engineers. The internal memo appears the weakest of the samples because of its unprofessional register and deviation from standard formatting and opening and closing salutations that would not typically be included in a memo. Perhaps the awkward tone and register in the memo is indicative of his still "trying on" his social roles as engineer and writer within the organization.

ACQUIRING RHETORICAL KNOWLEDGE

The genres Tim was using in his engineering work of course have their rhetorical aspects: the proposal's intent is to create consensus on a path of action and the technical reports he wrote also had action-directed purposes. What I will look at here are both the global issues in persuasive writing in engineering, and specific audience needs Tim encountered in school and workplace settings.

Then/In School

After you work on a project for a while, you forget what people know and what people don't know. You know all this stuff so you read, you can say a sentence, and it assumes half a dozen things, and they're all clear to you. It's hard to kind of pull yourself out and look at it from afar.

***

What you have to do is convince 'em that you thought of every point by showing that you talked about every point, giving the results . . . it's in the appendix where the actual nitty-gritty kind of arguing about, oh, you made this assumption and you can't make that assumption . . . you sometimes have to include things, you know, this is a point, but it's not important and this is why. So 'cause otherwise they assume you haven't thought of it.

***

This {referring to Red Rover report} is just the kind of stuff that just tend to get done the night before 'cause you feel like you've done the work already . . . it's like this isn't the real work, this is just writing it up . . . you have to manufacture this stuff, they have that all-important grade you know.

—Tim, senior year

In school, even though two of Tim's projects were in response to external engineering companies' needs (soil moisture and down converter), the predominant rhetorical situation was that of getting the assignment done for a grade. There was no direct contact with the companies he was doing the work for, so the "real" audience was the professor. As others have found, it is nearly impossible to simulate a real-world task in a school context (Dias 2000, Freedman et al. 1994). School takes precedent: it is more immediate, so the more distant target audience cannot be fully imagined. In the process of understanding the professor's expectations, though, Tim started to pick up on some of an engineering audience's needs and think about how best to meet those needs. For example, he understood that the reader needed to be convinced that all possible solutions to an engineering problem had been considered, and that the proposed solution was the best. He thought about audience needs in terms of how much information was needed, and how a proposed solution to an engineering problem could be written persuasively.

Tim's weakest attempt at persuasion was in his first project—the soil moisture project. As we have seen, in the conclusion to his proposal he stated he made his recommendation because (a) he thought of it and (b) he understood it. Apparently, Tim felt safe admitting his novice status to his professor. It's unlikely he would have been so candid to a client or boss. His senior project, the down converter for cellular phone transfer stations, relied on a more thorough and interlocking set of arguments. The design had to meet criteria given at the outset: reliability, safety, durability, and cost-effectiveness. In the body of the proposal, Tim explains the process of eliminating alternative solutions, the recommended design, the ways it will meet design specifications, and finally, the costs—lower than the next best solution. There is a clear progress in the reasoning and a clear attempt to persuade. And the tone is more professional than in his soil sensor proposal, done in school.

Given the constraints of the social context in school, however, Tim had limited opportunities to learn the intricacies of the rhetorical situations he would encounter in the workplace. It is also worth noting that he separated the critical thinking part of the school projects from the writing, the former being the "real work" and the latter just an obligatory function of being in school and the professor needing something to grade.

Now/In the Workplace

What is interesting about Tim's perspective on the rhetorical aspects of writing in engineering after he had been working for two years is the more specific understanding of both audience needs and the types of arguments that needed to be made in almost every communication, i.e. safety first, profitability second. The legal ramifications of doing thorough work and making decision that were rooted in concrete data, not just opinion, were clear. Tim understood, as he put it, "at deeper levels," the admonition his professor had given him in school to question his own assumptions. Since the company he worked for manufactured medical equipment that would be surgically implanted in patients, he had a ready understanding of what was at risk if work was not done well—and that included careful written documentation of work.

Only the internal memo Tim showed me has an overtly persuasive aim: he wanted to convince his colleagues to do a more thorough analysis of standards for physical appearance of the product than was being proposed. He begins the memo by congratulating his colleagues on what they have done so far, then points out the flaws in their proposal, based on a series of facts that Tim claims are relevant to the situation. About two-thirds through the memo, he states, "We need information instead of simply drawing a line in sand that is based on opinion and aesthetic appeal of a very select group of people—ourselves."

He then lists the categories of information he recommends should be gathered before criteria are set for the cosmetic appearance of the item being manufactured. In the closing paragraph, he goes back to praise: "I am heartened by the striving for quality that I see in the company. . . . I just would like to encourage us, making use of the resources of excellent people who have joined the company, to pursue quality critically and with rigor."

The other documents Tim showed me, the technical reports, are a mixture of straight information and some subtle forms of persuasion. The purpose of these reports is to explain what tests were run on new machinery to assure they would operate to the degree of precision needed. But there is a persuasive purpose as well: throughout the document (four pages), it is evident that Tim is also seeking to persuade his audience that he has run the right tests and has done a thorough analysis of the functioning of the piece of equipment. To bolster his credibility as the engineer who has performed the tests, he explains why he used a glass scale instead of actual stent struts. He indicates the rigor of testing through documentation of the testing procedures used. He addresses what is typically done in the industry to bolster the credibility of his procedures. And he refers to a previous technical report's recommendations to bolster his own argument.

But the more dynamic aspects of the rhetorical situation and how Tim learned to handle them are found in the interview transcripts. Here is an excerpt:

Anne: So who are the people you have to convince?

Tim: Well, it'd typically be other engineers. . . . I wanna convince them if I think we should do it this way. I don't wanna say, this is the way we're gonna do it.

Anne: So how do you convince your colleagues?

Tim: We have policy meetings.

Anne: So it's not in writing?

Tim: A lot of it is you talk to a few different people, just kind of on the run, and when you've found a common language, then you kind of take it to a more formal . . . it could be in writing or a larger, sit-down meeting.

Anne: So you don't sit down as a rule?

Tim: Sometimes you sit on the floor (laughs). Yeah, you don't get as much done when you sit down.

Anne: So you negotiate the ideas orally?

Tim: Usually, yeah.

Anne: Before you put it in writing.

Tim: Yeah, because you might be off base for one thing, and if you are you don't wanna have your name on it (laughs). You wanna kind of check, check with some people.

This bit of dialogue indicates the interplay of oral and written communications in the workplace discourse community and the kinds of rhetorical work done orally, before texts are produced. As I have seen in another workplace setting, delicate negotiations are often handled orally, rather than in writing, and what gets written reflects the agreements that have been reached (Beaufort 1999). Notice the delicate power negotiations: "I don't wanna say, this is the way we're gonna do it." Also, the statement "when you've found a common language," is perhaps figurative, suggesting not the need for terminology and verbiage per se, but for a common understanding of what is involved and what the best course of action might be.

Here is another excerpt from my conversation with Tim when he's been in his job two years that portrays, quite vividly, just how much argument and persuasion are part of the engineer's "job."

Anne: In engineering, what's the basis for an argument?

Tim: Safety, yield, reliability, reliability. Safety's probably the biggest one, both safety for operators, safety for patients. Pretty much everything revolves around that. Cost, not really. . . . If it's the right way to do it, it will be worth it.

A study . . . evidence . . . always the question, when must you, before you act, insist on a study that's absolutely tailored to your specific instances and when is it okay to reason based on a similar

> situation . . . Everything is questioned . . . you can question any-
> body . . . yeah but, have those machines been calibrated, what's
> the actual data you got from those machines, and how do you
> know what that data means, does it mean a rivet . . . have you ever
> tested this machine under similar conditions with and without
> rivets . . . we had a dispute recently about how we're gonna go
> about deciding what's acceptable and what's not for the cosmetic
> appearance of the product . . . I had to think carefully about what
> people's assumptions, what's their knowledge, so it's kind of like
> stripping away variables that aren't relevant.

As others who have written about the rhetoric of science have indicated (Bazerman 1982, Fahnestock 1986, Latour and Woolgar 1979),
empirical evidence is a strong part of the rhetorical context, but human
judgment and logic are also factors in building arguments in scientific
fields. The discernment regarding when a new study is needed, or when
arguments can be made on the basis of the claim of analogous situations
reported in previous empirical studies is an example of walking the fine
line between facts and reason that Tim is learning to negotiate. But the
predominant issue in terms of rhetorical knowledge for Tim, suggested
by his comments, is questioning all assumptions, and getting as much
empirical evidence to support an argument as possible.

Tim also had to learn to deal with multiple audiences in a single text
in his workplace writing, unlike the single audience (teacher) that he
had to assuage in student days. He says:

> It seems to me, OK, I'm in an engineering world, everyone will understand
> what I write, but they don't, I mean, a lot of them are from different enough
> disciplines that they don't know what you're talking about, so you do have to
> explain a lot . . . someone who's responsible for regulatory affairs is basically
> concerned with OK, when an auditor comes, what is he or she gonna be look-
> ing for, so you read it with that auditor's eyes and say oops, red flag, what do
> you mean by this . . . everyone else's feedback is more or less predictable . . .
> when engineering looks at it, they just have a completely different viewpoint
> . . . you have to write to the audience of the operator. You also have to write
> to the audience of the auditor.
>
> —Tim, two years after college

The need for a single document to address differing needs of different readers was the second big challenge Tim faced in writing on

the job. So the rhetorical challenges were more difficult in the work-place than in school.

In sum, it appears that Tim was at least somewhat aware of the rhetori-cal challenges of creating successful texts in his workplace environment and he was facing new challenges to his rhetorical skills not faced in school. While I do not have a means of assessing his growth or compe-tency rhetorically in his work environment, nonetheless, his being able to articulate an awareness of rhetorical issues is a positive sign.

WRITING PROCESS KNOWLEDGE

In the interviews with Tim in his senior year and two years after school I did not explicitly ask about the ways in which he approached the writ-ing tasks in engineering, so my information regarding Tim's growth in handling the actual process of writing is limited. However, a few com-ments showed up in the transcripts that demonstrate that Tim definitely had some different means of approaching writing tasks required in engineering courses than he used in writing for history classes.

Then: Writing Processes in School

As we saw, the process for writing in history was one of reading, note-taking, categorizing notes to find themes and a core idea, and drafting. In engineering, Tim used a different set of writing processes. Here are a few of Tim's comments that reveal what he did:

Bullets helped me kind of limit and clarify and put borders on things. So I know that I don't have to tackle everything . . . just have to tackle one piece at a time and then I fire and do another one. They break it up for me to see where I'm going 'cause I can get pretty lost if I use paragraph form.

***

In the engineering stuff, they gave us the outline. I actually volunteered to follow it. . . . by using that and not worrying about, you know . . .

***

The biggest challenge was working with two guys. . . . This {design} is the one that we finally selected. So we had a knock down drag out about that. [We were] working on appendices, then deciding where to reference them in [the] main document . . . [it was] not a linear composing process.

—Tim, senior year

When I asked what he'd learned about writing in the context of his engineering classes, the first response was "bullets." As the quote above reveals, using bullets was not just a stylistic device. They aided his thinking/writing process: "I don't have to tackle everything . . . just . . . tackle one piece at a time." Writing with bullets apparently allowed Tim to get detailed information down, one piece at a time, without being overwhelmed by the entire body of information that needed to be conveyed.[37] Another aid to the writing process that he mentioned several times was the set structure for proposals—each section could be written as a task in itself. Only at the final stages did the larger task of synthesis, connecting all the parts and deciding if information was best in one section or another, become of concern. One other reference to the writing process—assembling the information for appendices, and then deciding where in the main texts appropriate referencing to those materials should be made—suggests that the composing process was not linear, but iterative: information was written down and then added to as necessary in stages, rather than all at once.

But as has been reported in the literature on workplace writing (Couture and Rymer 1991, Doheny-Farina 1986, Ede and Lundsford 1990, Witte and Haas 2001), writing in engineering is most often a collaborative process. His first project, on soil sensors, Tim did alone. But the Red Rover and down converter projects were collaborative efforts. In the school context, Tim's only observations on the collaborative process concerned the social dynamics—one person not doing enough work (and there was no "boss" to supervise), and a group member being too intuitive a thinker and unable (or unwilling?) to do the objective analysis required for the task. Different members of the team wrote different sections and one person edited for consistency among the parts. And in spite of differences of opinion on the best solution to engineering design problems, the writing part of the collaborations did not become problematic for Tim.

Now: Writing Processes in the Workplace

Tim: I write memos, email, some of those that require some thought and preparation and peer review, some of them are quick, dirty, disorganized, get the main points out there, let people organize them themselves . . .

Anne: So how much do you write, what percent of your time?

Tim: Uh, may be 5 or 10, probably ten. That'd be a day every two weeks or an hour a day.

Anne: What's it like?

Tim: It's very frustrating. It's very detailed. There's many more drafts than I've ever done before, much more exhaustive peer review, and the peers are not very stable . . . you show the thing to them once and they'll have their comments; if you show the same thing to them the next day they'd have different comments. So when you incorporate the comments and send it back to them, it's still not done.

—Tim, two years after college

The social context of the workplace added some new elements to the mix of factors Tim had to deal with in getting writing tasks accomplished. The press of getting work done, for one, made writing tasks get prioritized. Turning out a well-crafted memo was less important than expeditiously getting information in colleagues' hands. On the other hand, as Tim indicates, technical protocol documents required a long, collaborative process before being signed off by the five or six people representing different interests within the company. Writing processes varied according to the relative importance of the documents in relation to the other activities of the company, as was the case in the non-profit agency I studied (Beaufort 1999).

There is one other point worth noting: what appeared to be difficult in the writing process on the job for Tim was the precision required in certain genres and the task of synthesizing different points of view. Tim told me at one point that he was not a detail-oriented person, so these aspects of the writing process were challenging. But on the other hand, as he indicates, having others' review one's writing was a form of social and emotional protection as well.

The difference between the school context and workplace context, in terms of effect on the writer's process, was also evident in this comment:

The peer review seemed kind of artificial in class, you know. In school, sure it makes it better, but how much do they really know about what I'm writing or how much do they really know what good writing [is], but . . . now . . . you don't want to be done with it until other people have read it . . . I might not like what they say but you want people to read it to protect yourself for one thing . . . you're too involved in it to read it the way someone else would . . .

—Tim, two years after college

How successful Tim was in adapting writing process knowledge from college to the workplace cannot be assessed from this limited data. However, it is clear that the workplace setting did change the way Tim went about getting writing done. In school, Tim's professors tried to simulate the collaborative writing processes that take place frequently in the workplace. But as Tim's comments show, the dynamics of that collaborative process were much more complex, and for higher stakes of course, in the workplace. Purposes and processes for completing engineering logs, even, were vastly different in school and in the workplace. There can be no doubt that social context influences all aspects of a writer's performance. Tim was learning to adapt to contextual factors that resulted in handling writing tasks in a variety of ways.

In sum, then, what can be said about Tim's learning to write like an engineer? Clearly, there were significant differences between writing for history and writing in engineering. Tim was able to learn from his professors and his environment what the expectations were in writing for engineering and to follow those expectations well enough to graduate and gain employment in a small manufacturing firm. Those differences encompassed not only subject matter, but different ways of thinking, different social purposes and values in the discourse communities, different genres, different kinds of rhetorical issues and even, different writing processes between writing for history and writing in engineering or, for that matter, writing in his freshman writing courses with Carla.

Tim's writing in school, however, was still far from that of an experienced engineer. As my engineering colleague said, "I've seen these problems [Tim's] before. This is very familiar" (Kincaid, personal communication). And, as Kincaid also pointed out, there is little room for a novice engineer to make mistakes in his written communications on the job. Fortunately, Tim was an astute learner in the informal learning environment of the workplace. In only two years time and without any formal coaching on his writing by his employer, Tim could articulate many of the social constraints on written texts and the necessary processes and conventions for written communications in that engineering environment. He was writing important documents—in particular protocols for testing new equipment or protocols for using equipment that needed to be precise, in order to ensure a safe work environment and reliable products.

What remains for reflection and discussion in the final chapter is a review of what Tim gained across the four years, writing in three different contexts, and what might have led to greater gains in writing skills than what he did achieve. Tim had syntactic fluency when he began his college career. In freshman writing he gained an awareness of the need to consider his audience's needs. By the end of his senior year, he had at least some conceptions regarding the differences between writing in history and writing in engineering. The question is, what, in the four years of his university experience, could have led him to be better prepared for the workplace writing he would do?

6
NEW DIRECTIONS FOR UNIVERSITY WRITING INSTRUCTION

As I begin this final chapter, I wish first to honor the acts of courage and integrity of all of Tim's teachers to teach him well, as well as Tim's own dedication to learning and to making a meaningful contribution to society. I am privileged that these individuals have allowed me to get to know them and to try, through this research, to provide suggestions for how we all might teach writing better. And to all who read this for the sake of this same enterprise of teaching well and learning well, I say, we are in this inquiry together. Knowing readers will make their own connections and draw their own conclusions from this work, I offer final thoughts only as catalyst for furthering the inquiry we are in together.

It seems to me that three things need to be noted at the end of this case study.

First: a developmental model for understanding writers' growth, for designing curriculum and assessment measures and for training teachers (whether writing teachers or teachers in other disciplines) and tutors needs to encompass the five knowledge and skill domains used here to frame the analysis of a writer's growth. To focus on one or several aspects of writing expertise to the exclusion of the others represents less than a full view of the developmental process for gaining writing expertise. This theoretical lens can be useful not only in designing curriculum and understanding what the causes are for individual students' writing problems, but also in designing tools for assessing writing development.

The theoretical model of discipline-specific writing expertise employed in this analysis of data (see Figure 1, page 18) has enabled a complex view (both broad and up-close) of one writer's skills. Since Brannon's (1985) review of what was then known about writers' developmental processes, we have traveled a considerable distance in refining our understanding of this thorny issue. Each aspect of the model employed here showed yet another dimension of what was going on. Other models of writing development—declarative versus procedural knowledge (Berkenkotter et al. 1988), knowledge-telling versus knowledge transforming (Bereiter and Scardamalia 1987), discourse conventions versus writer's mental representations (Flower 1994) or subject matter versus rhetorical knowledge (Geisler 1994)—would have shown some but not all of the aspects of the writer's development documented here.

At the same time that I have tried to be inclusive of all knowledge domains writers must draw upon, I have also tried to break down into discrete pieces the various aspects of expertise in order that we may refine our lenses of analysis. For example, the model used here parses Geisler's conception of rhetorical knowledge to include both the situatedness of genres, the overarching aims of a discourse community or activity system, and the particular situation of an immediate act of composing—three interrelated but different aspects of rhetorical context. The same is true for recent explications of genre theory (Bawarshi 2000, Devitt 2004), which include not only textual features but also the situations in which genres act and are acted upon. These theorists fully explore the ways in which genres interact with social contexts and writers' composing processes. But the more precise explication of the social scenes affecting writers that discourse community theory affords again suggests the value of theoretical parsing of the knowledge domains important to writers. The data here also challenge Geisler's claim that subject matter knowledge develops first, then rhetorical skill. In Tim's case, both subject matter knowledge and rhetorical knowledge were factors in the writing task, even in his freshman essays, and gains were seen, though modest, in both of these aspects of his writing across the four years.

In operationalizing this model, differing aspects of subject matter knowledge have also been parsed: factual and conceptual knowledge as well as the critical thinking skills necessary to selectively use that knowledge. Accounting for the influence of subject matter knowledge and critical thinking skills on written products accounts for an often-neglected element in discussions of acquisition of disciplinary writing expertise (Jolliffe 1995).

As I was initially acknowledged, the aspects of disciplinary writing expertise parsed here are interrelated and interactive. Subject matter knowledge affects the skill with which the content aspects of a genre are handled. Discourse community knowledge can inform the rhetorical purpose of both a given genre and a specific rhetorical instance. Critical thinking skills, which I chose to discuss in relation to analysis of subject matter, are present in all aspects of figuring out a writing project—the rhetorical aspects, the procedural aspects, etc. Likewise, genre knowledge could inform the writer's process for completing the task and influence the shaping of subject matter knowledge. Genre knowledge is intertwined as well with the social dynamics of rhetorical acts within the discourse communities. But in spite of these overlaps and interactions, the operationalized definitions of each knowledge domain (see Table 10 p.221) do lead to fuller explorations of what's going on when writers seek to gain new skills.

In terms of Tim's progress in gaining expertise in these knowledge domains, the data here suggest that in college Tim did not advance beyond the first stage, acclimation (i.e. possessing limited and fragmented knowledge), according to Alexander's (2003) general schema for a developmental continuum in gaining expertise in a domain of knowledge. The interview with Tim after two years of working in a manufacturing firm suggests at that point, perhaps, he was approaching Alexander's second stage, competence:

> Competent individuals not only demonstrate a foundational body of domain knowledge, but that knowledge is also more cohesive and principled in structure . . . Moreover, these knowledge and strategy changes in competent learners are linked to increases in individuals' personal interest in the domain and less dependence on situational features of the environment (p. 12).

For example, at that time Tim spoke to me of the interrelatedness of different genres in the discourse community he was working in; he discussed with me the ways in which the genres of his work related to the tasks to be accomplished; and he understood the social roles of a "writer" in that particular discourse community. As for the second aspect of Alexander's notion of "competence"—increased interest and self-motivation—Tim came across in my final interview with him as fully engaged with his work and fully cognizant of the important role of writing in the company's survival. There was a seriousness of purpose in the writing as he described it that was not present in any of his accounts of school writing tasks.

As others have reported in other research studies, what was the most difficult for Tim in school—in freshman writing, in history and in engineering—was to grasp the "real' social context for writing in those disciplines, beyond the context of "doing school." Kaufer (1995) says, "We are still at square one when it comes to defining legitimate social goals of a writing program." In spite of a decade more of work since Kaufer's pronouncement, I believe we are not much further toward this end. In freshman writing, Tim did not really have exposure to how journalists or environmentalists write for the multiple discourse communities they address. The one "authentic" writing task in freshman writing, his community service writing project for an environmental organization, did not succeed for Tim because he did not understand the discourse community he was writing for. So the experience was one of frustration rather than learning.

I would add that the problem Kaufer names also exists in writing-in-the-disciplines initiatives. In history, one paper would receive praise and another criticism; it did not become clear to Tim what was acceptable writing and what was not (except that he knew religious topics had to be handled differently in history than in, say, religious publications). The genres of history writing he could only describe in fuzzy terms at the end of his coursework, and when he tried to appropriate history to a current social need in Russia and wrote passionately about it, he was rebuffed with a lower grade. So other than "flapping" (his jargon) or just "playing" with ideas, Tim did not approximate the "real" work of the discourse community of historians in any of his undergraduate history essays. If that was his professors' aim (which I suspect was not the case), the attempts were not successful.

Engineering writing in school came the closest to being an authentic writing task for Tim, attached to the enterprises of engineering discourse communities: the projects assigned were from "real" clients, and the reports written went back to those clients. In engineering, the problem to be solved through writing was clear and the surface conventions of the genre of engineering proposal were spelled out in assignment instructions. But still, the genre forms were followed by rote, without an understanding of the values and aims of the discourse communities that necessitated those conventions. When the professor wanted one design proposal submitted for an award, Tim and his classmates thought doing so was "a joke." As he said, referring to the project, "It's just a lid."

Lack of understanding of discourse community norms and values also inhibited deeper levels of understanding of subject matter, genre expectations, and rhetorical strategies. As I have said, these knowledge domains, or sub-skills in the composing process are interrelated. Since the writer's own ideas were the primary subject matter in freshman writing and the subject matter presented in the readings—the natural world and environmentalism—were secondary to Carla's focus on the writer and the writer's process, Tim did not delve deep into these subjects. In history, what seemed to be missing for Tim was knowledge of appropriate analytical lenses with which to view various historical texts. In engineering, there was a major shift for Tim with regard to critical thinking skills. His means of analyzing ideas in history, or religion, or environmentalism would not work in designing mechanical objects and solving the associated problems of cost, safety, and marketability. Fortunately, an engineering professor named Tim's problem to him and the proverbial light bulb went on. Tim made marked improvements after that in his engineering courses at least in his analytical skills in the discipline.

Considering genre knowledge across the three contexts Tim was exposed to in school for academic writing brings up some interesting points. His knowledge of specific genres and the associated discourse communities remained superficial, but exposure to more genres and genre differences was eye-opening. In freshman writing, as he said, he felt unshackled from the five-paragraph essay: he learned the purposes of writing, acceptable content, and forms for writing were numerous. In history, he floundered with unclear genre expectations and much haziness on the other aspects of writing for history. In engineering, he was confronted with genres and conventions radically different from anything else he had been exposed to. The seemingly small formatting issue—use of bulleted points instead of narrative—was actually huge for Tim. He came to realize that the bulleted format allowed a different sort of thinking and processing of information than lengthy prose narratives, a difference that suited readers in an engineering environment. His realization in his first job of the critical role of logbooks for an engineer (and for the engineering company) also represented a growing awareness of the inter-connectedness of form and function in genre.

As far as I could tell, Tim had no formal instruction in any of the discipline-specific genres he was asked to write in school or after school in his job. He did figure some things out on his own, which would cause some to argue that there is no need for explicit genre instruction (Freedman 1993). To that argument I would say, Tim was probably more astute than some novice writers would be, and secondly, as Devitt (2004) and Johns (2002) also argue, Tim—and other novice writers—would probably produce writing at a much more expert level, more quickly, if they are explicitly taught genres in relation to social contexts in which they function.

Added together, the five knowledge domains as applied to this case of one writer working in three different contexts yield a complex picture of development toward expertise. His development was uneven. He broadened his notion of what "counts" as writing, he learned to adapt at least to some of the differences in the expectations of the different discourse communities he encountered, he probably became more adept at handling the process of composing, given the volume of writing he had to produce and the "method" he could articulate to me at the end of his senior year for getting writing done. But there was no smooth upward curve toward expertise. Rather, the line of progress toward expertise moved in fits and starts, fluttered, stopped, started.

This is fairly typical, particularly in situations where there is little formal coaching of writers or clear progression of writing assignments that will reinforce previous learning and add new skills. Bereiter and Scardamalia (1993) say, "The career of the expert is one of progressively advancing on the problems constituting a field of work, whereas the career of the non-expert is one of gradually constricting the field of work so that it more closely conforms to the routines the non-expert is prepared to execute" (p. 11). If Tim had had better and consistent instruction across all four years of college, I am convinced he could have progressed farther. There is too much evidence of guesswork and confusion on Tim's part about the writing tasks he encountered and lack of a clear progression of increasingly challenging writing tasks to suggest otherwise. What he figured out was the "routines" that worked for a non-expert.

But on the other hand, Tim's views of writing were expanding and becoming more complex, as he explained in our conversation at the end of his senior year of college:

> Uh, well, shoot . . . Four years ago, before taking classes here, I would have said, well that's not really writing . . . realizing that . . . it's not like a particular genre that qualifies as writing. Okay, now you can use style or you pay attention to this, but it's like, you know, whenever you scribble something down, I mean anytime you sit down at the keyboard then that's writing. Even if it's one, two, three, four.

And what is most important for those teachers, administrators, and researchers reading this is not how far this one writer progressed toward any form of writing expertise, but rather, the mental note we should make: look at the whole picture—the five knowledge domains in writing expertise—not one part or two when trying to help writers or to assess them. Each aspect of the knowledge involved in writing expertise is important, each affects the other areas in which the writer is seeking mastery. Appendix A offers suggestions for explicitly working with students in the five knowledge domains.

I would add a particular note about the role of subject matter knowledge in a successful writing performance. Both the literature in composition studies and the particular circumstances of Tim's writing experiences point to a lack of clarity about the degree to which subject matter knowledge affects writing performance. "Reaching" to find something to say is a major hurdle when one is new to a field of inquiry and yet must write on demand. This flies in the face of conventional wisdom about teaching writing (i.e. that subject matter, other than the writing process itself and rhetorical issues, is of minor concern) and only adds to the difficulties of a teacher who want to work on students' writing skills. The subject matter concern also raises the programmatic issue of where or when writing instruction should occur: within a particular discipline, or as part of a writing program.

I do not have easy solutions to offer. When I teach writing courses, I strive to define a sphere of intellectual inquiry that we will undertake as a group, one that our readings and class discussions and writing projects will help us to understand even just a little better by the end of a short 10- or 14-week course. Wiggins' (1987) definition of "essential questions" has been a most helpful tool in my design of necessarily brief intellectual inquiries so that there is a serious exploration, hopefully, rather than a superficial treatment of a subject matter through the reading and writing we do.

And in light of the issues I raise here, institutional issues of when and where writing courses should occur have no one answer either. I know from experience in three very different institutions of higher education that particular local circumstances (variables such as budget constraints, the pool of available teachers and their qualifications, makeup of the student population, and departmental politics) all play a role in such decisions. In the best of all worlds, I lean toward a freshman seminar model, as long as the seminar teachers have a thorough grounding in principles for designing and evaluating writing assignments. These seminars would begin a process that courses in upper-level majors could add to, with carefully designed writing requirements and appropriate faculty support (professional development, small classes, etc.) for those teaching such courses. (For an excellent model of a sequenced writing curriculum in a major, see Kovac, *Writing Across the Chemistry Curriculum*).

Second, teachers in all disciplines should employ techniques that aid transfer of learning for writers. As Premack (1989) says, "The objective of both education and (in a sense) intelligence is transfer. We commend teaching that enables the student to perform correctly in situations different from those in which he was trained" (p. 239). In light of the issues presented in this case study, I would argue that all faculty should acknowledge and make clear the socially situated aspect of the writing they assign, so that students understand the connection between writing conventions and the work those conventions are meant to accomplish in given discourse communities. Two recent additions to the literature in composition studies, Devitt (2004) and Smit (2004) make this same plea. I add my voice to theirs, but with a more specific appeal.

Smit (2004) says,

> Writing teachers get what they teach for, instruction in particular kinds of knowledge and skill and not broad-based writing ability. If we want to promote the transfer of certain kinds of writing abilities from one class to another or one context to another, then we are going to have to find the means to institutionalize instruction in the similarities between the way writing is done in a variety of contexts (pp. 119–120).

I would argue that we are looking to teach not similarities in the ways writing is done in different contexts, but rather, to teach those broad concepts (discourse community, genre, rhetorical tools, etc.) which will give writers the tools to analyze similarities and differences among writing situations they encounter.

We have seen in this case that Tim was given little explicit instruction in the particular socially based writing conventions of the three writing contexts he encountered in college. If that had been the case, he most likely would have adjusted more readily to the changing expectations for writing as he moved from one discourse community to another. There was one exception: Carla emphasized the importance of considering audience in any act of composing. So Tim tried to consider audience when writing to his history professors or his engineering professors. But the concept of "audience" as traditionally defined in rhetoric does not go far enough toward illuminating a complex web of social relations, values, and conventions a writer must take into consideration. So, for example, Tim thought the history professor who had young children would resonate with an introduction to his history topic that drew an analogy to raising children. But what Tim did not understand was that discourse community norms in history required altogether different strategies for connecting with one's readers; as a result, his rhetorical strategy was ineffective.

Or, in the case of genre conventions, Carla favored the more literary, exploratory form of the essay and did not name this particular "sub-genre" of the essay to her students. So, Tim did not readily adjust to the more hierarchical, linear form of logic and structure for the academic essay that his history professors wanted from him. Nor did his history professors explain what conventions were to be followed in a historical essay compared to essays in other discourse communities.

All faculties can benefit from being grounded in the research on transfer of learning and in genre and discourse community theories, the two most important organizing frameworks for understanding writing in multiple social contexts. And this theoretical background is especially critical for teachers and tutors of writing. Writing teachers and tutors are in the unique position of preparing students to enter others' discourse communities. Writers would benefit greatly if careful attention were given in classroom and writing center instruction to key concepts that will help them to become skilled learners in other social contexts for writing.

The research on transfer of learning has yielded some key principles that can apply in any context of learning. I summarize those principles briefly here and demonstrate how they apply specifically to facilitating transfer of learning with respect to writing.[38] Perkins and Salomon reviewed more than two decades of research on transfer of learning and concluded that "To the extent that transfer does take place, it is highly specific and must be cued, primed, and guided; it seldom occurs spontaneously" (Mikulecky et al. 1994). They are referring in particular to "high road transfer," those types of situations in which "mindful application of abstract concepts to new situations" is required (Perkins and Salomon 1989) In particular, they suggest what teachers can do to facilitate transfer:

> learners are shown how problems resemble each other; learners' attention is directed to the underlying goal structures of comparable problems; . . . examples are accompanied with rules, particularly when the latter are formu-lated by the learners themselves; . . . learning takes place in a social context (p. 22).

In another article, they refer to "mental grippers" for organizing general domains of knowledge that then can be applied in local circumstances(Perkins and Salomon 1989). The concepts of "discourse community" and "genre" can be two such "mental grippers" for writers, and well as the model for writing expertise I have drawn, which includes subject matter knowledge, rhetorical knowledge, and writing process knowledge as well.

Flower (1989) makes a similar argument. She says the most worthwhile thing we can teach is "rhetorical knowledge and principles of rhetorical problem-solving that will transfer across different writing tasks." She refers to "writing plans" (what I refer to as genre knowledge) and "topic knowledge" (what I call subject matter knowledge) in addition as helpful tools in transfer situations. And she points out a key problem with transfer of learning in school contexts for writing:

> In school writing the social, rhetorical context is often buried and the student is used to dealing with assignments, not problems . . . when the writer sits down to compose, his or her old assignment-driven strategies for producing text leaves no room in the writing for rhetorical problem-solving (p. 20).

This was clearly the case for Tim in all three school contexts—freshman writing, history, and engineering. Writing tasks were mostly assignments, i.e. responses to an authority figure's need to evaluate the learner's competence, not rhetorical problems to be solved within the context of a network of discourse community members whose texts existed for multiple social purposes. Rhetorical problem-solving became a reality for him only when he moved into his first job and the relation of texts to social action was immanent and clear.

What is clear in all of the literature on transfer of learning is *first, that learners need guidance to structure specific problems and learnings into more abstract principles that can be applied to new situations.* As Gick (1987) says, "Experts shift their basis for categorizing problems from relatively surface attributes of problems to more abstract, structural attributes that cue principles relevant to the solution" (p. 39). These are the "mental grippers" Perkins and Salomon refer to and this is where conceptual knowledge of discourse communities and genre knowledge becomes useful. If students are led to see the features of a discourse community represented in a particular course and understand the properties of discourse communities in general, and ideally, have opportunities to analyze (with guidance) several discourse communities, they can then take that skill in analyzing a discourse community into new social contexts for writing. And likewise with the concept of genre: we cannot possibly teach all genres students might need to know in the future, but we can teach the concept of genre and ask students to apply the concept to analysis of several text types.

I have also just exemplified the *second principle for aiding transfer of learning, namely, giving students numerous opportunities to apply abstract concepts in different social contexts.* Teachers often assign different types of genres in a course, but and if there were also a discussion of the similarities and differences among the genres, applying the concept of genre to those genres assigned, students would learn how to use the concept of genre to analyze new text types they need to read or write. And along with multiple examples of genres in action (rather than mere writing assignments), teachers can acknowledge both the immediate social dynamics of a given course—the temporary discourse community of the course—and through case studies, or examples from their own work in various discourse communities, they can acknowledge and exemplify to students "real" rhetorical problem-solving in multiple discourse communities.[39]

And there is a *third principle for increasing the chances of transfer of learning that runs throughout the literature: teaching the practice of mindfulness, or meta-cognition.* Literally "thinking about thinking," meta-cognition implies vigilant attentiveness to a series of high-level questions as one is in the process of writing: how is this writing task similar to others? Or different? What is the relationship of this writing problem to the larger goals and values of the discourse community in which the text will be received? These and other reflection-in-action types of questions, if a part of the writer's process, will increase the ability to learn new writing skills, applying existing knowledge and skills appropriately (i.e. accomplishing positive transfer or learning).

In sum, to aid positive transfer of learning, writers should be taught a conceptual model such as the five-part schema I have laid out here for the "problem-space" of a writing task, i.e. the five knowledge domains they will need to draw from to complete the task. Then, they can work through each aspect of the writing task in a thorough manner, looking for what in the current situation for writing is similar to past writing tasks, or analyzing new tasks with appropriate "mental grippers" for understanding. And teachers and tutors should also assist in what

Perkins and Salomon refer to as "bridging," i.e. "[mediating] needed processes of abstraction and connection-making" (1989). Acquainting students with the need for bridging and the tools I have laid out here for doing so will teach them to learn for transfer. This is meta-cognition on the teacher's part. (Appendix A gives further examples of ways to teach or tutor for transfer of learning.)

The third recommendation I make here, based on this case study and my experience as a writing program administrator, is that *depart-ment chairs, writing program administrators, and deans would greatly increase the "return on investment" in writing instruction if they foster opportunities for faculty to create sequential, developmentally-sound writing sequences that extend across courses in a major.* I would urge the same for those who propose composition texts to publishers and to the editors at those presses who specialize in composition rhetorics and readers. The sample assignments in such texts, I suggest, would aid writers to a much greater degree if they followed the principles laid out here.

Bereiter and Scardamalia (1993) say, "For many, the effect of years of practice is simply to produce increasingly fluent bad writing" (p. x). And Young and Leinhardt (1998) say "[there is a need for] models for systematic instruction of disciplinary writing." If we are going to foster advanced levels of writing literacy in students we graduate from higher education, we cannot assign responsibility for this goal solely to a single course or even two; nor can we expect that any type of writing task will do. Smit (2004) echoes my plea:

> To insure that students do generalize certain aspects of writing, colleges and universities will have to make writing in different courses more related and systematic, so that instructors can build on what students have learned previously. They will have to implement what Arthur Applebee calls an integrated curriculum ". . . Somehow we have to break down the barriers between writing classes and the barriers between the instructors of those classes; we have to get over the notion that instructors are mini-dictators of their own private domains" (p. 193).

Sequencing should occur both within courses and across courses and departments. John Williams, a history professor, realized that requiring a single major paper at the end of an upper-level history seminar, a typical practice in the disciplines, would have yielded better results if, in the early weeks of the course, he had built in smaller writing and critical thinking tasks that introduced the skills needed to accomplish the capstone essay for the course (Beaufort and Williams 2005). Lower and upper division courses and even graduate courses should be accompanied, no matter what the discipline, by a sequence of writing tasks for students to undertake that will gradually increase the challenges in the tasks assigned and move students along in critical areas of writing expertise: discourse community goals and values, genre conventions in the community, and interpretive/critical thinking skills that are necessary companions to subject matter, rhetorical skills, and writing process skills.[40]

The data presented here point to this need for continuity of writing instruction across the college curriculum. Assignments Tim received, both in freshman writing, in history, and in engineering did not evidence a clear sequential path that would allow both repetition of skills in order to refine them and gradual, linked assignments requiring new writing skills.

The sequence of assignments in Tim's first course in freshman writing sought to introduce a series of different but related rhetorical problems to the students. But the jump from personal, expressive genres (letters, journal entries, first-person narratives) to the community service writing project (a newsletter article reporting on an unmet market need) was a shift of great magnitude: Tim missed the cues from the newsletter editor on what was expected and also became self-critical for writing something that he felt did not uphold his romantic notions of writing for self-expression that had been unleashed in the same course in earlier assignments. So he bridled at the community service project and had to write several drafts to produce both the content the newsletter editor wanted and a style the editor wanted.

In the second freshman writing course, the sequence from field research (an interview), to rhetorical analysis of a single source, to the major research assignment could have fostered an awareness of the multiple sources of information on a topic and how different sources might yield different sorts of data. The assignment to analyze one text was intended to teach critical reading skills that could then be applied in the longer research assignment. But the bridges between these assignments—the principles I have spelled out here—did not become evident to Tim as far as I could see. And in Tim's case, the lack of perception of any continuity between the three assignments was exacerbated by the fact that he took the option of writing on three very different topics (Vatican II, genetic engineering, and ecology in Russia) for each of the assignments.

In the six history courses spanning three years from which Tim showed me work, I could see only one shift in the assignments: in his freshman year, he was working mostly with secondary source material (he did work with a couple of primary source texts—Benedict's *Rule* and Augustine's *Confessions*) but starting in his sophomore year he was working almost exclusively with primary sources. But the types of intellectual tasks he was asked to take on—the scope of reading and analysis or synthesis of materials, the interpretive tasks, even, the genres—were either similar throughout the three years of coursework in history, or in one case, harder in his freshman level course than some of the tasks in subsequent sophomore and junior-level courses. Mostly, he was still writing five-to-seven page essays in his upper level seminars and the tasks were the same as the tasks given in his freshman-level courses: analyze a historical text or a historical period. It is not surprising, then, that his skills in writing history did not show noticeable improvement.

There was less writing in Tim's engineering courses: he gave me only a literature review and three product proposals—two from his junior year and one from his senior year. The only variations apparent in the product proposal assignments were in the subject matter of the proposals. He did get repeated practice in writing project proposals (and as a result, the language became more appropriate to the genre), but the assignments were virtually the same across courses.

As noted earlier, there is little documentation of discipline-specific writing sequences at the college level. And Haswell (1991) likens most composition textbooks to "default cookbooks." He says, ". . . although the cookbook method may help clinicians assess and find material, it does not diagnose individuals or lay out a plan for therapy" (p. 292). While I would not want to liken writing curricula to therapy, nonetheless, Haswell's point—that there is a dearth in the literature of plans for writers' developmental processes—is valid. Even within composition studies, there is not enough emphasis on developing curricular sequences across writing courses. Teacher autonomy should not be the primary criterion for curricular decisions when students' developmental progress is at stake. And within writing courses, the model derived from Moffett (1983) for sequencing assignments from the personal essay to more abstract arguments (based on Piaget's child development theory), needs to be revisited. At least, in my own teaching I have found two problems with starting students with expressive/personal writing: 1) without an intellectual framework for analyzing personal experience, which hopefully the course will provide, students generate a superficial narrative without substantial intellectual content and 2) in college settings, this type of discourse is generally an anomaly, so students tend to dismiss the importance of the assignment in relation to their other work. I still offer students the opportunity for personal exploration of the course theme, but generally in ungraded freewriting done in class.

The conceptual model of the knowledge domains in disciplinary writing articulated here could enable curriculum developers to conceptualize course sequences, assignment sequences, and even course content that would maximize students' opportunities to build subject matter and critical thinking expertise, as well as awareness of discourse community norms and norms for key genres employed in the discourse community. And in addition to style guides, which many disciplines use and are helpful for sentence-level and documentation issues, departments could provide students with tips about the specifics of rhetorical situation and composing processes useful in a given discourse community. A few in composition studies (Kiniry and Strenski 1985, Rose 1989, Spear 1983) have begun to articulate general sequences of assignments that build on Bloom's taxonomy of critical thinking tasks. Work is needed as well in specific content domains. For example, in history, some have begun studies on the critical thinking skills and rhetorical knowledge needed to work with texts as sources for historical analysis that can inform the design of history curricula (Gunn 2000, Hall 1987, Walvoord and McCarthy 1990, Woodman 1988).

Others also offer useful frameworks for conceptualizing curricular sequences at the college level: Berryman (1992) gives a useful framework for creating what he calls cognitive apprenticeships: considerations of content, sequencing of content, and methods of instruction, including the social factors that influence learning.[41] Kiniry (1985) argues for sequencing expository and persuasive writing assignments taking into account the intellectual hierarchies developed in cognitive psychology and Kovac (2001) instantiates such a sequence of assignments across four years of a college-level chemistry curriculum.[42] And Russell (2001), unlike Kiniry and Kovac, makes explicit the need to combine not only the cognitive apprenticeship aspects of learning to write for specific discourse communities, but also the social dimensions.[43] Others (Beaufort 2000, Lave and Wenger 1991, LeFevre 1987) echo the social apprenticeship aspect of learning, a dimension that should be added in curriculum design.

As with most matters in education, there is no one "right way" to build a sequential writing curriculum. But certainly the research and the principles I have referred to here should be considered in developing comprehensive, well-sequenced writing curricula in all disciplines. And it should be noted that the evaluative climate of schools can sabotage even the most well-thought-out writing curricula and pedagogies and undermine efforts to introduce students, as apprentices, to disciplinary practices (Greene 2001, Nelson 1990). Methods of assessing students' writing development is another critical factor in aiding maximal learning.

In addition, setting writing assignments at an appropriate level of difficulty, providing some but not too much scaffolding to assist students in their zone of proximal development, as Nelson's research attests, is not easy. Tim did not try as hard with assignments that seemed to him ill-conceived. Factoring in students' backgrounds and personal interests in conceiving of curricula that will motivate and inspire a sincere effort is yet another complication of designing successful writing curricula (Alexander 2003). Tim sometimes was thinking beyond school in his creative approaches to assignments. When an assignment allowed him to tap into his personal interests (the Stalinism essay is an example), he expended more effort. As Bazerman says, if we want motivated writers, we need to assign problems they want to solve for more than the grade.

In spite of these significant challenges, our task as educators is to give our students the very best writing instruction, based on the sound principles that research has demonstrated can increase individuals' writing literacies in multiple discourse communities. Additional longitudinal, comprehensive studies of the development of writing expertise in a variety of discourse communities and the influence of curriculum and instruction on that development would aid our efforts in this area.

CODA

When an administrator asks, "Are students learning to write better in these courses?" usually the answer cannot be a simple "yes" or "no," as this case study demonstrates. When a teacher sits down to plan a course or to grade a set of essays, no matter how many times the task has been done in the past there is a certain feeling of needing the fortitude of Hercules yet again. When a tutor meets with a writer who is stuck or uncertain, the question is, "Where to start?" Because of all the factors in a writer's growth I have outlined here, one must consider multiple variables all together. To each—administrator, teacher, tutor—I would say courage is needed, and patience, and compassion. These must come from within. What I have hoped to supply here is the added element of what to consider as curricular or evaluative decisions with regard to writing are made.

If we return to the questions raised in Chapter 1, I trust the reader has found at least partial answers here:

- *Why can't graduates of freshman writing produce acceptable written documents in other contexts?* In part, because each context requires specialized or "local" know-how. And in part, because we have not yet become experts at teaching for transfer.

- *How can we expend dollars for writing programs wisely? How can we apply the research in composition studies to re-conceptualizing writing programs and teacher/tutor training?* Coach faculty to assign serious intellectual questions for exploration in writing courses and instantiate the inquiry in particular discourse communities. Create developmentally sound linkages in writing curriculum across disciplines and within disciplines. And teach for transfer.

- *How can we set students on a life-long course of becoming more expert writers?* Let them know what is entailed in gaining expertise—continuously tackling more and more difficult writing challenges. Let them practice learning new genres and the ways of new discourse communities and point out the ways in which they have learned these things. Challenge them to apply the same tools in every new writing situation.

Jeff Davis (2004) says there is a source beyond reason where truth originates. I have tried to apply reason here. I hope I have also touched truth.

EPILOGUE
A Conversation Ten Years Later

I sweated through the work of this research project alone. But I always knew I must go back to Carla, Tim's freshman writing teacher, for two reasons: Her read of the manuscript would be another means to triangulate the data, and I owed her the right to comment on my analyses and interpretations of her courses. So I sent her the manuscript when it was a solid second draft. What resulted was a five-hour conversation that we agreed to tape and use as the basis for this epilogue. Here, you may read the edited version of the transcript, which we collaborated on. The italicized portions represent those sections I felt were most germane to the arguments of this book.

Anne: What were some of your thoughts when you read the manuscript?

Carla: Tim was atypical in some important ways. He was really good at expressive writing. That was where his talent was. Each student has his own particular strengths and weaknesses as a writer and usually you need their strengths to find their weaknesses as well. So, yeah, he was not uniquely talented as an expressive writer, but talented, and really enjoyed it. So it doesn't surprise me that he ran into some conflicts as he got further into his majors.

A: Why do you think he didn't enjoy his community writing?

C: Because it was constrained and defined by audience, purpose, genre. And it wasn't an open-ended project in which there was room for him and his personality and his writing style. I think that's another thing that identified him as a certain type of writer. There are certain types of students who are horrified at open ended-ness and who crave to disappear and become just a kind of medium for the genre. Students have different kinds of experiences with writing.

A: And that links to your saying his strength was expressive types of writing and that also defined his views.

C: I don't think that every student has the kind of experience that Tim did as he moved into his major, but every student has some degree of conflict. For some of them, their conflict happens in first year writing, where they're asked to often just think more originally, to draw analytical conclusions of their own — the humanities model. I guess we're still somewhat attached to that bias in teaching academic genres in first year writing.

A: Right. You're absolutely right. And then—

C: *Genre is—I mean getting a grasp on academic genres, whether it's in history or engineering or human biology or philosophy or anything else—is a question of understanding audience and purpose.* The paper you told me about that Tim had written, that complex paper in his history class about the orphanage and so on, I think that at the time you were involved in my classes, ten years ago, I still hadn't really integrated academic writing and community service writing very well. They were just more or less side-by-side. The more I thought about it, the more I realized it was really all about audience and purpose. And you said that was something that Tim recalled and took with him from my class. I encourage my students to understand that, including understanding the context in which they're writing. If that involves writing an academic essay in a particular course context, they're obliged to understand what the reader's expectations are. In other words, the professor's expectations, the conventions of writing in that particular field. If they have an idea that's kind of out of the box . . . I encourage them to think about that risk and decide what their purpose is and what's most important. Was it more important for Tim to get that down? To connect his experience in Russia with political theory he was encountering in this class, even though he was disappointed with how it was received? He may well have decided that was a risk worth taking. I don't know. And if he didn't, if he thought that approaching it that way would be automatically okay, then he wasn't thinking about audience and purpose. You know, when I came to Southern, my first class here was teaching a writing focus in a physics class.

A: Oh really?

C: Yeah. It was the nascent writing in the majors which, at that point, was voluntary on the part of teachers in the disciplines. They could elect to put a writing focus in their classes. If they did they were assigned a writing coach.

A: Coach?

C: Yeah, an instructor, tutor, whatever. So that was my first experience teaching at Southern, helping students in an upper division physics class with their writing in physics. And, boy, that was a challenge. I went out immediately and got a thick dictionary of terms (laughter) in electrical engineering and physics and studied the conventions for writing these reports. And then once I had a grasp of that, but not feeling particularly qualified, I tried to help them with clarity. And really, if they could make it clear to me then they were doing well.

At any rate, I started teaching at what was then called freshman English, in 1995, 10 years ago. And it was very, very much teaching from a literary criticism model. We would teach the research paper as well, and depending on the instructor, that was wide open. *But a lot of what we were teaching in the way of analysis was literature-based. And the freshman writing program was . . . housed within English. And that just in itself says a lot. I never thought that it should be in the English department. I think it gave a mis-impression that we were trying to create English majors,* at least humanities majors, and I have always thought that we should offer a more flexible approach in teaching all students, hopefully giving them the tools that they can use flexibly within the various disciples that they go off to. It was very difficult to teach in a program that had very little coherence. Some people taught it this way, some people taught it that way. But there was really a lot of room for me to develop my own curriculum within some very loose expectations of conferencing, teaching the research paper . . . teaching analytical writing. Students were more or less just assigned randomly to sections of this class, regardless of the interest or lack of interest in the course theme for that section.

A: *What are some typical assignment sequences now?*

C: *The sequence is rhetorical analysis, contextual analysis and the documented research essay. And there is a lot of freedom to invent versions, interesting ways of going about these assignments. The important thing for me is that students encounter, that they recognize that there are many kinds of writing, depending on purpose. It's very challenging and usually produces interesting, sophisticated essays.*

A: Like the paper I was describing to you that Tim wrote in his . . .

C: Yeah I know. When you were talking about that, I thought that. You know I think it's also important to talk about goals at this point. The purpose of our writing program currently is to teach students flexible skills.

A: So maybe it would be good to talk about how you have been able to think through the continuum between academic writing and community writing.

C: *Every piece of writing has an audience and it has a purpose. It may be an academic purpose and within that it may have an analytical or argumentative purpose, as in, say a humanities essay. In other academic genres, the writer may be asked to disappear in any explicit way as in writing a report of some sort. The genres that exist in community based writing are also various, depending on audience and purpose: grant proposals, brochures, web-based writing, fact sheets, position statements, training materials, educational materials. And I think you're asking, "Are composition teachers qualified to teach genres that have to do with disciplines and professions that they can't possibly be fully versed in?" One of the things I like about community writing is that the agency mentor, the community mentor becomes the rhetorical authority. My job is to manage the situation, to understand as much as I possibly can about the audience, about the purpose, about the assignment, to have access to models, and to coach.* And the mentor—even if I do make a suggestion, I put it in very qualified terms, you know, like tell the student to ask the mentor if this or that would be a better approach. And sometimes the mentor says yes and sometimes the mentor says no. And when it comes to writing for an agency, the mentor at the agency has the final word. But my students do have to trust me to understand the assignment well enough to know what I am doing in basic terms, in terms of the genre. Since I have been doing this for fifteen years, I do know how to write a grant proposal at this point and I do know what a good brochure looks like and reads like, including the design elements and the argument it can make. But it can be tricky.

But as for the classroom, that becomes more of a working place and less of a theoretical place. *I frame the work we do in class according to the rhetorical principles that we're dealing with, like, for example, what kinds of appeals are you making in this document? To what degree is this an argument, to what degree are you simply reporting or analyzing or persuading? The classroom is the place where we put it in the larger rhetorical context.* And share the work. And talk about issues that exist out there in the community and the assumptions around academic approaches and very pragmatic, let's-get-down-to-business approaches. There are real differences, for example, between an academic argument and a grant proposal. So even though clarity and organization are really important in both, with a grant proposal you're in a situation where no one is obliged to read you. If they glance at something and it isn't clear, or it doesn't capture them, it goes in the trash. It's gone . . . and you have unambiguously failed to achieve your purpose.

A: Maybe we can shift a little bit . . . going back to your reading of my analysis of things that you did ten years ago in your class. Were there are any surprises for you?

C: In reading this?

A: In reading this. Or we can start with a more general question: What were your reactions?

C: What do you mean by surprises? Like was I was surprised that I did do things a certain way or surprise that you interpreted them as you did?

A: What caught your attention what made you say "oh," whatever that "oh" means. "Oh" interesting or . . . "Oh" wrong or . . .

C: I think one of the surprises was a question of how broad the conclusions can be, based on this one guy or this one teacher. And that is part of the challenge as teachers we face. We set our curriculum but we have a classroom full of very different students headed in very different directions. How do we set a curriculum for all of them? What's our mandate in teaching? Why do we teach? What are our goals in teaching first year writing to this hodge-podge of people? So in a way I have the same sort of challenge as a teacher as you do as a researcher. I have to have an answer to the question, who is my model going to be? Who is the student I am directing myself to? Or is it inherently a custom-built enterprise, teaching such a range of students to write? I think that the way I run conferences it is to an extent tailored to each student, but I have to make the class coherent. It's a challenge. How do we do that?

Let's see. There was a place here. You say,

There's no meaningful activity one might engage within the context of freshman writing that connects it explicitly to any other discourse communities students might be in presently or in the future. For the majority of students freshman writing is not a precursor to a writing major; it is an isolated course, an end to itself a general education requirement to be gotten out of the way.

Well the fact is that even though lots of first-year students say they know what their major is going to be, most of them change their minds after the first year anyway. *So, most students don't know what their majors are. How can we connect what we're doing with specific discourse communities? I don't think we can. Not only because we are not qualified as experts in all these genres. I don't think it's our job. But I don't think this means that we shouldn't expose students to different genres and modes of writing. To make them aware of how they might adapt to a huge range of writing situations, audiences, and purposes. I think it's our job to teach them rhetorical flexibility.* And this, for me, is what community-based writing in an academic context accomplishes.

A: So what you're saying is their community writing context becomes a second discourse community that they bring back into the freshman writing context.

C: Yeah, and that's a premise of service learning; it's not a one-way thing. There is reciprocity in what students take out into the community and what they bring back in. One set of circumstances and kind of knowledge informs another. You write here, let's see,

> Students are ill-prepared to examine questions or understand the literacy standards of discourse communities they are encountering in other disciplines, in the work world or in other social spheres they participate in. This results in negative transfer of learning. What worked for the freshman writing essay is inappropriately applied to the writing of history or social sciences or in business. The student must learn to fail attempts at such transfer of supposed "general writing skills" how to adapt to the standards and purposes for writing in their discourse communities.

I wanted to ask you what you meant by general writing skills. I know you put it in quotations but what do . . .

A: Well, what I mean by that is, I think it's a somewhat vague concept that a lot of people hold. Most academics who are not writing teachers think there is this set of "general writing skills." That's what they say, that is how they will refer to it.

C: How would they . . . Grammar and usage, is it?

A: Yes. With teachers in other disciplines that is what I get. I get an answer that is basically talking about sentence level skills: grammar, usage, punctuation, spelling. That's what others usually mean by "general writing skills." And then in terms of writing teachers, most that I have worked with certainly go beyond the level of grammar and sentence level skills, but they add . . .

C: Organization?

A: Yeah, I hear organization, I hear thesis, I hear purpose, voice. But again, even though they say the words "audience" and "purpose" I don't feel there is a deep interrogation of what that means in the context of their classroom or in the larger context. I think there are a lot of assumptions there.

C: Yeah, there are a lot of assumptions . . .

A: And I want to break through a lot of those assumptions and say, "Hey, let's look at this more closely."

C: Yeah. Definitely, me too. I teach, for example both deductive and inductive strategies for organizing writing, and through that we work on thesis for all kinds of writing, and the thesis is not one thing. Sometimes we talk about thesis questions instead of thesis statements. But you know, in the progressive essay I was telling you about, students' essays come out differently because they take it in whatever direction they want in the end, depending on what they decide is their primary purpose. One student's essay might be more formal, mostly analytical with a deductive thesis. Another student's might be primarily narrative and that thesis will be inductive. An example of how and when and why an inductive thesis might better than deduction, what if you sat down to read a detective novel, and at the end of the first chapter the author wrote, "The butler did it." *I think just exposing them to the idea that in various contexts one fundamental approach toward thesis and organization will work well and another might fall completely flat—it's really important to them to know they have these choice to make, and if you get across the idea of audience and purpose clearly enough they can make judgments about how to apply it. And sometimes they do it well and sometimes they don't. But what else can we teach them in the first year?* And yes, my classroom is a discourse community itself, but then I say that right from the beginning. This is a community.

A: *And how do you name what the features of that community are to them? Or get them to think of the classroom as a discourse community?*

C: *In one course I teach, where the community writing component is very large, we talk about what communities are. We define it. What is a community, what brings people together in a community? What's inclusive about a community and, by definition, what's exclusive about it? And then we talk about language groups, what happens in the exchange between two different communities, the conversation that evolves and where it might go wrong just through the use of language. So, I define the discourse community of the class as educational, basically. And to some extent, personal, because students do relate to one another personally. I define it by asking students to consider what their common interests are and one of common interests is to write better.* So that becomes a serious, identifying trait of this group of people who come together twice a week and then in conferences and so on. So there is a lot of emphasis on having a common understanding of each writer's goal in each rhetorical situation, whether they are writing an academic paper or working on a brochure or a grant proposal. There is a lot of peer review. The first question is: Who's your audience, what's the desired result, and then practicing putting ourselves in different heads. So it's an educational community of writers, with common interests and different values. It's a safe place.

A: *What do you think about my suggestion that comes in Chapter Two, my comments that, yes it's a classroom discourse community, but given the theme of your course at that time, and given your particular philosophy of teaching writing, the discourse community you were introducing them to was creative non-fiction, or literary journalism, or it could have been a subset of creative non-fiction . . .*

C: *I don't think it's my job to teach any one of those genres. One thing that I do disagree with early on is when you are saying something along the lines of there not being an emphasis on research and that assigned writing seemed to be short. You mentioned three pages. I think the précis that I taught might be around that, but the progressive paper is five to seven pages and it asks students to use sources. And the research paper is 12–15 pages. I didn't ask students to write a research paper at the time you observed me. So in the first quarter of the two-semester sequence, as you observed, I did spend a lot more time with the personal essay because I was working with students mostly on organization, on levels of generalization, paragraph level work, sentence level work, because those students generally needed that. Tim was a very good writer in these terms. Then in the second course of the sequence, I exposed them to different kinds of research possibilities, including primary research. In the courses I teach now, personal writing is only one aspect of the contextual assignment. I feel the personal perspective is important to get students connected with the subject matter and with their places as researchers. So I hold on to a part of that.* But specifically you asked me what I thought of . . .

A: Well naming . . . I mean I do think we agree that the classroom itself is a discourse community and that needs to be acknowledged upfront, that the educational context is a discourse community.

C: Yeah. And we're not pretending here. We are here for an actual purpose.

A: And we can't pretend that we are generalists or whatever.

C: *You had asked me why not teach a course in creative non-fiction or environmental writing . . .*

A: *Or explain that those are discourse communities your course at least touches on, and has some connections with.*

C: *Because it's too narrow. The environmentally-themed course that I teach touches not just on environmental writing . . . in fact it doesn't really focus on environmental writing as a specific genre at all. . . . I mean people aren't doing environmental reports, they're doing . . .*

A: *Environmental journalism maybe?*

C: *Maybe early on in the course, while they are learning about their relationship to writing and learning about voice and so on. But by the time they are writing their research papers they are definitely writing an academic paper, but it isn't in a field or discipline per se. It's within the context of learning how to do research, how to draw analytical conclusions based on research.*

A: *Some people say this is the dilemma: can we teach some kind of generic academic writing in freshman writing that is actually useful and is good preparation for their moving into the disciplines, into their professional writing? That is one of the big questions for the field right now. I think it is a very thorny issue. And some institutions have said, "No, we can't and so let's just do away with freshman writing" and they go directly to writing in the major.*

C: *Well, I think that really undercuts the liberal arts mission. You know, the idea that part of what you do is you build a fire under the mind and open people up early on to a broader view of human experience and ways of looking at things. One of the things I like about the course themes I've developed is that they are inherently interdisciplinary—looking at things as a philosopher, as a biologist, as a geologist, as a literary person, a historian, as someone interested in business or economics.*

A: How do you get to that interdisciplinary way?

C: Well, environment is a really good theme for all of those things. Students over and over again in their course evaluations say, "I had no idea that the ways this one idea, this one question—which is where do human beings fit in the scheme of things? The natural world? "Who are we ?—connects with every conceivable discipline at the university." So given that, you have students pursuing their interest within that theme, and sharing ideas, sharing rhetorical problems. It has taken me a really long time, my whole career so far, to get a better and better handle on that, and what the rhetorical umbrella is that brings the whole works together in a coherent way.

A: And for you that umbrella is rhetorical situation.

C: Yeah it is. It's most essential. Trying to make it real and variable for students as much as possible.

A: *See, another part of my claim, and this is a theoretical issue, is that traditional rhetoric and even more contemporary rhetoric still has a hard time fully accounting for all of the dynamics of social context. And what I am arguing is more from an anthropological perspective than a rhetorical point of view. There are certainly elements of rhetorical theory in the view I'm espousing, but it's a broader, anthropologically-based view that is looking at communities as discourse communities. Considering things like what is the social hierarchy as that affects writing? What is the role of text within the social dynamics of that community? What is the epistemology of that particular community? A whole series of questions that, at least in my understanding of rhetoric, don't necessarily get asked.*

C: *No, they don't.*

A: *And I feel they are very important because they affect the immediate rhetorical decisions.*

C: *Oh, absolutely.*

A: *So I'm trying to create a frame that is a little broader than audience and purpose.*

C: *Or a little more focused.*

A: *However you want to say it.*

C: I think that is what WAC should be about. That is what writing in the majors should be about. It should provide the theoretical, anthropological basis for writing in that field. It's like, what are we doing and why are we doing it? What does it say about this community of professionals or scholars or whatever? I don't think there is any way, if our goal is to provide sort of a general education in an introductory writing course, to do that. I mean yes, we bring up all sorts of ideas around discourse communities, including with the reading that my students do. I don't know if you know June Jordan's essay "Nobody Mean More to Me Than You."

A: No.

C: . . . and "The Future Life of Willie Jordan?" That's the first reading we do in all my classes because it brings up so clearly the reality of discourse communities, of language identity—in this case, primarily ethnically based. Identity politics and the language around them, it personalizes the choices people make about who they are talking to and why. *So yes, bringing up ideas around discourse communities is part of what I do in first year writing—and no doubt ten years ago I was not as clear about that as I am now. That's a long time to develop one's teaching practice.*

A: What's helped you to get clearer?

C: Well, community-based writing for sure has helped. What else has helped me? Well, you know, the kind of rhetorical focus now in my program; that kind of coherence has helped. Having the institutional support for a series of writing requirements has helped tremendously. It clarifies what you are doing. I think at the time that you observed there was a feeling that I had to do everything, that this was all these students were going to get in the way of focused instruction. I was the only person who was going to sit down with Tim and tell him that he was a wonderful writer and give him the credit he deserved for what he was especially good at. I couldn't help him apply it two years down the road in his history class or in his engineering class, but, well now someone else is going to be doing that in writing in the majors for every student. And I have a much more coherent way to explain what I'm doing, to put the history of rhetoric behind it and to apply it in novel ways because of the context in which courses exist now in our program.

A: *And that context, that rhetorical context wasn't as clear to you ten years ago?*

C: *Oh, hell no. It wasn't.*

A: *. . . because you didn't have training in it.*

C: *No, I did not. And that's changing, at least where I am. Since I was trained as a writer, not in composition and rhetoric, it's been a very steep learning curve. We're getting much more training now, more opportunities for professional development. It was a challenge for me, but it was close enough to what I was after all those years. Although it's hard, I welcome it. There is also the whole language, just studying and reading about rhetoric. I mean a lot of my understanding was intuitive, because I was a writer and I faced these situations, working through them on my own. And so I knew intuitively, even a long time ago, how I wanted to do it. The working it through in practical terms without any institutional support was very difficult and now I have a lot more institutional support, but I also have an understanding and a language to put to it that, well, it's professionalized what I do.*

A: *Let's just go back to the any-more-surprises question, and what did it feel like to be the subject of the research study, you know, both in* terms of the time of, and now, reading this . . . This hasn't been easy?

C: *No.*

A: *Just tell me, honestly. Because I think this is something of value to me and of value to the research community, and I hope to the larger community, to hear what it's been like to be a subject of close analysis.*

C: *Um . . . it has been hard. Um . . . I'll just start putting out reasons. . . . I think there are ways in which it is hard that are rational, and, you know, make sense; there are also ways in which it is just kind of, uh, you know, "Oh yuck." You know, the way you respond when you see yourself on videotape or hear your voice.*

A: *Right.*

C: *Um . . . I think that, I . . . it was hard because I feel like I bear a heavy weight here, not just scrutiny. The critical conclusions that you draw, because I'm providing the occasion for them, it therefore feels heavy. There's a part of me that has hurt feelings in a way because I, of all people, was trying at that time, ten years ago, to address exactly the sorts of issues that you raise without a lot of support institutionally. And, um, I remember feeling when you asked me if I was interested in participating, and if I would participate, I . . . well, first of all I said yes because I respected, I got a good feel from you, you know, and that you were very sharp; we have a lot in common—what we value about education. I felt incredibly enthusiastic and turned on in my teaching at that point, and I felt it was kind of remarkable that, not just I, but several of my colleagues, how, given the lack of guidance that we had, and certainly the lack of status, we were nonetheless really, really, really committed, and giving our students the best of what we had, and I, you know, I still feel that way.*

    But I think of . . . well, I felt that I was trying as hard as maybe one or two others in our department were, to bring the real world in, to bring all the thinking and research and writing that is entailed into the mix. I . . . oh, just as an aside, in terms of goals for teaching, I really don't know in what combination my goals are to teach students in a first-year writing course how to be flexible writers, so that they can write well in the rest of their education career, or, to prepare them for writing beyond. Probably both, but I don't know to what extent each is important . . .

Anyway, I think, my feelings were a little hurt and I felt kind of unrepresented, partly because there wasn't a lot of discussion of community writing, my efforts to bring that into the classroom so that my students could experience the difference between that and academic writing. I think I was doing better than most teachers in being aware that that was a gap, and that teaching so-called academic writing was a seriously limited approach.

A: Yeah.

C: So it was that. It was also one hell of a long time ago. Ten years ago. And although most of the basic premises of my teaching are the same, they have evolved in, I think, productive ways. So you feel just a little foolish, looking back, saying to yourself, "Oh, wow." Actually, you asked what surprised me. A little over two years ago when you were presenting at 4C's San Antonio, I don't remember whether you said that you were working on this book and that it was getting there. If you did, I spaced it out. So I was just surprised when this manuscript showed up. Tim and I are so in it. *The focus is uncomfortable combined with the broad conclusions about what's wrong with first-year writing institutionally and how we teach it. Because I felt proud then and I feel even more proud now about how far I'd come and I feel self-conscious about that burden of representing all teachers. Of course, when you were in my classroom, I felt really good about you being there because I wanted to share whatever I was doing because I thought it was exciting. I had no idea the study would become public after such a long time had passed and even if I had, I wouldn't have been able to envision how that would feel or what changes would transpire at my university or in my own teaching practice. It just feels very odd to be focused on so minutely and critically when my impetus was to invite you in order to share. I guess this is . . . how could I have known what you were going to do with the material? You didn't know what you were going to do with the material.*

A: *Right*

C: *So that was a lesson in being a research subject. It's not about that moment, but it's about a lot of different moments and a lot of different moments with theoretical and institutional contexts changing along with the teaching.*

A: *I think that is a very interesting point.*

C: *I tended to see it as that moment without context, I mean that was your job, to give the contexts. But it was kind of shocking, and not to have been involved in the process all that time.* I imagine Tim feels differently because he's had many conversations with you over the years. And more recently . . .

A: Well, he hasn't shared in the process of the analysis, certainly, but I was fortunate that I did not lose touch with him, because there were gaps in my data that I thought were critical to fill in by talking to him, if I could. I think I sent him the history chapter when it came out. I can't remember, to tell you the truth. And I will send him the whole thing, but . . . I think his interest in it will be marginal. He's not in education now.

C: Yep. Well, I have a lot at stake here.

A: Yes, of course.

C: In terms of professional pride. It's a unique position to be brought back to life after ten years and read yourself on the page.

A: So it's been hard.

C: Yes, I think there were some things missing that I wish had been there. Yes, more on community writing, definitely.

A: What else?

C: What I was trying to work through: the side-by-side assignments that I was trying to bring together, in order to look at academic writing and "real world writing," the differences between them, the similarities. How to view them together in a relevant way and bring the rhetorical coherence to the course. You know, I was very much in process with that. And I would work it out—better and better.

A: I would imagine that given that you've only had a month or a little more to digest this, it is probably too soon for you to reflect on . . .

C: I haven't fully digested it, I haven't. I'm very much in the process of doing that.

A: That makes a lot of sense. So if . . .

C: *I feel in an awkward position in terms of, suggesting what I feel is missing or you know . . . questioning some conclusions or some premises, because obviously I don't want to say, "You should change that."*

A: *Yeah.*

C: *As a writer and a teacher of writing my impulse is to collaborate and participate. It's hard to know what the boundaries are, so although I've been very honest in my responses and telling you what my responses have been, I don't know quite what to do with this.*

A: *What your role is.*

C: *Yeah. So retrospectively I guess I have a role right now, but I'm not exactly sure what it is, even though its been explained to me [laughs] in general terms. For example, did I really say that, because it's so different from what I feel now, and not being altogether certain. Not remembering how my teaching philosophy actually progressed from year to year.*

A: *Do you want me to send you the tapes?*

C: *[laughs] No, please don't! I'll give you anything. God . . . that would be horrible.*

A: There is another form of research. That is, it's a more collaborative model where you are teacher-researcher along with the researcher and we're constantly interacting at every stage.

C: This wasn't that sort.

A: No, it wasn't. So basically what you're telling me is that would have been preferable to this.

C: I'm not sure. It's just challenging to have been . . . suddenly here's a full-blown manuscript. I had no idea I would be featured or to what extent. I knew you were talking to other people and other classes. Just the intensity of the focus was difficult. It made me self-conscious.

A: Yeah. I guess I have to think about, you know, in other classroom-based research projects, would I do it in the same way? I will really have to think about that. At the time that I was working on this, it didn't occur to me to do it the other way. To be honest, ideally, I wish it had occurred to me, so that . . .

C: You weren't at that place.

A: Yeah . . . so I could have weighed the pros and cons. And maybe had some discussion with you. So that's something that I take from this.

C: So maybe as you followed Tim you might have followed the teacher as well.

A: Yeah, right.

C: Over a longer period of time. Because teachers learn too.

A: Is there anything else you feel like I missed, I didn't capture . . .

C: Well, I think some background information. I guess exploring some of the premises, like what is the goal in teaching first year writing or what are the ranges, the range of goals? How have they changed? And where, and under what circumstances? As you said they haven't changed in most places all that much. You know, things like, well a modes approach to teaching writing was very popular and now it's not so much. It's more, more based on audience and purpose and the way I envision that now.

A: *What have you been mulling as you've read this?*

C: *It gives me faith in myself that I was definitely on the right track all those years. I feel good about that. And the fact that the curricular changes, the institutional support I have received in terms of personal development and in terms of work situation, our status, our pay and so on. That, you know, I hung in there and I kept working at it and it's been vindicated because I see my approach reflected in the way things are changing, at least where I teach. And I feel very fortunate in that.*

A: *Well, in the short period of time you've had to react to this, what are the things you think you'll continue to think about? This particular study, and the time lapse and the institutional changes you've experienced helps you reflect on the influence of the institutional context on your teaching?*

C: *Totally. It also just gives me a perspective on what took form from ten years ago until now, the heart of my career, the core of my career. It puts it in brackets and it's very interesting to look back in a structured way. To be provided a structure, even if the conclusions I draw are different from the ones you draw.*

A: *Yeah*

C: *And how things in our field do change. It's hard to see those changes. At my institution they have been fairly dramatic at times, but that was preceded with years and years and years of change at a snail's pace. So change is possible.*

There are changes in the field and they can be productive. And, basically, I like the direction in which I am seeing things go and that is encouraging. I think it helps me see a way in which to contextualize what I did. Because the reason we connected all that time ago was because of genre-based, or real world writing, or whatever you want to call it—who writers are and what they do in different contexts. And so, having your point of view around that over time, as well as my own and certain of my colleagues', is great, it's interesting.

POSTSCRIPT

Readers will draw their own conclusions from this conversation and what further light it sheds on both the challenges of teaching writing to college students and the challenges of classroom-based research. For my part, I have mixed feelings about this conversation.

On the one hand, I am once again so grateful to Carla for her honesty, integrity, and courage to reveal her thoughts and feelings to me and our readers. She could have easily declined this occasion once again for dialogue and going public. I feel her efforts to do so make this report that much stronger. That she does not agree with my interpretations in some respects is important to note.

On the other hand, I feel a certain sadness, for two reasons. For one, I regret the discomfort I caused Carla for having conducted a one-way research project that left her feeling surprised and vulnerable in the end. Even though I followed proper human subjects procedures and was up front with Carla about my purposes, as she said, "I tended to see it [the data collection] as that moment without context." In hindsight, I think it would have been better, if time allowed and the teacher were interested, to do a collaborative research project, like the fine work that Steve Fishman and Lucille McCarthy have done over the years. Such efforts can yield unexpected synergies and lessons for both researchers, even though, as Fishman and McCarthy (2002) point out, there is no guarantee of an altogether smooth working relationship. But there is no hierarchy. The process is more egalitarian.

The second cause for sadness or concern as I read the transcript of our conversation is the gut feeling that Carla and I were talking past each other. Every time Carla mentioned "rhetorical situation" I was thinking "no: discourse community." In some ways, that is the whole point of this work—that the more fully we can understand and take into account all of the ramifications of social context (not just matters of audience and purpose and genre) on the teaching and learning of writing skills, the better the chances that learning in school will be for life, not just for the rhetorical moment. I don't think Carla and I are just having semantic problems. Rather, there is a viewpoint that I hope I have conveyed that takes issue with a long tradition of using rhetorical theory as the primary framework for the teaching of freshman writing. This difference, I think, is not a small one. Based on more recent interdisciplinary research and dialogue, I see enormous possibilities for a radical re-conceptualization of one of higher education's major endeavors—to produce more literate citizens. I hope readers will see the possibilities I am proposing, and together we will find better ways to do this important work.

APPENDIX A
From Research to Practice: Some Ideas for Writing Instruction

Here I briefly lay out a few of the teaching strategies I and my graduate student and collaborator, Dana Driscoll, have developed and tested in the classroom to put into practice the principles laid out in Chapter 6—principles that enable writers to become more flexible and learn writing requirements in new contexts more readily. I also draw on the excellent work of Amy Devitt, Mary Jo Reiff, and Anis Bawarshi in *Scenes of Writing: Strategies for Composing with Genres* (2004). And if ideas I think are mine were in fact borrowed from others but I no longer remember, I trust those individuals will let me know so that I can express gratitude and give proper acknowledgement.

TEACHING FOR TRANSFER

As I explained in Chapter 6, writers will not automatically bridge, or bring forward, appropriate writing strategies and knowledge to new writing situations unless they have an understanding of both the need to do so and a method for doing so. In other words, writers, if they want to gain expertise in multiple genres and discourse communities, have to learn to become lifelong learners. The developmental process for writers never ends.

So teachers and tutors who teach for transfer are doing a great service to their students. I would encourage all to read the articles I have cited by Perkins and Salomon (1989) for a deeper understanding of the research on transfer of learning. Keeping in touch with one or several students over the course of the students' education and entry into the work world to see what writing situations and difficulties they encounter and how they handle them can also enrich one's perspective on teaching writing. The ideas presented here will also guide teachers and tutors to aid their students in developing what Smit (2004) calls "rhetorical flexibility" and I would refer to as multiple writing expertises.

1. Teach learners to frame specific problems and learnings into more abstract principles that can be applied to new situations.

Expert knowledge is not just a head full of facts or patterns, a reservoir of data for the intellect to operate upon. Rather, it is information so finely adapted to task requirements that it enables experts to do remarkable things with intellectual equipment that is bound by the same limitations as that of other mortals (Bereiter and Scardamalia 1993, p.30).

The model of writing expertise (see Figure 1, page 18) as well as the concepts within the framework that are specific to writing situations—discourse community, genre, and rhetorical situation, are the kinds of "abstract principles" that can be taught explicitly and may help writers to frame their knowledge in ways that aid transfer to new writing situations. Generally, I begin with the concept of genres, and then, after students have read, discussed, written in several genres and we have talked about the nature of each, I bridge to the discourse communities students know and participate in. These "meta" discussions and activities are interwoven with the normal course activities of reading, discussing, and analyzing core readings and working on writing projects. Here are just a few of the ways these concepts can be introduced:

Ways to Teach Genre Awareness

- Type up a horoscope in poem format (short lines/verses). Ask a student to read this "poem." Ask for comments on the features that make it a "poem." Then reveal the true genre and discuss how one's mental schema for a genre influences the way one reads and interprets texts.

- Ask students to make a list of 10 genres they regularly read. Have them pick three and describe how they read them differently. Do the same exercise with 10 genres students regularly write. Then hypothesize how the genre prescribes or influences the processes entailed in reading or writing them (from *Scenes of Writing*).

- Collect multiple samples of a short, simple genre: for example, obituaries, wedding announcements, news briefs, postcards, abstracts of journal articles. Using a matrix like the one on the next page (acknowledging its simplified format for describing genres), ask students to identify key genre features. Then discuss the social actions and values represented in these genre features.

- Give students a short reading selection without disclosing the source. Ask them to infer the genre, then discuss its properties and how that influences the meaning of the text. Some possible sources: newspaper or magazine editorials, song lyrics, advertising copy.

GENRE FEATURES

	obituaries	journal abstracts
Rhetorical purpose(s)		
Typical content		
Structural features		
Linguistic features		

- Assign a brief topic and a genre students will use to write on the topic (for example, an ad to sell something in the newspaper). Then assign the same topic to be written in a different genre (a bulletin board notice? a listing on eBay?). Compare treatments of the subject in the two genres and how rhetorical purpose, content, structure, and linguistic features change (or not) in each genre (from *Scenes of Writing*).

- After students have collected multiple examples of a genre, analyzed the genre, and have written in that genre, have small groups write a "how to" guide for composing in this genre that other writers can use (Coe 1994).

Ways to Teach the Concept of Discourse Community

- Introduce the concept with a definition such as this: "A discourse community is a social group that communicates at least in part via written texts and shares common goals, values, and writing standards, a specialized vocabulary and specialized genres." Then present numerous examples of texts from very divergent discourse communities and ask students if they can discern which discourse community "owns" or uses the text (for example—the baseball scores reported in the daily newspaper, or lyrics from a rap song). Based on these text samples, students may speculate on what the features of the discourse community are, using the definition as a heuristic.

- For a given discourse community the students know (one's major, or a social group one is associated with), brainstorm a list of all of the genres one uses in the discourse community.

For each genre, ask students to identify common elements
that are found in all of the genres that reflect on the discourse
community's goals, and norms for good writing. Have them
compare the relationships between the genres.

- Ask students to bring to class sample texts from discourse communities they are members of. Remind them of the definition
  of discourse community. Have them do a brief freewrite on the
  ways that discourse community defines itself via its shared texts.
  Discuss their examples.

- Do a matrix such as the one below for the discourse communities of different academic disciplines. Have students who are
  familiar with (or majoring in) the different disciplines complete
  the matrix for their discipline. Have a whole group discussion of
  similarities and differences in the features of different academic
  discourse communities.

	Natural Sciences Discourse Community	Social Sciences Discourse Community	Humanities Discourse Community
Discourse community goals & values			
Typical genres (oral and written)			
Norms for genres (standards for good writing)			
Writers' tasks/roles in the discourse community			

- Show students two texts on the same topic, but written for different discourse communities (for example, a science report
  in *The New York Times* and one on the same topic in a scientific
  journal such as *Nature*). Ask them to list the differences they
  see. Refer back to the definition of discourse community and
  ask students to infer what the discourse community that "owns"
  each text values, based on features of the sample genres.

- Have students join a listserv or newsgroup and "lurk" for two
  weeks (a virtual discourse community). Observe special terminology used, or common terms that are given special meaning.

Observe who the members are. Answer these questions about the discourse community: What do you think the goals of the community are? How do the community's goals and values shape what they write? What else do you notice about the writing of this group? What content is important to this group? What themes are expressed across multiple texts? Are there dissenting voices? (from *Scenes of Writing*)

- Assign an ethnography of communication for a discourse community of the student's choice (an academic community, a social organization, a volunteer group they work for, a workplace setting, etc.). Teach the skills for taking field notes and conducting interviews and gathering written artifacts. Assign a library research component as well—what others have written about this discourse community. Discuss ways of parsing the definition of discourse community for analysis of the data. Have students prepare a final report on their research to describe the discourse community to an outsider. For examples of ethnographies of discourse communities, see Beaufort (1991), Fishman (1988), Heath (1983).

2. Give students numerous opportunities to apply abstract concepts in different social contexts

If knowledge is just items in a mental filing cabinet, then it is easy to acknowledge that an expert must have a well-stocked filing cabinet, but that is like saying that a cook must have a well-stocked pantry. The pantry is not the cook, the filing cabinet is not the expert. What counts with cooks and experts is what they do with the material in their pantries or memory stores (Bereiter and Scardamalia 1993, p.45).

Once students understand the frameworks for analyzing writing in different social contexts, they can be given tasks that invite comparisons, and using the concepts to "decode" what is happening in new writing situations. For example:

- Have students compare texts assigned in a given course they are taking for genre features and relationship to the discourse communities represented.

- Ask students to collect writing assignments from different courses and different professors. Students can analyze the assignments for genres assigned and inferences in the assignment about the discourse community represented.

- Assign students a writing task in a given genre for a given discourse community. Then ask them to write about the same content for a different discourse community. Afterwards, ask them to reflect on the differences in how they approached the tasks (writers' roles), what values and goals of the discourse communities they had to keep in mind, and what norms for genres they needed to change for a different discourse community.

- Assign a community service project or an internship in a field related to the subject matter of the course. Prepare students to analyze the social context using the theoretical lenses of discourse community knowledge and genre knowledge and rhetorical situation as they are working on the assignment. Bridge back to the academic context with a discussion of differences between the academic discourse community and the discourse community of their field work.

3. Teach the practice of mindfulness, or meta-cognition, to facilitate positive transfer of learning

In its fullest sense progressive problem-solving means living an increasingly rich life—richer in that more and more of what the world has to offer is taken into one's mental life. But that increasing richness, because of its time and cognitive demands, requires the judicious reduction of peripheral problems. Sages like Henry David Thoreau have been telling us that for a long time (Bereiter and Scardamalia 1993, p.).

This principle is an extension of the familiar step in the writing process of reflection after the project is completed. What is important for transfer is constantly connecting new and already-acquired knowledge. Here are some suggestions for fostering meta-cognition about writing knowledge that will also aid transfer of learning.

- In the write-ups for writing assignments, make explicit to students the ways in which the new work connects to skills already practiced.

- Have students keep a process journal. At the end of each writing project, they can answer a series of questions such as these:

  1. *What did I learn in doing this writing project about writing itself?*

  2. *How did I learn what I learned in this project?*

  3. *How does this new knowledge about writing connect to what I already knew about writing?*

  4. *What do I want to remember to apply to the next writing project or situation?*

  5. *How did this project add to my understanding of the concepts of discourse community and genre?*

  6. *Which knowledge domains did I struggle with the most in this writing project: discourse community knowledge? subject matter knowledge? genre knowledge? rhetorical knowledge? writing process knowledge? What could I do better in the next project in one of these knowledge domains?*

- Have a general discussion with students after all have completed their process journal for a project—a meta-discussion about process. At the end of the discussion, have students add to their process journal anything else they want to remember for the next project as a result of the discussion.

- Midway through a new writing project, encourage students to look at their process entry for the last project to see what they need to remember to do in this project.

- When students receive written feedback on their work, have them respond to that feedback in their process journal.

- Format grading rubrics in ways that highlight the specific concepts about writing you want to reinforce with students. Use the same rubric consistently on multiple assignments. At the end of the course, ask students to analyze these feedback rubrics for changes/growth in their writing skills.

BUILDING DEVELOPMENTAL ASSIGNMENT SEQUENCES

> Expertise is not simply about problem-solving. Experts, we propose, tackle problems that increase their expertise, whereas non-experts tend to tackle problems for which they do not have to extend themselves (Bereiter and Scardamalia 1993, p.78).

Bereiter and Scardamalia conclude, after extensive research on the nature of expertise in many domains of knowledge, that the single most distinguishing characteristic of those who gain expertise in a variety of skill domains are those who continually assign themselves more and more complex problems to solve. For educators, this translates to a need for students to experience sequenced writing assignments within and across courses in which skills required to complete the task build upon previously acquired skills.

Berryman (1992) reminds us of the multiple dimensions of knowledge and skill in which teachers must simultaneously foster increasing complexity: domain knowledge (conceptual and factual), problem-solving strategies, cognitive management strategies (how to get the writing done), and learning strategies (how to cope with new challenges in a project). In addition, Berryman offers these *principles for sequencing*:

- global skills before local skills (developing an overall sense of the terrain before moving into details),

- increasing complexity,

- increasing diversity.

The five-part model of writing expertise used in this study is another good guide for considering all dimensions of writing expertise that must be built into a curriculum.

For those writing center administrators responsible for training tutors and writing tutor-training guides, I would suggest considering a series of more detailed heuristics, based on materials I have presented here, for global revisions of texts that could aid tutors and their students in thinking through the multiple dimensions of any piece of writing. The materials presented here would also assist tutors working in a campus writing center in generating, with their clients, more awareness of context-specific features of a particular writing task either in the pre-writing or revising stages of work.

For those responsible for developing curricula for writing intensive courses in the disciplines, I would suggest developing heuristics for thinking through the subject matter, genre, discourse community, rhetorical, and writing process aspects of the discipline. Such heuristics could serve to guide faculty as they design writing projects for their students. In addition, department chairs and deans would do well to fund faculty initiatives to think through and design a sequenced writing curriculum in given majors or concentrations. Some of the teaching suggestions offered below, for writing courses, could be adapted to discipline-specific writing courses as well.

For those responsible for developing curricula for general writing courses, I offer the following outline of a writing curriculum, with its associated assignment sequence, as an example of such a curriculum. In addition to a careful scaffolding of skills from one assignment to the next, there are feeder assignments that develop the sub-skills needed in each major writing project.

The course is also theme-based, so that a cohesive intellectual content is built along with practice and instruction in basic writing skills. While some may counter that students bring a subject matter with them—their lived experiences—this curriculum is based on the assumption that a focused theme and joint intellectual inquiry can facilitate creating a community of learners, a temporary discourse community, that in some small way approximates other discourse communities (Jolliffe 1995). For this particular course, the theme "Writing as Social Practice" serves the dual purposes of a topic for investigation and as a reinforcement of fundamental principles about the nature of writing. (David Smit, in *The End of Composition,* also proposes a similar theme for a first-year writing course.) In what follows, I designate which pieces of the curriculum are shared with students and which are for the teacher's benefit.

COURSE OVERVIEW: WRITING AS SOCIAL PRACTICE (FOR STUDENTS)

Who do you write for: self? family? partner? friends? teachers? social or political groups? colleagues? And why do you write: to handle emotions? to think? to connect with others? to gain some course of action or a specific result?

For all of these audiences and all of these purposes, we write. Some of our writing is private, some is public. Vygotsky, a Russian psychologist who wrote in the early 1900s, argued from his studies on language acquisition that even "inner speech" is social in the sense that we internalize the language around us and re-appropriate it for our selves.

So, the premise of this course is that writing is a social act—an act of connecting with others and with our worlds for multiple purposes. Together, we will explore how our writing is shaped by and shapes these multiple social worlds. We will examine the literacy practices that thread through our lives and the ways in which our social relationships are maintained or extended through what we write (or do not write). And we will examine the ways in which we can expand our social networks through writing.

Here are the *essential questions* that will guide our inquiry in this course. They have no "right" or "wrong" answers. We will revisit them on a frequent basis as the course progresses. And, we may add new questions to our list.

- How does writing change from one social context to another? How can we explain those changes?

- What's at stake in one's ability to express thoughts well in writing? How does writing skill impact social relationships? Power relationships?

- What practices can best help us in learning to add new writing skills to our repertoires?

COURSE OUTLINE (FOR TEACHERS)

The curriculum consists of five interconnected units intended for a 15–week semester. Each unit focuses on a different aspect of writing within and about a discourse community or multiple discourse communities. In Unit 1, students will be introduced to discourse community theory and explore their own literacy practices, as well as receive coaching in managing the writing process. They are also introduced to the genre of the autobiographical essay. In Unit 2, students will complete a textual analysis of two pieces of writing on the same topic written in different genres for the same or different discourse communities. They gain a working understanding of how to think of texts as genres and genres as social acts that embody discourse community values, goals, and norms, and learn the norms for an academic essay as it would appear in most discourse communities in the humanities. In Unit 3, we add ethnographic research into the mix, having students collect and analyze texts from a discourse community to reinforce and deepen the learning in Units 1 and 2 about these key concepts, as well as beginning to do both field and library research in a university setting. They again write an academic essay, with a rhetorical purpose of either informing or persuading their audience of some key finding in their research.

Unit 4 is an optional unit (depending on pacing of the course and student needs) to extend research skills. Topics for the second research project may vary, but we encourage continuing to build on the theme of the social dynamics in writing practices. Students might extend their ethnography from Unit 3 or pick related themes: exploring another discourse community, or a topic such as censorship, intellectual property issues, language policy issues, language and identity, propaganda campaigns, political rhetoric, etc. Unit 5 is a short unit focused on revision, in which students will be asked to revise their essay from either Unit 2 or Unit 3. This final project, a major revision after students have gotten some distance from the earlier draft, enables them to deepen and affirm what they have learned in the course about all five aspects of expert writing knowledge: discourse community knowledge, subject matter knowledge, genre knowledge, rhetorical knowledge, and writing process knowledge.

Here are the assignments for Units 1, 2, and 3, feeder assignments that lead up to the major essay, and readings for the units.

Unit 1: Literacy Autobiography (for teachers)

The literacy autobiography is a way for students to get their feet wet with writing a literary essay, using subject matter they are familiar with. At the same time they are introduced to key concepts that frame the course: meta-cognition of writing processes, discourse community theory, and genre theory. Rather than just a recounting of events, the assignment will require that they analyze their own literacy practices using discourse community and genre theories. The assignment will also facilitate their understanding how their past experiences have shaped who they are as writers now. Teachers are encouraged to share their own literacy histories and writing practices with students as well. In addition to using the feeder assignments below, teachers can use any of the activities described in the "Teaching for Transfer" section that precedes this section.

Focus Skill Areas

Discourse Community Analysis: Understanding of discourse community concepts; analyzing one's own membership in various discourse communities.

Meta-cognition: Reflection and analysis of individual writing practices, how those practices were formed, and how those practices were shaped by the social context in which a writer is situated.

Autobiography as a Genre: Learning the literary genre of the autobiographical essay.

Unit Readings

(Note: all readings except for one reading in Unit 2, the McCloud piece on comic strips, are taken from the essays available in the Bedford/St. Martins Custom Reader package)

"How to Tame a Wild Tongue" by Gloria Anzaldua

Anzaldua's autobiographical piece reflects on her struggles with language and identity as a bilingual of English and Spanish (and several other cross-varieties she identifies). It is a very interesting piece of writing in that "how" it was written is almost as important as "what" is being said. So this can do double duty in terms of both a look at language/literacy and a piece for rhetorical analysis.

"Why I Write" by George Orwell

In this piece, Orwell talks about how historical events he witnessed and took part in helped shape himself as a writer. He analyzes the reasons that people write, finally ending with his own political motivations. The essay has strong connections to writing as a social practice and the evolution or stages that each writer goes through as he or she is developing.

"Mother Tongue" by Amy Tan

In this piece, Tan describes her mother's "broken English" and struggles with the notion of cultural identity as it relates to language. Tan's essay truly demonstrates the struggle of assimilation of generations of Chinese immigrants in terms of language acquisition.

"Power of Books" by Richard Wright

Another type of literacy autobiography, this piece brings in how much culture has an influence on the literacy practices of the author. As a struggling American in the early part of the 20th century, Wright demonstrates how books gave him a sense of power and authority. With this piece one can make greater connections to how literacy itself is a social act determined not only by an individual writer but that individual's larger culture.

Feeder 1.1 Discourse Community Map adapted from *Scenes of Writing*

Using a large piece of paper, construct a discourse community map that outlines the different discourse communities you belong to and the different literacies you must have in order to be a member of each discourse community. Use posterboard or tape several smaller pieces of paper together.

Consider the following areas when creating your map:

- What are the conventions of this discourse community? i.e. What are the purposes and goals of the community and norms for "good writing?"

- Texts: what are the typical genres use by members of this discourse community

- Topics: what subjects are written on in this discourse community?

- Terminology/lingo: what specialized language is used and why is it used? Provide examples.

- Joining the discourse community—how does one become an insider? What are the writing activities and roles of discourse community members?

Here is an example:

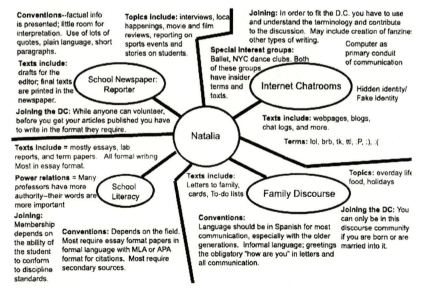

Feeder 1.2 Writing Rituals adapted from *Professional and Public Writing*

Each writer develops a set of "rituals" when she writes (even if she does not realize she's doing it!). These rituals can be helpful and effective (such as organizing your notes before you write or finding a quiet place) or not as helpful (such as stopping writing every 15 minutes to check your email). It is very important to help develop rituals that maximize your effectiveness as a writer. This journal entry will help you start become aware in a meta-cognitive way of your own writing process, i.e. how you get writing done.

Task: In your class journal, write a page on your own writing rituals answering some of the following questions:

- What rituals do you practice when you write?

- How do you think these rituals started?

- Have they changed over time or do they change in different places or when doing different kinds of writing?

- For example, has your use of a computer formed or changed your rituals?

- Have your writing rituals changed since you have come to college?

Feeder 1.3 Genre Features of an Autobiographical Essay

For the first essay assignment you will be asked to write a literary essay on your own literacy practices. In this unit, you have read literacy autobiographies by several authors, each with his or her own style, but each also following genre conventions of the literary essay. Go back to the literary essays we have read, and pick out at least six key features that define the genre of literary essay (and the sub-genre of personal essay) from other genres.

Here are some suggestions for discovering the genre features:

- Rhetorical purpose: what seems to be the author's purpose in writing about these experiences, in this genre? What do you think the author intended the reader to experience?

- Content: What types of evidence are used? Examples? Quotes? Hypotheticals? Primary research? Secondary research? What seem to be typical themes in these essays about literacy?

- Structure: How is the text organized? (in terms of paragraph organization, overall organization). How does each piece begin? How does it end? Are there any consistent conventions regarding structure among the autobiographies?

- Linguistic features: Think about what types of language are used in the texts—is it formal or informal? Is there any specialized vocabulary used in the texts?

Create a two-column chart similar to the example below. Be sure to correctly cite page numbers and authors for the provided examples.

Genre features	Examples
Rhetorical purpose (s):	
Content: The first person is used frequently in Autobiographical works	"I remember being caught speaking Spanish" (Anzaldua, 658) "I weighed the personalities of the men on the job" (Wright, 1622)
Structure:	
Linguistic features:	

Literacy Autobiography Essay Assignment

Overview and Purpose

Throughout this first unit, we have been exploring different aspects of personal writing—ourselves as readers, as members of a larger discourse community, and as writers and responders to texts. It is now time to put the pieces together and examine our larger literacy practices through a literary essay that takes the form of a literacy autobiography. This assignment will allow you to examine yourself as both a reader and writer of texts in multiple contexts. This will deepen your understanding of how you have been a member of, or influenced by, various discourse communities. It will also give you an awareness of the genre of a literary essay (in contrast to an academic or scholarly essay) and the rhetorical skills associated with the genre.

Task

Write an autobiographical essay (four pages minimum) using the conventions of the literary essay we have studied in the unit readings and Feeder 1.3. For this essay, focus on those turning points or most meaningful events that have shaped who you are today as a reader and writer. Consider the discourse communities you described in Feeder 1.1

as they bear on your literacy autobiography. Analyze how those discourse communities have shaped you as a writer and analyze your writing rituals (Feeder 1.2) in order to gain greater insight into the things that have influenced your development as writer/reader.

As you shape the overall point of your essay, keep in mind your rhetorical purpose in writing this piece in this genre. Look for the theme in your experiences and analysis that will surprise, stir, delight, or educate the reader. Shape the details of your essay around this theme once you have discovered it. Note: If you are literate in more than one language, feel free to discuss your literacies in multiple languages! Do not feel that you must only discuss literacy practices in English! But for the sake of your English-speaking readers, write your final draft in English.

Getting Started

Here are some things you can do in addition to reviewing the feeder assignments as you prepare to do your first draft:

- Expand your mind map of discourse communities you belong to, now that you have greater understanding of the concept of "discourse community." Include in your mind map specific literacy events that were turning points for you as a reader and writer.

- Were there individuals important in these critical events/ moments that shaped you as a reader/writer? Make a list of those people. Pick three. Mind map specific memories associated with those individuals related to your development as a reader/writer.

- Try writing ten sentences, rapidly. Start each sentence: " I am . . ." Finish the sentence with a few words that describe you as a reader/writer. What do you discover?

- Go back through memorabilia—old papers? Journals? Early drawings? Old favorite books? Letters sent or received? Ask your parents or siblings if they have any of this memorabilia they can share with you. Go thru these artifacts and see what memories are stirred, what you learn from them.

- Pick the autobiographical essay from our readings that you liked the best. Read it again and see what writing techniques you can borrow from this writer as you write your essay.

Tips for a Successful Essay

Organization

- You should organize your essay thematically rather than give an account strictly based on a chronology. Look for the overarching point/theme that ties two or three prominent experiences together. Then develop each experience, thru anecdote, rendering, story-telling to subtly support your overarching point.

- Do not begin your essay with a thesis statement laying out your overall point. The literary essay as a genre depends on extensive descriptions and details to build to the point, which is usually revealed at the end of the essay.

Rhetorical Strategies

- Specific examples are always better than generalizations. If you are going to generalize, be sure you provide specific evidence and examples to support your generalization. Thru careful selection of telling details, put your reader in the scene, i.e. able to form a visual image of what you describe.

- No four- or five-page essay can tell a person's entire history (even in a select area such as literacy). Therefore, you will have to be selective and choose only the most memorable experiences. Make your words count.

- I encourage you to include other types of media in your literacy autobiography. These types do not count toward the four pages, however. (In other words, if you include photocopies of your first short story, you still have to write four pages of text.)

Evaluation Criteria

Rhetorical Purpose

- Essay shows a clear focus—answers the "so what" question for the reader

- Essay fulfills reader's genre expectations

Content

- Essay shows ability to apply theories of discourse community and genre to a concrete situation, as tools for analysis

- Essay shows insight, creates interest through descriptive and narrative rhetorical skill

Structure

- Essay parts follow a logical, thematic sequence that lead up to the overall point of the essay

- Essay's point is either implied or stated at the end of the essay

- Paragraph breaks are logical and facilitate easy reading of the essay

Linguistic Features

- Essay shows careful choice of language appropriate to its intended audience

- Essay is virtually free of sentence-level errors (spelling, grammar, etc.)

Unit 2: Genre Analysis (for teachers)

The second unit introduces the students to genre analysis. While traditional writing classes often assign textual analyses, having students look at texts in terms of genres and how they are written allows them to build more transferable skills to carry into other writing environments. The comparison of two texts should be less difficult than analyzing a single text. In addition to the feeder assignments that follow, the activities for teaching genre awareness in the "Teaching for Transfer" section can be used.

Focus Skill Areas

Critical Thinking: Ability to compare and contrast genre feature of two texts.

Discourse Community: Deepening understanding of discourse community concepts by looking at two texts within or across discourse communities.

Genre Analysis: Understanding the concept of genre; being able to recognize different genres; being able to recognize the features that differentiate one genre from another.

Rhetorical Analysis: Understanding of the different rhetorical devices, ability to recognize and interpret how those devices are functioning in a piece of writing

Unit Readings

"Setting the Record Straight" by Scott McCloud

McCloud's essay, in the genre of a comic, is a textual analysis and historical overview of the world of comic books and should provide a solid foundation to begin to discuss "genre" within this unit.

"Rewriting American History" Frances Fitzgerald

An historical analysis of the changes of history texts (mostly content, but some rhetoric) over the last 50 years. She challenges the notion of "history" and "truth" and demonstrates that both are socially constructed. She also addresses the notion of tokenism within history textbooks. This will give students an example of one type of textual comparison, although these texts are all within the same genre. Should provide a very interesting class discussion as well!

"Journalese as a Second Language" by John Leo

This is a great "insiders" look into the specialized language of journalism as a genre focusing on the way which journalists use language to distort or pacify readers. This would be a good piece to introduce genre analysis or the concepts of genre and can serve as a bridge to bringing in other types of genres with their own specialized discourses.

Feeder 2.1 Images in advertising

Choose two genres in advertising that include visual and verbal images (magazine ads, billboard ads, ads on product packaging, etc.) The two ads should be for the same product, or general category of product (i.e. do not compare ads for wrist watches and cars; rather, compare ads for one of these products in two different print media). Write a two-page analysis after you have used the genre matrix chart to describe the key genre features of each ad. (Note: you may need to look at several examples of each genre in order to see clearly what features are typical of the genre.) You can use the following questions to guide your analysis, but your analysis should be written in standard paragraph form, with transitions between paragraphs, an overall point, etc. (Note: include copies of both ads—Xeroxed or snapshot images of the ads are fine.)

- What are the key features that define each genre you have chosen?

- What are the assumed audiences for each genre?

- Are there any specific conventions used in one genre that isn't found in the other?

- How are the two genres similar?

- What are the reasons for what is conveyed visually? For what is conveyed via text? How do the visual and verbal texts in the ad interact?

Feeder 2.2 Context of Meaning

In "Learning the Language," Peri Klass discusses (see p.200) her transition to learning a new language in a discourse community. Locate an article from your chosen field of study or in a discourse community you are a member of. Choose one word in the article and investigate its meaning within your field or discourse community. Now, go outside of your discourse community and see if the word (or similar renditions of the word) is used elsewhere. What are the differences in meaning? How do these change based on the genre?

Example: In the field of linguistics, there is a term called "grammar." This term refers to the unconscious knowledge that individuals have about language. In the general sense, however, "grammar" refers to specific rules you have to learn in English class or can even imply issues of sentence-level written competence. While the two terms may seem similar on the surface, they are used for very different purposes. Grammar in linguistics is innate, unconscious knowledge that every native speaker of a language has and uses. Grammar in the general sense is the prescriptive rules that you have to study, learn, and apply so that your own language more closely fits the accepted standard.

Feeder 2.3 Says/Does Chart for Rhetorical Analysis

By this time, you should have chosen the two articles you will be analyzing for the second unit. Construct a says–does chart (about a page each) for each of the two articles. In the "Says" column, briefly summarize the key point of each paragraph. In the "Does" column, describe what or how the writer is rhetorically moving the reader through the piece—the use of logic, repetition, transitions and other organizational strategies, etc. (for more information on the says/does exercise see Elbow and Belanoff, *Sharing and Responding*).

Genre Analysis Essay Assignment

Overview and Purpose

In this unit, we have been working on analyzing texts in different genres. For this assignment you will be finding and comparing two or more texts written on the same subject in different genres. The purpose of this essay is to allow you to gain a better understanding of the importance of genre and discourse community knowledge to writers. It will allow you to better understand the ways writing differs among genres and allow you to strengthen your skills in writing in the genre of a textual analysis (a form of academic essay).

The Task

Locate and photocopy at least two texts on the same subject from different genres (see the examples passed out in class). For example, you could find an article within a scholarly journal (whose audience will be knowledgeable in the field) related to your major or field of interest and then find an article on the same topic that was written for a general audience. Alternatively, you could look at an editorial on a political issue, a government report on the issue, and several message board posts or letters to the editor in response to the editorial.

After you have analyzed each text, do a comparison of the texts considering each of the four genre features we have been analyzing with sample genres. Once you have done the genre analysis, consider how you could generalize your findings about these genres in a five- to six-page academic essay. Include the two articles you are analyzing and bibliographic citations to these articles in your completed project.

Getting Started

- Create a matrix that shows the similarities and differences of each of your texts considering the four areas of genre analysis we have discussed in class. Use the heuristic below to aid you in developing your matrix.

Heuristic for Analyzing a Genre

Rhetorical Issues: Audience and Purpose Questions

- Who is the intended audience?

- What discourse community (or communities) is this audience in?

- What are these readers likely to know? want to know? Why?

- How much time will this audience want to spend reading this document?

- What is the writer's purpose?

- What does the writer want the reader(s) to do after reading?

Content Questions

- How does the writer select content material to achieve his/her purpose with this particular audience?

- What types of information are considered appropriate in this genre?

- What types of information would be considered inappropriate in this genre?

- What types of evidence are acceptable to support claims?

Structure Questions

- How much information is considered appropriate?

- What is a typical sequence for information in this genre?

- How is the structure serving the audience's needs and the writer's purpose?

Style/language Questions

- How formal or informal is the language?

- What specialized vocabulary is used?

- How long/short are sentences and paragraphs?

- What other language features do you notice?

Evaluation Criteria

Your essay should follow the conventions of an academic essay in the humanities, with a clear focusing thesis in the introduction and supporting points developed in the remainder of the essay. The structure will follow a logical, thematic progression from the thesis statement. Paragraphs will generally begin with a transition word or phrase to provide continuity with the previous paragraph, and have a summarizing topic sentence at the start of the paragraph. The conclusion to the essay should summarize key points and point the reader toward something to ponder, or what "next step" might be called for in relation to your subject.

Unit 3 Ethnography of a Discourse Community (for teachers)

The third unit allows students to build on their analysis skills from the previous two units while introducing a new type of research—ethnography. Not only will students gain valuable experience in learning more about discourse communities, which will translate to their own academic fields, but they will also gain an understanding of how one type of primary research is done.

Focus Skill Areas

Discourse Community Analysis: being able to identify, understand and analyze discourse community conventions.

Research Skills: Primary research skills—observational data, collection of text samples, interview skills, ethics of research, library research.

Analysis Skills: Learning how to integrate different types of raw data into a written format.

Unit Readings

"Boring from Within: the Art of the Freshman Essay" by Wayne Booth

This essay is an analysis of the freshman essay from a teacher's perspective. This kind of piece will be a great opportunity for students to analyze their own past works and perform an overall meta-analysis of what freshman writing is or isn't. It also gives advice to writing students on how to make their own essays come alive. In using this essay in class, students can also analyze whether their writing class constitutes a discourse community.

"Sex, Lies, and Conversation" by Deborah Tannen

Tannen addresses in this work how speech and gender roles themselves are socially constructed and hold power. Teachers can extend this concept into the realm of discourse communities as well.

"Learning the Language" by Perri Klass

This is the short reading on learning the language of the medical profession and can be used concurrently with the Journalese piece. It makes powerful connections to the political nature of language and vocabulary choices and how new members in the medical professions must learn a new way of speaking and behaving in order to be accepted in the medical discourse community.

Feeder 3.1 Who Do I Want to Study?

Write a page on two potential discourse communities you are interested in studying. Be sure to answer the following questions:

- What discourse community you are interested in studying?

- Why you are interested in studying it?

- Your biases and assumptions surrounding the discourse community (i.e. what opinions do you have about them.) Do you see them in a positive or negative way and why?

- How you plan on gaining access to the discourse community and their written texts?

Feeder 3.2 Research Question

Most research starts with a question (or in the sciences, a hypothesis). Formulate at least three key questions about the group you are interested in studying. The questions should be open-ended (not simple yes or no questions). These questions will help you better organize your own observations and research findings. Here are some sample questions:

- How do the particular writing practices of this discourse community reinforce and achieve the group's goals and purposes?

- Why does this particular discourse community place more value on _____ than on _____?

- What are the most common genres used by the discourse community and why are these particular genres the ones utilized?

- What roles to writers take? What social status do writers have?

- How do individuals gain entrance to this discourse community and achieve "insider" or "expert" status?

- What about this discourse community would be of interest to people who are not members of the community?

Feeder 3.3

Once you have chosen your discourse community to research, decide how you will gain access to the group if not a member. Collect samples of as much of the writing in as many of the genres the community uses as possible. If the group meets in a physical space and in a time frame in which you're doing this assignment, do at least one observation of the group or a few group members in order to begin to shape your research question(s). During the observation, use a double-entry method of note-taking. If you cannot have face-to-face contact with the discourse community, contact several of the group's members by email or telephone and do preliminary interviews in order to find out something about the community and begin to refine your research question(s). Bring your results to class and be ready to give a short report of your results.

Feeder 3.4

Use the library's online databases and/or stacks to locate two articles that provide background on the discourse community you are researching. Be as specific as possible, but understand that there are limitations to the articles available. For example, if you are going to conduct a discourse community analysis of the local poetry club, it is very unlikely that you will find articles on that specific club. But you certainly will find articles on the larger poetry reading movement. Note: if you cannot find any references that talk about the discourse community (and you have consulted a reference librarian for help), then find two published documents from the discourse community and, based on what you observe about these texts, further refine your research questions.

After you locate your two articles, write an annotated bibliography of the two articles. In the annotation, summarize the articles and state what you have gleaned from them to help you further refine your research question(s). Bring your annotated bibliography, along with the two sources you found, to class.

Unit 3 Essay Assignment

At this point in the course, we have explored ourselves as writers (Unit 1) and the texts from two different discourse communities (Unit 2). It is now time to take this exploration a step further where we further our research and analysis skills by looking at a discourse community as a whole.

Skills you will learn in this assignment:

- Collecting primary observational data or interview data

- Synthesizing research into a written format

- Categorizing raw data and looking for themes

- Writing in a new genre (ethnographic report)

- Ethics of research involving human subjects

- Genre analysis skills

The Task

In this assignment, you will be conducting an ethnography of a discourse community. Ethnography is essentially a study of a group of people and is a methodology and genre used typically in anthropology. In doing ethnographic research, you observe a group, take notes, and report on your findings. For this ethnography, you will be observing and analyzing a discourse community that you belong to or one that is new to you. In other words, you will be focusing primarily on the writing practices within a specific social group. The focus of this research should not be solely on social dynamics or oral discourse, but rather on how written texts work within the group.

What types of discourse communities can you observe? The possibilities are endless, but here is a short list to get you thinking:

- Any sort of club or organization that produces written texts: for example: a non-profit organization that produces a weekly newsletter; a club that has weekly meetings and produces information on their website; or an online group that produces fan fiction.

- A group that regularly attends a particular type of event, such as convention or concert or theatre performance. There are lots of these happening on campus; alternatively, you can find tons of things happening in the place where you live—you could observe an environmental group protesting at city hall and then look at their "texts" at their website, or you could attend a conference in your field of interest and then also look at the written products, handouts, abstracts, etc.—of the discourse community.

- A group associated with a particular job or profession that produces some sort of written product: groups such as teachers, contractors, journalists, public relations people, an advertising agency, or the executive board at the local bank.

- A group related to your field of study—graduate students in a lab, professors, people working in the industry, etc.

Getting Started

- Be sure to collect written texts and other "artifacts" from the group for further analysis.

- If you are not a member of the group, contact a group representative to arrange your visit. Explain your purpose—this research assignment. Reassure the group that anything which is confidential you will either write about using pseudonyms or not reveal. You may want to put your agreement in writing to the appropriate member(s) of the group.

- If it is not possible to observe or have a face-to-face meeting with the group, arrange for several interviews with group members by phone or email.

- Be careful to separate your actual observations from information you assume or your opinions and reactions to what you observe. To help you facilitate this type of "objectivity," use a double-entry notebook. We will be discussing the double-entry notebook more in class.

- Some observers interact more with the group they are observing than others. If you plan on having some interaction, be sure you still have time to write and take notes.

- Give people some time to get accustomed to you before starting your note taking. Individuals who know they are being watched will behave differently than those who are in their natural environment without observers. But they tend to forget their observers after a while.

- Revisit your notes and organize as soon after as possible. Or, if you did an interview in which you were not able to take notes, write up the conversation as soon as possible afterwards.

- Be sure to pay special attention to the speech and literacy practices and language use of the group members that you observed.

- Look for patterns in language, behavior, writing practices. Also, consider people who don't fit the pattern or the norm.

What to Observe?

When you are observing, it is impossible to focus on everything. For the purposes of this assignment, you should focus your observations on the discourse community's writing practices. You may also note what gets communicated through other channels—oral? visual?

- For what purpose(s) are texts produced?

- How important is writing to the group as a whole?

- What genres are used in the discourse community?

- How are texts produced within the discourse community?

- Who produces texts? Do all community members produce or just a select few?

- What guidelines does the community have for what counts as "good writing" in the community, i.e. what are the norms for genres?

- How are individual genres related to each other in the discourse community?

- How do the genres and the purposes for the discourse community relate?

- What types of specialized vocabulary or "jargon" do they use?

- How do this group's writing practices fit into what we have conceptualized as a discourse community? How is oral discourse used to complement written discourse? Or vice versa?

Assignment Requirements

The essay (six pages minimum) will present your findings as a research report or researched argument. Here are some guidelines for a successful essay:

- You should organize your essay thematically, not chronologically. Do not give a report of what you did while researching—instead, group your data and focus on reoccurring themes of interest in your data that give answers to your research questions.

- You should also utilize some of the data you have collected directly in the essay—direct quotations or observations make great examples!

- Regardless of format or organization, each essay should have a primary focus on the writing practices, written texts and language of the group in question.

- Your research should include appropriate primary or secondary sources to support or amplify your field research. You may use sources from popular magazines, newspapers, non-scholarly Internet sites, or other sources, but you need to include at least three scholarly sources, as this is an academic essay.

- Use American Psychological Association (APA) citation guidelines for in-text citations and the works cited list at the end of your essay. (APA is generally the citation style used in the social sciences.)

Submit all field notes, interview notes, and library or on-line sources you are including in your works cited list in your project folder.

A SUMMARY OF APPROACHES

These, then, are some resources for applying the theoretical framework and principles that I argue for here for developing effective writing instruction at the university level—in writing centers, in discipline-specific courses, and in general writing courses. Of course, I'm sure there are other approaches that would embody the principles for teaching for transfer and for teaching to all five skill domains beyond the ones I have outlined here. In addition to considering the activities and assignment sequences here, I encourage readers to review the articles by Kiniry (1985), Rose (1998), and Beaufort (2000) for other examples of sequential learning. Also Kovac's (2001) sample curriculum for chemistry majors is an excellent example of moving majors through the different levels of critical thinking in Bloom's taxonomy and for introducing them to the range of genres chemists use in developmental fashion. Smit's (2004) broad outline in Chapter 9 of *The End of Composition* for three linked writing courses that build disciplinary writing expertise systematically can also serve as a guide for sequential curriculum building across several courses.

Teaching writing is one of the most complex tasks I know of, because multiple cognitive and social factors must be taken into account at once. For teachers and tutors, then, the dilemma is what to work with students on first, second, third, etc., as tasks must in some ways be broken down into manageable chunks. The old models for writing instruction broke the task down by units within a text: vocabulary/spelling; sentence patterns; paragraph structure; essay structure, etc. These, we know now, are not the most useful building blocks either for learning or for motivating learners. The urge to communicate, to solve meaningful writing problems, as Bazerman (1997) says, is the most powerful motivator for learning to write better. The best curricular approaches, then, give students meaningful intellectual challenges and provide the scaffolding (Applebee and Langer 1983) for them to achieve success in the lifelong path of learning. I would hope others will build on the ideas presented here.

Here are two essays Tim wrote in his freshman year of college: one, a textual analysis of an article by an ethicist, written for Freshman Writing, and the other, a historical essay interpreting events and texts for a western civilization course, also Tim's first year at the university.

RIGHT AND WRONG IN GENETIC ENGINEERING: A CHRISTIAN'S PERSPECTIVE (FOR EGL 102)

The last decade's discoveries in genetic science have opened discussions at the dinner table, laboratory, and Congress on questions that ten years ago existed solely on the pages of science fiction. Their relevance is now real, casting confusion over the decisions of birth, illness, treatment, and death. Is it morally justified, many ask, to read a fetus' genetic code, allowing the parents to abort a handicapped child? Is it right to consider altering the DNA, the very map of life? Isn't the integrity of life threatened by manipulating genetic traits?

Answers given to questions of right and wrong in genetic therapy range widely. Many fear that people who altered the genetic makeup of individuals would be "playing God." Other invoke the experience of the Nazi era in Germany and oppose any development of gene-altering processes, concerned that it will lead to similar atrocities. Still others suggest that any new technology that is useful should be put into practice.

Dr. Lewis Bird, professor at Eastern College, where he teaches medical ethics, responds to these solutions with a different framework. As the Eastern Regional Director of the Christian Medical and Dental Society, Dr. Bird has had the opportunity to spend a great deal of effort investigating the complexities of genetic research, testing, and therapy. In an article for the *Perspectives on Science and Christian Faith* quarterly, he answers those afraid of "playing God" by pointing out that taking antibodies for a sore throat also intervenes in the natural progression of human life. If it is justifiable to heal by performing invasive surgery with a knife or laser, to halt the spread of illness by administering antibodies, and so on, then it is likewise acceptable to use genetic technology. This solution is acceptable to many people, but it leaves at least two questions: First of all, as those sympathetic with Christian Scientist and Amish persuasions would ask, are modern medicine's techniques acceptable at all? Secondly, some wonder, doesn't genetic technology's deeper penetration into the fabric of human life set it apart from other forms of medical treatment?

Dr. Bird also allays the concern that genetic engineering will lead to abuses similar to those of Nazi Germany's medical community. There is no basis, he believes, for the assertion that use of genetic technology will inevitably lead to atrocities offensive to respect for human nature. Certainly, some crackpot in an unregulated laboratory may take it into his head to perform some evil deed, but he could just as well cause harm to people by using widely accepted technologies such as the surgeon's scalpel or the radiologist's X-ray. Dr. Bird recognizes the risk of powerful technologies like genetic therapy and recommends using caution and supervision to ensure the proper use of genetic engineering.

To those who think "if it can be done, it should be done," Dr. Bird has a simple response: Not necessarily. For him, if it can be done, it may be done. How to decide? To lay out a map for determining the path of ethical medical practice, he researched both the Eastern and Western traditions for common, universal principles of medical ethics and found five that relate to genetic engineering.

First of all, we must do no harm. This Dr. Bird derives from the Confucian Silver Rule: "What you do not want done to yourself, do not do to others." Because there is the chance that someone may disregard the harm done to patients of genetic treatments, he urges thorough regulation and caution in approving genetic therapy techniques.

Geneticists must honor the sanctity of human life taken from the belief that man was created in the image of God. At each step, we must ask, "Does this process ultimately enhance or degrade human dignity?" The answer will direct our steps. God as known in the Old and New Testament does not require a "hands-off" policy, Dr. Bird believes, but we must use caution in assessing the consequences of our work for human life.

Medical technology must be used to alleviate human suffering. The Hebraic-Christian tradition repeatedly calls to our sense of compassion and provides examples of healing as a ministry. The Golden Rule extends the Silver Rule in exhorting us to "do for others what you would have them do for you." To know to do good and not to do it is sinful, in Dr. Bird's view. God gave us the knowledge we now possess; we must rely on Him to guide us in using it for ultimate good.

The patient and his or her family must always preserve the right of confidentiality. Outside intrusion on the privacy of the family violates numerous historical codes of ethics. The Hebrew Oath of Asaph and the Greek Oath of Hippocrates both emphasized privacy, and the modern Declaration of Geneva gave it further sanction. Medical personnel must protect right in all cases.

The responsible patient also has the right to consent to the treatment based on truthful information about the treatment, its risks, and real potential. The sacred value of the human free will is underscored in the New Testament numerous times. The first line of the Nuremberg code of ethics [word unclear] response to the Nazi atrocities reasserts the patient's right to [word unclear] against willful disregard for the patient's human rights.

This enumeration of Christian guidelines for medical ethics invites two responses: first, is this list both complete and correct? If not, what principles have been overlooked or misunderstood? Based on the new list, is genetic therapy at all justified? Second, if Dr. Bird's principles do capture the guidance of scriptures, does genetic therapy indeed pass their scrutiny?

A satisfying response to the first question will result only from exhaustive research of scriptures and history. Dr. Bird's findings, however, seem to provide a universal basis for ethical decision-making. If one accepts these principles, the categorical denouncement of genetic technology is out of the question. The only alternative is fundamental rejection of all healing arts and reliance on spiritual healing alone.

In general, ethicists like Dr. Bird refuse to condemn technology, while focusing their scrutiny on motives and consequences. To a Christian involved in genetics, concern for the patient should be a top concern. The great potential of genetic technology for curing genetically transmitted diseases encourages Christians in scientific professions. Taking careful stock of the risks and nature of the technology now in discovery, they hope to make the most of technology's new promise while staving off abuse. Dr. Bird, at least, does not intend to ignore this God-given opportunity to fulfill his mission of ministering deeds of good will.

In the medial ethics essay, Tim is mostly summarizing and reporting what this particular philosopher had to say about the ethics of genetic engineering. At two points Tim stands outside the text as questioner: First, in his introductory paragraph, he raises viewpoints of those opposed to genetic engineering. He then summarizes the author's answers to these objections and presents, in order, the author's detailed guidelines for ethical medical practices. Tim's second point of questioning comes at the end of his essay: he asks how thorough and convincing the author has been. But the question is not explored, nor are the argument strategies the author used analyzed or evaluated. (See chapter 2 for further analysis of this essay)

Here is an essay from Tim's HIS 101 course, written in the same time frame that he was completing the essay on the ethics of genetic engineering for his freshman writing class.

AUGUSTINE TO BENEDICT: THE RELIGIOUS JOURNEY (FOR HISTORY 101, WESTERN CIVILIZATION)

One of the recurrent questions of religion is the explanation of change in religious belief. Christianity has repeatedly altered its character according to the needs, desires, and outlooks of believers, taking on widely varying forms through the centuries. In St. Augustine's *Confessions* and the *Rule* of St. Benedict, fundamental differences appear in concepts of good, evil, God, man, Christ, a Christian's purpose, lifestyle, the secular and spiritual worlds, and finally the writers' approaches to spirituality. These variations pose the question: What were the causes and effects of these changes? Viewed in the context of history, we see in *Confessions* and *Rule* how the destabilizing effects and moral crisis of the fall of Rome widened the gulf between Eastern and Western Christianity.

The Roman Empire of Augustine's day was much more closely related to the Greco-Roman tradition than the world Benedict wrote his *Rule* for. In 400 A.D., at the completion of *Confessions*, Rome was still a united empire. The new capital of Constantinople was 70 years old, the ties between the East and West were very close. Christianity had been the official religion of the empire for 19 years, providing a significant unifying force.

The new imperial policies of Constantinople had begun to sow seeds of downfall, however, and life was changing. The transition to Constantinople brought problems to the empire. Squabbling began between the priesthoods of Rome and Constantinople over primacy. As the capital, the Greeks felt themselves the rightful leaders of the faith. As the city of Peter, Roman clergy did not want to relinquish the spiritual reign. Distance from the West complicated relations with new settlements of Goths in the empire, resulting in unrest in the Balkans and Gaul. Theodosius, the emperor, responded by trying to integrate the newcomers but succeeded only in placing Rome in an ever more alien environment.

After the writing of *Confessions*, the social and political developments underway progressed quickly, creating a less Roman and less stable society, topping the tables of power from the emperor toward the clergy. In 410 A.D., the Gothic king Alaric sacked Rome. Attila the Hun attacked Italy in 451–452 A.D., followed two years later by the Vandals' attack on the empire. Finally, the Romans for the first time acknowledged conquest in 476 A.D. to Odovacer, who rose uncontested to the Roman throne and was even recognized by Constantinople. In 483 A.D., the Byzantine emperor supported a coup installing Theodoric as Western emperor. During this entire time barbarians settled all the Western provinces in great numbers (Western Heritage, pp. 206–207). Since the adoption of Christianity in the fourth century, the social stature and influence of Christians had been ever increasing, leading to moral dilemmas for many Christians, as it appeared that Christians were sacrificing their faith for profit on Earth. The decline in royal power automatically enhanced the papacy's political power, allowing them to come to the fore as a force balancing against kings. In 455 A.D., Pope Leo announced the doctrine of Pontifex Maximus, by which he asserted his role as the highest priest. Further in 494 A.D., Pope Gelasius introduced the theory of papal primacy, changing the relationship of spirituality and secular life, preparing the venue for St. Benedict.

In considering the development of Christianity from a unified church through Augustine to Benedict, a central question revolves around the nature of God. The acute legal crisis in the fifth century spurred the departure of Benedict from the views of Eastern Orthodoxy and Augustine. St. Augustine's picture of God does not vary greatly from the Eastern view, where the two principal themes are his loving and all-powerful goodness. St. Augustine concurs (Augustine, p. 102) adding that God is "supremely" good and therefore incorruptible (Augustine, p. 161). He is omnipresent, and He leads His children to Him.

In the *Rule* a different image emerges. Between Augustine's completion of *Confessions* in 400 A.D. and Benedict's writing of the *Rule* in about 530 A.D., the structure of the Roman society had come into crisis. The empire had suffered five major military defeats. The national security difficulties took the place of primary importance, and legal affairs suffered. More and more residents, soldiers, and principal rulers were non-Roman, place the way of life in a state of flux with uncertain outcome. Social needs boosted the importance of the Western concept of Christianity as a legal relationship between God and man. God remained for Benedict good and benevolent (Benedict, p. 44), but he increasingly took on the role of a parent who commands his children and of a judge who is approachable only through intercessors including abbots. Benedict's "frequent inspections" (Benedict, p. 92) by abbots (who fill the role of God in the monastery) foster an image of an untrusting, vindictive God as judge and parent, rather than as loving Creator. The people's need for justice and stability in such times gave increasing importance to the thought that what man overlooks in judgment of wrongdoing, God will not.

Augustine explores the question of wrongdoing and evil in *Confessions*, discussing various theories of man's nature, finally deciding that man's will is ultimately good. He describes two human wills (Augustine, p. 196) present in one human nature (Augustine, p. 197). He says that each of man's sometimes conflicting wills and his nature are good (Augustine, p. 160); "not even Cataline himself loved his crimes" (Augustine, p. 71). Although man's nature is "spiritual"

(Augustine, p. 355) and his will is good, it is not supremely good, and is therefore corruptible. For this reason it needs to be "enlightened by another light," God's work in men's hearts (Augustine, p. 109), This enlightenment sets man free from evil, the privation of good (Augustine, p. 172). "Liberty [is] proper to man's nature, and servitude [is] introduced by sin" (City of God, Ch. 15) therefore, God restores the liberty of man's nature. Refuting any claims that man's will and reason must be suppressed before God, Augustine declares: "faith is the liberator of human reason" (Augustine, p. 197), which is created by God and is good.

The Benedictine answer to wrongdoing and man's will reacted to the contemporary fear of new evils facing Roman society and Westernized the church. Benedict does not spend time wondering if human will is good or bad; he writes based on the premise that it is evil. Based on his judgments that self-denial (Benedict p. 80), obedience and labor (Benedict, p. 43), are the greatest of virtues, then gluttony, disobedience, and laziness personify human nature. The crisis of virtue and disillusionment with Christianity "of the world" in the Roman empire explains well the sweeping change toward the condemnation of man as the incarnation of evil.

A revelation of the forces of good and evil and of the natures of God and man's natures sets the state for resolution of the conflict between them. The most evident divergence in the paths of Western and Eastern Christianity lies in this resolution: salvation through justification by good works and the purpose of human life. Augustine's reason for being a Christian expands the Eastern simple desire to receive God's love through His grace (Benz, E. *The Eastern Orthodox Church: Its Thought and Life*, p. 48) by adding why man wants this love, the primary element of the faith (Benz, p. 31). Man desires happiness in life (Augustine, p. 248) through rest—knowing God (Augustine, p. 117)—and inner peace (Augustine, p. 369). God gives man this inner peace and rest. This is Christianity. Augustine ventures slightly further in later works, asserting that the whole of human history is meant to separate God's people from those who choose evil (Benz, p. 47). This marks a departure that, in subsequent centuries, leads to the doctrines of good works and life as amnesty, which eventually is expanded into the afterlife to include the Western conception of purgatory. These ideas remained ever strange to Eastern Orthodox Christians.

The doctrine of justification by good works grew out of protest against unfaithful worldly Christianity and represents continued growth of the importance of the legal relationship between God and man. Benedict's *Rule*, as compared to Orthodoxy and Augustine, pursues the definition of justification by good works, extolling the emulation of Christ in self-denial (p. 80) and obedience as the greatest virtues and raison d'etre of Christian belief and living. Whereas in Augustine and Eastern

Orthodoxy one can live a good life in service and love through faith and God's gifts (Augustine, pp. 369–370), the *Rule* allows a Christian a life of love, faith and charity (Benedict, p. 20) only if he or she first follows the path of virtuous obedience (Benedict, p. 19). This attained, love and charity were regulated by the abbot (Benedict, p. 20). An example of the obedience ethic is Benedict's implicit writing that the Christian who is more obedient will be more loved and higher ranked by God (Benedict, p. 43). This step led to the doctrine that although the abbot "can err in commanding," the monk "cannot err in obeying" (Benedict, p. 22).

In practice of good works, someone must command, and someone must judge the Christian's obedience. This role was conferred upon the abbot, creating fertile ground for the development of future doctrine in a direction ever further from the Eastern Orthodox belief. As "commander," he received responsibility for each child's soul (Benedict, p. 21), creating a doctrine of authority and leading to the Western clergy's power to forgive sins, as witnessed by the priests' words, "Ego te absolve" after confession (Benz, p. 50). This new responsibility, coupled with the filoque clause added in the ninth century, strengthened the dogma of intercession and hierarchy, utterly unknown in the East.

The emphasis on obedience and lifestyle was natural to Christians of the day. Contemporary Christianity was very much invested in political life, which was greatly corrupt. The shortcomings of Christians in and of the world were visible in their deeds and lifestyle. Accordingly, the solution to the problem seemed to be likewise in deeds. Only through humble good conduct through suppression of the evil human will could lie the path to salvation. Thus, the resolution was that God must reward good behavior and condemn bad behavior, strengthening the case for a legal covenant of salvation in exchange for good works.

The reconciliation of the importance of lifestyle and spiritual values raises the question for the roles and natures of the secular and spiritual worlds. The condition of the Roman state brought about its medieval condemnation. Whereas the Eastern Church and Augustine professed the distinctive responsibilities and abilities of each, Benedict presupposed the evil nature of the state. Augustine did not condemn the state (Tierney, p. 9).but by the time of Benedicts' writing of the *Rule*, Pope Gelasius had already proposed the theory of papal supremacy: "There are two swords," royal power and moral authority. Since moral authority, vested in the priesthood, answers for the king's salvation, the priest's power is "more weighty" than that of kings (Tierney, p. 13). This new and contested doctrine clearly affected the writings of Benedict, who counseled man to turn away from the state to a better way of living.

The final question of dogma concerns each writer's concept of Christ and His role in the life of Christians. This point illustrates well the effects of human needs on people's concept of God. In the Eastern faith, which has always placed great importance on Christian love, He is most frequently seen as Savior Son of God and Pantokrator, or all-powerful (though merciful) judge. Augustine, whose life path occupied an intensely intellectual search for spiritual rest, refers to him primarily as Teacher (Augustine, pp. 283, 287), Enlightenment of Man (Augustine, p. 343), and as the incarnate God and Word of God. Finally Benedict, who sought an example of a perfect life in the tumultuous time of spiritual crisis (Benedict, p. 13), describes Him as the greatest good on Earth and the most unselfish Being, pointing the way to a life of self-denial.

Beyond the various points of belief illuminated by these texts, the reader gains an overall impression of the values of the writer through the language used, structure of writing and focus of attention. In general, Augustine's *Confessions* leave an impression of the importance of the individual search for truth, and in Benedict, the reader gleans from the pages the monk's concern with unity. Throughout, Augustine's writing focuses on the soul whereas Benedict occupies himself with material life with man on Earth. Augustine examines substance of belief (Augustine, p. 1118) whereas Benedict discusses form of its communal practice. Augustine searches for meaning, warning against "[serving] the creature rather than the creator" (Augustine, p. 116), whereas Benedict holds up a symbol for the flock to follow. Augustine includes human reason in the search for truth whereas Benedict requires only unwavering obedience to the community father. Augustine's thoughts and writings are intellectually complex whereas Benedict strives to simplify. Augustine values the individual search and choice whereas Benedict promotes stability through community supremacy (Benedict, p. 20) and the new vow of stability (Benedict, p. 32).

In Augustine and Benedict's treatment of the many issues of humanity, God, a Christian's goal and life, Christ, and the secular and spiritual worlds, it becomes clear to the historian that the unstable conditions of Rome's final years and the moral dilemma in Christianity provided the impetus for the momentous change in the belief structure of early medieval Christianity. This episode in the history of Western Europe illustrates the role history and society have in shaping religious belief while exposing as well the origins of our concepts of religion state, justice, and spiritual and material values. Early Western Europeans interpreted religion in order to satisfy the needs of their time and relate to their experience and environment. Through their efforts we are granted a penetrating look at the heritage of Western culture and a better understanding of the world we have become.

(For a detailed analysis of this essay, see chapter 4.)

APPENDIX C
The Research Methodology

To assess systematically what is or isn't working in any program of writing instruction is difficult because longitudinal studies of writers are difficult. Equally difficult is data-driven theorizing about writing expertise and the developmental processes of writers, given the number of variables at work, many of which are hidden from a researcher's scrutiny. Case studies are difficult to generalize from with absolute certainty. And, as this is the case of a mainstream student (i.e. middle class and white), cases involving students of diverse backgrounds are needed to determine the usefulness across a broader spectrum of writers of the theoretical framework presented here. With these difficulties in mind, I urge other researchers to test the robustness of this theoretical framework of writing expertise in capturing the nuances of what in fact is going on in disciplinary writing at the undergraduate level and in other contexts for writing. For those interested in case study methodology, I offer in more detail here how data collection and analysis were handled.

A case study does afford the opportunity to look at multiple variables in a given writer's performance over a long time period. Others have embedded case studies in large-scale studies (Carroll 2002, Sommers and Saltz 2004). That can be an effective method for getting both in-depth and far-ranging data. I would add one further general comment before getting into the particulars of this study. A case study that is rooted in ethnographic methods is ideal; otherwise, the data gathered in the case can be "thin" or one-sided. Interviews, while extremely important and relied on heavily here, cannot tell the whole story. Seeing the subject "in action"—either by field observation or by interviews with others in the field of action—allows that critical element of triangulation: taking what the subject says and comparing it with others' views and with the subject's work. Ethnographic methods yield a richer set of means for gathering data than a simple interview–style approach to case studies, as will be illustrated in what follows.

PARTICIPANT AND SETTING

As the reader knows by now, the study focused on Tim, an undergraduate student at a major private university in the US in the mid-1990s. As part of a pilot study leading up to this study, I observed three freshman writing classes taught by three different teachers, and interviewed five students from each class. Tim was among the 15 initial students in the pilot study. When I invited him to continue working with me through the rest of college, he readily agreed to the project. He said he loved writing and enjoyed talking to me about it.

Tim had a double major in college—history and engineering. He focused first on history. By the end of his junior year, he had completed all of his history requirements and began taking the math, science and engineering courses he needed. Data were collected in Tim's freshman, junior, and senior years and then two years after he had graduated.

DATA COLLECTION

As I have indicated, there were six data sources: (1) interviews with Tim (both general and discourse-based), (2) writing samples (7 from freshman writing, 12 from history, 7 from engineering) (3) source materials used in the essays (4) evaluators' comments on the papers, (5) expert historians' and engineers' commentaries on Tim's disciplinary writing, which I solicited during the analysis of data and (6) observation of Tim's freshman writing courses. Time did not permit observation of classroom instruction in his history and engineering courses, and Tim's history professors either turned down or did not respond to requests from me to interview them regarding Tim's work in history.

Interview Data

Interviews were of several types: (1) a pre-established set of questions at the outset, in order to elicit information about literacy development before college, (2) open-ended interviews in order to elicit topics of importance to Tim rather than solely imposing my concerns (Briggs 1986) and (3) stimulated recall or discourse-based interviews that focused on specific essays and the particular theoretical concerns of the study in order to get at both tacit knowledge and the "whys" for particular textual features (Dipardo 1994, Greene and Higgins 1994, Odell et al. 1983). Interviews ranged from one to two hours in length, depending on Tim's availability and the extent of the conversation that developed. (Generally, I have found that the more open-ended the interview, the richer the yield of unexpected yet important data.) Interviews were tape-recorded and then transcribed for analysis.

In addition to interviewing Tim, I interviewed his freshman writing teacher, Carla, on four or five occasions during the study, as well as the director of freshman writing and two other teachers who participated in the pilot study.

Writing samples

Freshman Writing: journal entry, letter to movie producer, process essay, first-person narrative, newsletter article (community service project), reflective essay (on community service project), interview essay (on the effect of Vatican II), single-source essay (on ethics in genetic engineering)

History: five essays freshman year on Islamic history and the Middle Age, four essays sophomore year on colonial American history course and Muscovite Russia , one essay junior year on Stalinism and two essays on technology and society

Engineering: In junior and senior years, a literature review, irrigation process proposal, Red Rover proposal, cellular technology proposal. On-the job, an internal memo and two protocols

Original Sources

I tracked down as many of the sources Tim was writing from in freshman writing and history as was possible in order to assess the reading-to-write component of his writing literacy development. Where I could not locate an author mentioned (in many cases, sources were undocumented in Tim's essays), I asked Tim, who sometimes could fill in the missing reference, or I asked a historian whose expertise was in the particular time period Tim was writing about for help in identifying sources. With the majority of the original sources for Tim's essays in hand, I was able to assess the type of critical thinking Tim was doing (paraphrasing, summarizing, interpreting, etc.), i.e. how much of Tim's writing represented thinking not represented in the source texts themselves.

Teacher and experts' comments on Tim's writing

All of Tim's essays written for freshman writing were commented on at length by Carla. Eight of the essays from history that Tim showed me had teacher comments on them. Also, the history department's web pages gave some background on requirements for the major and typical syllabi for the courses Tim took or similar courses. In addition, I elicited comments on Tim's essays from historians with expertise in the specific areas of history Tim was writing on, so that historians' views of Tim's history writing are represented in addition to my outsider's view as a composition researcher. Engineering work Tim showed me did not have the benefit of Tim's teachers' or bosses' comments, but I did solicit expert opinion on his engineering work from engineering professors at Stony Brook University.

Observation Data

I observed and tape-recorded approximately half of Tim's freshman writing classes and two other freshman writing classes at the same institution in order to understand the context for Tim's work in these courses. Time did not permit observation in his other courses.

In all, I collected approximately 20 hours of interview material, 30 hours of classroom observation field notes (of freshman writing) and tapes, and 100 pages of writing from Tim as well as comments on his writing by evaluators. Table 9 (next page) represents the method of triangulation—the use of multiple data sources for obtaining a view of gains in the developmental areas under consideration.

DATA ANALYSIS

In this case, a theoretical framework (with a few added elements) that I had employed in an earlier study of four writers making the transition from school to workplace writing was applied to this dataset as well.

Interviews, writing samples and classroom observation tapes were analyzed using the aspects of writing enumerated in the conceptual framework for disciplinary writing expertise. Operationalized definitions were developed (i.e. naming how the knowledge domains of writing would be observed) both from a theoretical or top-down perspective, and inductively, based on the data, in order for this theory-driven aspect of the coding to be consistent and valid (Cronbach and Meehl 1955). Operationalized definitions of the coding categories are indicated in Table 10 (see p.220)and units of analysis are indicated below. Where data were relevant to more than one category, those overlaps were noted. In some instances units of analysis from similar research studies were used; in other cases, units of analysis were arrived at inductively. Given the nature of the research questions and to avoid skewed representation of the data (Greene and Higgins 1994), interviews were also read against each other for consistency or changes in Tim's views over time. And in order to triangulate the data, interview and class transcripts, the set of essays and source documents were then read iteratively for particular instances that confirmed or disconfirmed interview data

TABLE 9

Triangulation of Data

	Interviews	Student essays	Source documents	Teacher comments	Third reader comments
Discourse community knowledge	X	X		X	
Subject matter knowledge	X	X	X	X	X
Genre knowledge	X	X	X		
Rhetorical knowledge	X	X			
Writing process skills	X				

and for additional evidence in the texts themselves of various aspects of writing and critical thinking expertise.

Discourse community knowledge was assessed via content analysis—what Tim said in interviews and did in his essays and what his teachers' wrote in response to his work that indicated understanding (or not) of purposes and constraints of the discourse community of historians.

Subject matter knowledge was assessed by content analysis: I noted topics that were expanded upon in successive papers or references to historical concepts and patterns beyond the particular source materials.

To analyze critical thinking, which was considered primarily in relation to subject matter knowledge, I compared source documents Tim used to the content of Tim's essays in order to determine what cognitive operations were evident in his writing. Bloom's taxonomy (1971) was useful for identifying broad categories of thinking—summary versus analysis versus evaluation. Analysis of organizational structures at the whole text level was also useful to determine methods used for linking ideas (Calfee and Chambliss 1987, Freedman and Pringle 1980, Greene 2001, Kuhn 1999), as was an analysis of claims and evidence (Toulmin 1958).

Genre knowledge was analyzed using Slevin's four areas of genre knowledge: purpose, content, structure, and linguistic features (Sievin 1988). These aspects of genre knowledge were helpful in recognizing particular genre features in Tim's essays. To assist with the genre feature

FIGURE 2

Scientific American Essay
Junior Year

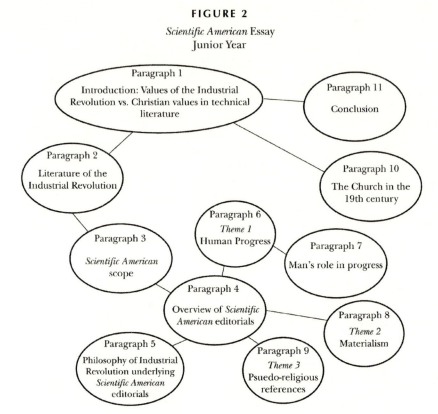

of structure, categories of expository structures developed by Calfee (1987) and Young and Leinhardt (1998), were applied to Tim's essays. To aid my "seeing" these text structures and the relations between ideas that these structures enabled, I used information mapping techniques (a combination of visual symbols and words—see Figure 2) to diagram the relationships between ideas in Tim's essays.

Analytical frameworks for assessing historical arguments in particular were also used—for example, looking at ways citations were (or were not) employed to build arguments (Greene 2001, Young and Leinhardt 1998). Genre knowledge was also assessed via meta-comments on genre in interview transcripts. Length of the essays and average T-unit length were also noted for additional indications of linguistic development.

Rhetorical knowledge was assessed via a content analysis of interviews, as the essays themselves were not indicative of the occasions for writing, choice of topic, etc.

TABLE 10

Operationalized Definitions of Five Knowledge Domains in Writing Experience

	Defining Features	Example
Discourse community knowledge	Knowledge of overaarching goals for communication; underlying values; and meta-discourses of the discipline	"Although your purpose is usually to discuss the past, some historians who probably are more comfortable being historians...would like to get at the future..." Tim, 2nd year
Subject matter knowledge	Knowledge of specific topics, central concepts, and appropriate frames of analysis for documents. Also, critical thinking skills to apply, manipulate, and draw from subject matter knowledge for rhetorical purposes.	"I missed some historical points...[that] inevitably happens when you don't study one thing deep enough..." Tim, year 2 "Your hypothesis is interesting and sophisticated. The logic with which you apply it to the readings is sometimes faulty." professor's comment to Tim, 1st year
Genre knowledge	Knowledge of standard genres used in the discipline and features of those genres: rhetorical aims, appropriate content; structure and linguistic features.	"There's so many different kinds of historical writing... there's the textbook, there's the Shrewbury type paper which just focuses on one little document and squeezes as much blood as it can out of that..." Tim, 2nd year
Rhetorical knowledge	Knowledge of the immediate rhetorical situation: needs of a specifi audience and specific purpose(s) for a single text	"It's aiming at popular audience like you know an intllectual audience I guess...when I was writing it, I was thinking of a *New York Times Book Review*." Tim, 4th year
Writing process knowledge	Knowledge of how to get discipline-specific writing tasks accomplished (meta-knowledge of cognitive processes in composing and phases of writing projects)	"I don't have my idea...So I get my fifteen sources on the table and go through them." Tim, 4th year

Writing process skills were noted via the writer's self-reports in interview transcripts.

For specific definitions and examples of the ways in which the definitions were operationalized in the data, see Table 10.

Analysis of the data, then, was both inductive and deductive, a combination of noting patterns and themes, making contrasts and comparisons, establishing linkages and relationships, and shuttling between data and larger categories (Bishop 1999).

IN SUMMARY

This, then, was the process for an inductive, data-driven approach to theory-building, and if this study is an indication, suggests the possibilities of a productive marriage of empirical study and theorizing.

NOTES

1.   For a history of the teaching of writing in the US, see Berlin, *Rhetoric and Reality: Writing Instruction in American Colleges, 1900–1985* (Carbondale: Southern Illinois University Press, 1987); Heath, "Toward an Ethnohistory of Writing in American Education," in *Writing: The Nature, Development and Teaching of Written Communication,* ed. Farr Whiteman (Hillsdale, N. J.: Lawrence Erlbaum Associates, 1981); and Miller, *Textual Carnivals: The Politics of Composition* (Carbondale: Southern Illinois University Press, 1991). For a critique of the last three decades of writing instruction in the US, see Harris, *A Teaching Subject: Composition since 1966* (Upper Saddle River, NJ: Prentice Hall, 1997).

2.   A number of key thinkers have being critiquing freshmen writing from within the system in the past 15 years. See Dias, "Writing Classrooms as Activity Systems," in *Transitions: Writing in Academic and Workplace Settings,* ed. Dias and Pare, *Written Language* (Cresskill, NJ: Hampton Press, 2000); Freedman, "The What, Where, When, Why, and How of Classroom Genres," in *Reconceiving Writing, Rethinking Writing Instruction,* ed. Petragalia (Mahwah, NJ: Lawrence Earlbaum Associates, 1995); Jolliffe, "Discourse, Interdiscursivity, and Composition Instruction," in *Reconceiving Writing, Rethinking Writing Instruction,* ed. Petragalia (Mahwah, NJ: Lawrence Erlbaum Associates, 1995); McLeod, "Cultural Literacy, Curricular Reform, and Freshman Composition," *Rhetoric Review* 8, no. 2 (1990); Petraglia, ed., *Reconceiving Writing, Rethinking Writing Instruction* (Mahwah, NJ: Lawrence Erlbaum Associates, 1995); Russell, "Activity Theory and Its Implications for Writing Instruction," in *Reconceiving Writing, Rethinking Writing Instruction,* ed. Petraglia (Mahwah, NJ: Erlbaum, 1995); Russell, "Rethinking Genre in School and Society: An Activity Theory Analysis," *Written Communication* 14, no. 4 (1997).

3.   I do not mean to imply that freshman writing is apolitical. In fact, educational institutions—and their benefactors—have appropriated freshman writing in a number of different directions to serve larger institutional or societal aims. It has served as gate-keeper when higher education was democratized. See Miller, *Textual Carnivals: The Politics of Composition*; as handmaid of the scientific industrial communities or as rebellious partner in the anti-establishment/expressivist movements of recent times Berlin, *Rhetoric and Reality: Writing Instruction in American Colleges, 1900–1985.* However, while these larger societal forces are important to acknowledge, I contain my focus on a more micro-level of discreet discourse communities that freshman writing concerns itself with—or could concern itself with.

4.   Some research has documented socially-driven syntax decisions that writers make. See Anne Beaufort, *Writing in the Real World: Making the Transition from School to Work* (New York: Teachers College Press, 1999); Broadhead and Freed, *The Variables of Composition: Process and Product in a Business Setting, Ncte Studies in Writing and Rhetoric* (Carbondale: Southern Illinois University Press, 1986); Faigley, "Names in Search of a Concept: Maturity, Fluency, Complexity, and Growth in Written Syntax," *College Composition and Communication* 31, no. 3 (1980).

5.   Several studies document difficulties transferring skills from one discourse community to another. See Bazerman, "What Written Knowledge Does: Three Examples of Academic Discourse," *Philosophy of the Social Sciences* 2 (1981); Beaufort, "Transferring Writing Knowledge to the Workplace: Are We on Track?," in *Expanding Literacies: English Teaching and the New Workplace,* ed. Garay and Bernhardt (Albany: State University of New York Press, 1998); Berkenkotter, Huckin, and Ackerman,

"Conventions, Conversations and the Writer: Case Study of a Student in a Rhetoric Ph.D. Program," *Research in the Teaching of English* 22 (1988); Carter, "The Idea of Expertise: An Exploration of Cognitive and Social Dimensions of Writing," *College Composition and Communication* 41, no. 3 (1990); Chin, "Learning to Write the News" (doctoral dissertation, Stanford University Press, 1991); Dias and others, *Worlds Apart: Acting and Writing in Academic and Workplace Contexts* (Mahwah, NJ: Lawrence Erlbaum Associates, 1999); Dias and Pare, eds., *Transitions: Writing in Academic and Workplace Settings* (Cresskill, NJ: Hampton Press, 2000); Greene, "The Question of Authenticity: Teaching Writing in a First-Year College History of Science Class," *Research in the Teaching of English* 35, no. May (2001); Kaufer and Young, "Writing in the Content Areas: Some Theoretical Complexities," in *Theory and Practice in the Teaching of Writing: Rethinking the Discipline*, ed. Odell (Carbondale: Southern Illinois University Press, 1993); McCarthy, "A Stranger in Strange Lands: A College Student Writing across the Curriculum," *Research in the Teaching of English* 21, no. 3 (1987); Prior, "Response, Revision, Disciplinarity: A Microhistory of a Dissertation Prospectus in Sociology," *Written Communication* 11, no. 4 (1994); Schryer, "Records as Genre," *Written Communication* 10, no. 2 (1993); Smagorinsky and Smith, "The Nature of Knowledge in Composition and Literary Understanding: The Question of Specificity," *Review of Educational Research* 62, no. 3 (1992); Teich, "Transfer of Writing Skills: Implications of the Theory of Lateral and Vertical Transfer," *Written Communication* 4, no. 2 (1987); Walvrood and McCarthy, *Thinking and Writing in College: A Naturalistic Study of Students in Four Disciplines* (Urbana, IL: National Council of Teachers of English, 1990).

6.   For a fuller description of the problems with subject matter in freshman writing courses, see Carroll, *Rehearsing New Roles: How College Students Develop as Writers*, ed. Brooke, *Studies in Writing and Rhetoric* (Carbondale, IL: Southern Illinois University Press, 2002); Durst, *Collision Course: Conflict, Negotiation, and Learning in College Composition* (Urbana, IL: National Council of Teachers of English, 1999); Jolliffe, "Discourse, Interdiscursivity, and Composition Instruction." in *Reconceiving Writing, Rethinking Writing Instruction*, ed. Petraglia (Mahwah, NJ: Lawrence Erlbaum Associates, 1995) , 197–216.

7.   An exception is the post-modernist or critical literacy compositionist's approach, which often reverses the emphasis: writing instruction is secondary to pursuit of inquiry into social inequalities.

8.   Cornell University, Georgetown University, and the State University of New York at Albany are three schools, among others, who use a freshman seminar approach to introducing students to academic writing.

9.   An exception is *Writing Across the Chemistry Curriculum* by Kovac. Kovac, *Writing across the Chemistry Curriculum: An Instructor's Handbook* (Englewood, NJ: Prentice Hall, 2001).

10.   The most specificity I could find in the tutoring manuals I surveyed on how to approach helping a student revise a draft was Clark's directive for tutors to ask genre-related questions of the writer. Clark, *Writing in the Center: Teaching in a Writing Center Setting, Third Edition*, 3rd ed. (Dubuque, Iowa: Kendall Hunt Publishing Company, 1998). But of the three manuals I consulted (all considered core texts in the field) only Clark's went as far as asking genre questions.

11.   Here is a sampling of the work, mostly in cognitive psychology, on the nature of expertise: Ackerman, "Cognitive Ability and Non-Ability Trait Determinants of Expertise," *Educational Researcher* 32, no. 8 (2003); Bryson and others, "Going Beyond the Problem as Given: Problem Solving in Expert and Novice Writers," in *Complex Problem Solving: Principles and Mechanisms*, ed. Sternberg and Frensch (Hillsdale, NJ: Lawrence Erlbaum Associates, 1991); Chi, Feltovich, and Glaser,

"Categorization and Representation of Physics Problems by Experts and Novices," *Cognitive Science* 5 (1981); Gott and others, "A Naturalistic Study of Transfer: Adaptive Expertise in Technical Domains," in *Transfer on Trial: Intelligence, Cognition, and Instruction,* ed. Detterman and Sternberg (Norwood, NJ: Ablex, 1993); "What Is an Expert Student?," *Educational Researcher* 32, no. 8 (2003); Sternberg, "Abilities Are Forms of Developing Expertise," *Educational Researcher* 27, no. 3 (1998).

12. Trimbur's *A Call to Write* is an exception. It is a genre-based rhetoric, with some reference to discourse communities that "own" the genres covered. Using genre as a mid-level, overarching concept gives a view of writing that is somewhat more socially situated and comprehensive. And Klooster and Bloem's *The Writer's Community,* though out of print, gives an excellent overview of discourse community theory as a way of organizing writing tasks. Klooster and Bloem, *The Writer's Community* (New York: St. Martin's Press, 1995), Trimbur, *The Call to Write,* 2nd ed. (New York: Longman, 1999). Two newer rhetorics organize their instruction around genre theory.

13. This conceptual model builds on work of others on the socio-cognitive and rhetorical dimensions of writing expertise, including notions of situated cognition. See Brandt, *Literacy as Involvement: The Acts of Writers, Readers, and Texts* (Carbondale, IL: Southern Illinois University Press, 1990); Flower, *The Construction of Negotiated Meaning: A Social Cognitive Theory of Writing* (Carbondale, IL: Southern Illinois University Press, 1994); mastering sets of genres embedded in particular discourse communities (Bizzell, 1982; Brandt, 1986; Rafoth, 1990; Walvrood & McCarthy, 1990), and understanding the rhetorical dimensions of a given communicative situation (Dias & Pare, 2000; Flower, 1979; Freedman, Adam, & Smart, 1994; Geisler, 1994; Greene, 2001; Sperling, 1990).

14. Devitt, *Writing Genres* (Carbondale: Southern Illinois University Press, 2004); and others take issue with a theory of discourse community. Devitt says that the definition of "community" must be something other than discourse, and she suggests that groups can share genres. She proposes looking at three different layers of groups in relation to genres and the ways genres function: communities, collectives, and networks. I would suggest that the operationalized definition of discourse community which I developed, based on an ethnography of communication in a non-profit organization. See Beaufort, "Operationalizing the Concept of Discourse Community: A Case Study of One Institutional Site of Composing," *Research in the Teaching of English* 31, no. 4 (1997) answers most of the objections raised to the concept.

15. Slevin's helpful definition of genre is as follows: "Genre is a received form, part of a cultural code, that synthesizes discursive features (e.g. subject matter, meaning, organization, style, and relations between writer and implied/actual audience) in recognizable ways." See Slevin, "Genre Theory, Academic Discourse, and Writing within Disciplines," in *Audits of Meaning,* ed. Smith (Portsmouth, NH: Boynton/ Cook Publishers, 1988).

16. There are a number of studies that examine the relation of genres to social contexts and the social actions accomplished by those genres Berkenkotter and Huckin, "Rethinking Genre from a Sociocognitive Perspective," *Written Communication* 10, no. 4 (1993); Devitt, "Generalizing About Genre: New Conceptions of an Old Concept," *College Composition and Communication* 44, no. 4 (1993); Johns, ed., *Genre in the Classroom: Multiple Perspectives* (Mahwah, NJ: Lawrence Erlbaum Associates, 2002); Miller, "Genre as Social Action," *Quarterly Journal of Speech* 70 (1984); Schryer, "Records as Genre."; Swales, "Re-Thinking Genre: Another Look at Discourse Community Effects," (Carleton University Conference on Genre: Unpublished Paper, 1992).

17. For a fuller explanation of the relationship between, and distinctions between

genre theory and discourse community theory as I see them, see Beaufort, *Writing in the Real World: Making the Transition from School to Work*. Chapter 3.

18.   As I have stated, this conceptual model encompasses the "stored" knowledge experienced writers have of how to approach writing tasks, but does not encompass the actual composing process itself. Rather, this model expands the "stored knowledge" aspect of the Flower and Hayes model of a writer's mental process in the act of composing.

19.   A majority of composition textbooks devote the bulk of their attention to these aspects of writing knowledge.

20.   For further discussion of outsider to insider paradigms of writers' growth, see Bartholomae, "Inventing the University," in *When a Writer Can't Write*, ed. Rose (New York: Guilford, 1985); Bizzell, "Cognition, Convention, and Certainty: What We Need to Know About Writing," *PRE/TEXT* 3, no. 3 (1982); Williams, "Afterword: Two Ways of Thinking About Growth: The Problem of Finding the Right Metaphor," in *Thinking, Reasoning, and Writing*, ed. Maimon, Nodine, and O'Connor, *Longman Series in College Composition and Communication* (New York: Longman, 1989).

21.   Beaufort, *Writing in the Real World: Making the Transition from School to Work*, (New York: Teachers College Press, 1999); Dias and Pare, eds., *Transitions: Writing in Academic and Workplace Settings*, (Cresskill, NJ: Hampton Press, 2000); Dyson, *Social Worlds of Children Learning to Write in an Urban Primary School* (New York: Teachers College Press, 1993); Hull and Schultz, "Literacy and Learning out of School: A Review of Theory and Research," *Review of Educational Research* 71, no. 4 (2001), Michael Rose, *Lives on the Boundary* (New York: Penguin Books, 1989); Russell, "Activity Theory and Its Implications for Writing Instruction.," in *Reconceiving Writing, Rethinking Writing Instruction*, ed. Petraglia, (Mahwah, NJ: Erlbaum, 1995); Smit, *The End of Composition Studies* (Urbana, IL: Southern Illnios Universtiy Press, 2004), Sperling, "Uncovering the Role of Role in Writing and Learning to Write: One Day in an Inner-City Classroom," *Written Communication* 12, no. 1 (1995), Swales, "Other Floors Other Voices: A Textography of a Small University Building". In *Rhetoric, Knowledge, and Society*, ed. Bazerman (Mahwah, NJ: Lawrence Erlbaum Associates, 1998).

22.   A number of studies of beginning writers are instructive about the holistic nature of acquiring new writing skills. See Dyson, *Social Worlds of Children Learning to Write in an Urban Primary School* (New York: Teachers College Press, 1993); Dyson, *Writing Superheroes: Contemporary Childhood, Popular Culture, and Classroom Literacy* (new York: Teachers College Press, 1997); Heath, *Ways with Words* (Cambridge: Cambridge University Press, 1983); Himley, "Genre as Generative: One Perspective on One Child's Early Writing Growth," in *The Structure of Written Communication: Studies in Reciprocity between Writers and Readers*, ed. Nystrand (Orlando, FL: Academic Press, 1986).

23.   Here are some of the pivotal developmental studies: elementary Dyson, *Multiple Words of Child Writers: Friends Learning to Write* (New York: Teachers College Press, 1989); Langer, "Children's Sense of Genre: A Study of Performance on Parallel Reading and Writing Tasks," *Written Communication* 2, no. 2 (1985); secondary Durst, "The Development of Analytic Writing," in *Contexts for Learning to Write: Studies of Secondary School Instruction*, ed. Applebee (Norwood, NJ: Ablex, 1984); Sperling and Freedman, "A Good Girl Writes Like a Good Girl," *Written Communication* 4, no. 4 (1987); and post-secondary DiPardo, *A Kind of Passport: A Basic Writing Adjunct Program and the Challenge of Student Diversity* (Urbana, IL: National Council of Teachers of English, 1993); Greene, "The Role of Task in the Development of Academic Thinking through Reading and Writing in a College History Course," *Research in the Teaching of English* 27, no. 1 (1993); Hays, "The Development of

Discursive Maturity in College Writers," in *The Writer's Mind: Writing as a Mode of Thinking*, ed. Hays and others (Urbana, IL: National Council of Teachers of English, 1983); Herrington and Curtis, *Persons in Process: Four Stories of Writing and Personal Development in College* (Urbana, IL: National Council of Teachers of English, 2000); Sternglass, *Time to Know Them: A Longitudinal Study of Writing and Learning at the College Level* (Mahwah, NJ: Lawrence Erlbaum Associates, 1997).

24.   The socially situated nature of cognitive activity has been demonstrated in a number of fields: cognitive psychology, composition studies, and linguistic anthropology, Lave and Wenger, *Situated Learning: Legitimate Peripheral Participation* (Cambridge: Cambridge University Press, 1991); Prior, "Response, Revision, Disciplinarity: A Microhistory of a Dissertation Prospectus in Sociology," *Written Communication* 11, no. 4 (1994); Scribner, "Studying Working Intelligence," in *Everyday Cognition: Its Development in Social Context*, ed. Rogoff and Lave (Cambridge, MA: Harvard University Press, 1984).

25.   Reading-to-write research has documented the tasks of critically analyzing text. Fisher and Scriven, *Critical Thinking: Its Definition and Assessment* (Point Reyes, CA: Edgepress, 1997); Freedman and Pringle, "Writing in the College Years: Some Indices of Growth," *College Composition and Communication* 31, no. 3 (1980); Greene, "The Question of Authenticity: Teaching Writing in a First-Year College History of Science Class," *Research in the Teaching of English* 35, no. May (2001); Rose, "Remedial Writing Courses: A Critique and a Proposal," *College English* 45 (1983); Voss, "Issues in the Learning of History," *Issues in Education* 4, no. 2 (1999); Young and Leinhardt, "Writing from Primary Documents: A Way of Knowing in History," *Written Communication* 15, no. 1 (1998).

26.   Studies of thinking about alternative views abound: Flower, Long, and Higgins, *Learning to Rival: A Literate Practice for Intercultural Inquiry*, in *Rhetoric, Knowledge, and Society*, ed. Bazerman (Mahwah, NJ: Lawrence Erlbaum, 2000); Greene, "The Question of Authenticity: Teaching Writing in a First-Year College History of Science Class," *Research in the Teaching of English* 35, no. May (2001); Kuhn, "Thinking as Argument," *Harvard Educational Review* 62, no. 2 (1992); Paul, "Dialogical Thinking: Critical Thought Essential to the Acquisition of Rational Knowledge and Passions," in *Teaching Thinking Skills: Theory and Practice*, ed. Baron and Sternberg (New York: W.H. Freeman and Company, 1987); Voss, "Issues in the Learning of History," *Issues in Education* 4, no. 2 (1999).

27.   The importance of metacognitive thinking has been documented in a number of fields: Flower, *The Construction of Negotiated Meaning: A Social Cognitive Theory of Writing*, (Carbondale, IL: Southern Illinois University Press, 1994); Kuhn, "A Developmental Model of Critical Thinking," *Educational Researcher* 28, no. 2 (1999); Perkins and Salomon, "Are Cognitive Skills Context-Bound?," *Educational Researcher* 18, no. 1 (1989); Salomon and Globerson, "Skill May Not Be Enough: The Role of Mindfulness in Learning and Transfer," *International Journal of Educational Research* 11 (1987).

28.   Note: some facts have been changed to protect the anonymity of those involved in the research project. These changes do not, however, alter the interpretation of data.

29.   In the Epilogue section of this book, Carla reflects on this report and how her teaching of freshman writing has evolved since the data were collected.

30.   For an example of students "doing school," thwarting a teacher's best-laid plans to engage her class in sociology, see Nelson, "This Was an Easy Assignment: Examining How Students Interpret Academic Writing Tasks," (Center for the Study of Writing, 1990).

31.   Though the term "belle lettres" had narrower connotations in the parlance of 18th

and 19th century rhetorics, today it usually connotes a very broad, general category of discourse within the humanities that is "elegant" or "tasteful."

32.   An exception is Jolliffe, "Discourse, Interdiscursivity, and Composition Instruction," in *Reconceiving Writing, Rethinking Writing Instruction*, ed. Petraglia, (Mahwah, NJ: Lawrence Erlbaum Associates, 1995) who has for a long time advocated students' digging deep in a particular subject matter as part of their acquiring critical thinking and writing skills.

33.   For an excellent overview of the evolution of the essay as a genre, and in particular, its forms in school assignments, see Heath, "Rethinking the Sense of the Past: The Essay as Legacy of the Epigram," in *Theory and Practice in the Teaching of Writing: Rethinking the Discipline*, ed. Odell (Carbondale, IL: Southern Illinois University Press, 1993).

34.   It was a requirement in the history department that all majors take a seminar in which they would be exposed to research methods in the field. Tim took this seminar (in his case, on Muscovite Russia) in his sophomore year.

35.   For two of the essays for the Muscovite history course, the professor typed responses—in one case, half a page, in the other case, a full page.

36.   It's not clear if he's referring to his work or others in this critique.

37.   An engineering colleague confirmed that engineers are fond of bullets, but there was a new recognition that bullets can hide too much information. "They're okay in a presentation or summary, but a whole proposal in bullets would be thrown out." (Kincaid, personal communication)

38.   A review of seminal findings and theories on transfer of learning is well worth the time for writing program administrators and others with oversight responsibilities for curricula. Brooks and Dansereau, "Transfer of Information: An Instructional Perspective," in *Transfer of Learning: Contemporary Research and Applications*, ed. Cormier and Hagman (San Diego: Academic Press, Inc., 1987); Foertsch, "Where Cognitive Psychology Applies: How Theories About Memory and Transfer Can Influence Composition Pedagogy," *Written Communication* 12, no. 3 (1995); Gick and Holyak, "The Cognitive Basis of Knowledge Transfer," in *Transfer of Learning: Contemporary Research and Applications*, ed. Cormier and Hagman (San Diego: Academic Press, Inc., 1987); Mikulecky, Albers, and Peers, "Literacy Transfer: A Review of the Literature," (National Center on Adult Literacy, University of Pennsylvania, 1994); Perkins and Salomon, "Teaching for Transfer," *Educational Leadership* 46, no. 1 (1989); Perkins and Salomon, "Are Cognitive Skills Context-Bound?," *Educational Researcher* 18, no. 1 (1989); Smagorinsky and Smith, "The Nature of Knowledge in Composition and Literary Understanding: The Question of Specificity.", Sternberg, "What Is an Expert Student?," *Review of Educational Research* 62, no. 3 (1992).

39.   See Appendix A for further examples of pedagogy to enact these principles for fostering transfer of learning.

40.   For an excellent example of an integrated, developmentally sound sequence of writing assignments across a subject area, see Kovac, *Writing across the Chemistry Curriculum: An Instructor's Handbook* (Englewood, NJ: Prentice Hall, 2001).

41.   Berryman (1992) suggests that content issues to be considered include domain knowledge, problem-solving strategies, cognitive management, and learning strategies. Principles for sequencing of curriculum and tasks include increasing complexity, increasing diversity, and presenting global issues before getting in details. Social factors to be build in, wherever possible, include intrinsic motivation, cooperative learning, and situated learning. And methods for instruction include modeling, coaching, scaffolding, and articulating otherwise invisible principles.

42.   Cognitive tasks which Kiniry (1985) suggests should be incorporated into a

sequence of writing assignments include listing, defining, seriation, classification, summary, comparison/contrast, analysis, and academic argument. He also points out that there are gradations of complexity within each of these categories of cognitive work.

43.   Russell (1997) highlights four key aspects of social apprenticeships, which, given the social nature of writing, must also be considered: designing writing tasks authentic to the discourse community; giving students agency, i.e. authentic roles as writers within the course and/or discipline; giving students authentic tools, i.e. genre knowledge for the target discourse community; and equipping students with discipline-specific writing process strategies.

REFERENCES

Ackerman, Phillip L. "Cognitive Ability and Non-Ability Trait Determinants of Expertise." *Educational Researcher* 32, no. 8 (2003): 15–20.

Alexander, Patricia A. "The Development of Expertise: The Journey from Acclimation to Proficiency." *Educational Researcher* 32, no. 8 (2003): 10–14.

Applebee, Arther N. "Alternative Models of Writing Development." In *Perspectives on Writing: Research, Theory and Practice,* edited by Roselmina Indrisano and James R. Squire, 90–110. Newark, DE: International Reading Association, 2000.

Applebee, Arthur N., and Judith A. Langer. "Instructional Scaffolding: Reading and Writing as Natural Language Activities." *Language Arts* 60, no. 2 (1983): 168–175.

Appleby, Joyce, Lynn Hunt, and Margaret Jacob. *Telling the Truth About History.* New York: W.W. Norton & company, 1994.

Bartholomae, David. "Inventing the University." In *When a Writer Can't Write,* edited by Mike Rose, 134–165. New York: Guilford, 1985.

Bawarshi, Anis. *Genre and the Invention of the Writer: Reconsidering the Place of Invention in Composition.* Logan, UT: Utah State University Press, 2003.

———. "The Genre Function." *College English* 62, no. 3 (2000): 335–360.

Bazerman, Charles. "Scientific Writing as a Social Act." In *New Essays in Technical and Scientific Communication,* edited by P. Anderson, 156–184. Farmingdale, NY: Baywood, 1982.

———. *Constructing Experience.* Carbondale, IL: Southern Illinois University Press, 1994.

———. *Shaping Written Knowledge: The Genre and Activity of the Experimental Article in Science.* Madison: University of Wisconsin Press, 1988.

———. "The Life of Genre, the Life in the Classroom." In *Genre and Writing: Issues, Arguments, Alternatives,* edited by Wendy Bishop and Hans Ostrom, 19–26. Portsmouth, NH: Boynton/Cook, 1997.

———. "What Written Knowledge Does: Three Examples of Academic Discourse." *Philosophy of the Social Sciences* 2 (1981): 361–387.

Beaufort, Anne. "Learning the Trade: A Social Apprenticeship Model for Gaining Writing Expertise." *Written Communication* 1, no. 2 (2000): 185–223.

———. "Operationalizing the Concept of Discourse Community: A Case Study of One Institutional Site of Composing." *Research in the Teaching of English* 31, no. 4 (1997): 486–529.

———. "Transferring Writing Knowledge to the Workplace: Are We on Track?" In *Expanding Literacies: English Teaching and the New Workplace,* edited by Mary S. Garay and Stephen A. Bernhardt, 179–199. Albany: State University of New York Press, 1998.

———. *Writing in the Real World: Making the Transition from School to Work.* New York: Teachers College Press, 1999.

——— and John Williams. "Writing History: Informed or Not by Genre Theory?" In *Genre across the Curriculum,* edited by Anne Herrington and Charles Moran, 44–64. Logan, UT: Utah State University Press, 2005.

Bereiter, Carl, and Marlene Scardamalia. *Surpassing Ourselves: An Inquiry into the Nature and Implications of Expertise.* Chicago: Open Court, 1993.

———. *The Psychology of Written Composition.* Hillsdale, NJ: Lawrence Erlbaum Associates, 1987.

Berkenkotter, Carol, and Thomas N. Huckin. "Rethinking Genre from a Sociocognitive Perspective." *Written Communication* 10, no. 4 (1993): 475–509.

Berkenkotter, Carol, Thomas Huckin, and John Ackerman. "Conventions, Conversations and the Writer: Case Study of a Student in a Rhetoric Ph.D. Program." *Research in the Teaching of English* 22 (1988): 9–44.

Berkenkotter, Carol, Thomas N. Huckin, and John Ackerman. "Social Context and Socially Constructed Texts: The Initiation of a Graduate Student into a Writing Research Community." Center for the Study of Writing, U.C. Berkeley, 1989.

Berlin, James A. *Rhetoric and Reality: Writing Instruction in American Colleges, 1900–1985.* Carbondale: Southern Illinois University Press, 1987.

Berryman, S.E., and T.R. Bailey. *The Double Helix of Education and the Economy.* New York: The Institute on Education and the Economy, Teachers College, Columbia University, 1992.

Bishop, Wendy. *Ethnographic Writing Research: Writing It Down, Writing It up, and Reading It.* Portsmouth, NH: Boynton/Cook, 1999.

Bizzell, Patricia. "Cognition, Convention, and Certainty: What We Need to Know About Writing." *PRE/TEXT* 3, no. 3 (1982): 213–243.

Bloom, B.S., ed., *Taxonomy of Educational Objectives Handbook: Cognitive Domain.* New York: McGraw-Hill, 1971.

Bohan, Chara Haeussler, and O.L. Jr. Davis. "Historical Constructions: How Social Studies Student Teachers' Historical Thinking Is Reflected in Their Writing of History." *Theory and Research in Social Education* 26, no. 2 (1998): 173–197.

Boquet, Elizabeth H. *Noise from the Writing Center.* Logan, UT: Utah State University Press, 2002.

Brandt, Deborah. *Literacy as Involvement: The Acts of Writers, Readers, and Texts.* Carbondale, IL: Southern Illinois University Press, 1990.

Brannon, Lil. "Toward a Theory of Composition." In *Perspectives on Research and Scholarship in Composition,* edited by Ben W. McClelland and Timothy R. Donovan, 6–26. New York: Modern Language Association, 1985.

Briggs, Charles L. *Learning How to Ask: A Sociolinguistic Appraisal of the Role of the Interview in Social Science Research.* New York: Cambridge University Press, 1986.

Briggs, Lynn C., and Meg Woolbright, eds., *Stories from the Center: Connecting Narrative and Theory in the Writing Center.* Urbana, IL: National Council of Teachers of English, 2000.

Britt, Anne M., Jean-Francois Rouet, Mara C. Georgi, and Charles A. Perfetti. "Learning from History Texts: From Causal Analysis to Argument Models." In *Teaching and Learning in History,* edited by Gaea Leinhardt, Isabel L. Beck and Caterhine Stainton, 47–84. Hillsdale, NJ: Lawrence Erlbaum Associates, 1994.

Broadhead, Glen J., and Richard C. Freed. *The Variables of Composition: Process and Product in a Business Setting, Ncte Studies in Writing and Rhetoric.* Carbondale: Southern Illinois University Press, 1986.

Brooks, Larry W., and Donald F. Dansereau. "Transfer of Information: An Instructional Perspective." In *Transfer of Learning: Contemporary Research and Applications,* edited by Stephen M. Cormier and Joseph D. Hagman, 121–150. San Diego: Academic Press, Inc., 1987.

Bruffee, Kenneth. "Collaborative Learning and The 'Conversation of Mankind'." *College English* 46, no. 7 (1984): 635–652.

Bryson, Mary, Carl Bereiter, Marlene Scardamalia, and Elana Joram. "Going Beyond the Problem as Given: Problem Solving in Expert and Novice Writers." In *Complex Problem Solving: Principles and Mechanisms,* edited by Robert J. Sternberg and Peter A. Frensch, 61–84. Hillsdale, NJ: Lawrence Erlbaum Associates, 1991.

Calfee, Robert C., and Marilyn J. Chambliss. "The Structural Design Features of Large Texts." *Educational psychologist* 22, no. 3–4 (1987): 357–378.

Canagarajah, A. Suresh. "Safe Houses in the Contact Zone: Coping Strategies of African–American Students in the Academy." *College Composition and Communication* 48, no. 2 (1997): 173–196.

Carroll, Lee Ann. "Rehearsing New Roles: How College Students Develop as Writers." In *Studies in Writing and Rhetoric*, edited by Robert Brooke, ???–???.Carbondale, IL: Southern Illinois University Press, 2002.

Carter, Michael. "The Idea of Expertise: An Exploration of Cognitive and Social Dimensions of Writing." *College Composition and Communication* 41, no. 3 (1990): 265–286.

Chi, M.T.H., P. Feltovich, and R. Glaser. "Categorization and Representation of Physics Problems by Experts and Novices." *Cognitive Science* 5 (1981): 121–152.

Chin, Elaine. "Learning to Write the News." doctoral dissertation, Stanford University Press, 1991.

Clark, Irene L. *Writing in the Center: Teaching in a Writing Center Setting, Third Edition.* 3rd ed. Dubuque, Iowa: Kendall Hunt Publishing Company, 1998.

Coe, Richard M. "Teaching Genre as Process." In *Learning and Teaching Genre*, edited by Aviva Freedman and Peter Medway, 157–169. Portsmouth, NH: Boynton Cook, 1994.

Couture, Barbara, and Jone Rymer. "Discourse Interaction between Writer and Supervisor: A Primary Collaboration in Workplace Writing." In *Collaborative Writing in Industry: Investigations in Theory and Practice*, edited by Mary Lay and William Karis, 87–108. Amityville, NY: Baywood Publishing Comapny, 1991.

Cronbach, L.J., and P.E. Meehl. "Construct Validity in Psychological Tests." *Psychological Bulletin* 52 (1955): 281–302.

Crowhurst, M. "Interrelationship between Reading and Writing Persuasive Discourse." *Research in the Teaching of English* 25 (1991): 314–338.

Davis, Jeff. *The Journey from the Center to the Page: Yoga Philosophies & Practices as Muse for Authentic Writing.* New York: Gothan Books, 2004.

Devitt, Amy J. "Generalizing About Genre: New Conceptions of an Old Concept." *College Composition and Communication* 44, no. 4 (1993): 573–586.

———. "Intertextuality in Tax Accounting: Generic, Referential, and Functional." In *Textual Dynamics of the Professions: Historical and Contemporary Studies of Writing in Professional Communities*, edited by Charles Bazerman and James Paradis, 336–57. Madison, WI: University of Wisconsin Press, 1991.

———. *Writing Genres.* Carbondale: Southern Illinois University Press, 2004.

Devitt, Amy J., Mary Jo Reiff, and Anis Bawarchi. *Scenes of Writing: Strategies for Composing with Genres.* New York: Pearson Longman, 2004.

Dias, Patrick. "Writing Classrooms as Activity Systems." In *Transistions: Writing in Academic and Workplace Settings*, edited by Patric Dias and Anthony Pare, 11–29. Cresskill, NJ: Hampton Press, 2000.

——— and Anthony Paré, eds. *Transitions: Writing in Academic and Workplace Settings.* Cresskill, NJ: Hampton Press, 2000.

———, Aviva Freedman, Peter Medway, and Anthony Paré. *Worlds Apart: Acting and Writing in Academic and Workplace Contexts.* Mahwah, NJ: Lawrence Erlbaum Associates, 1999.

DiPardo, Anne. *A Kind of Passport: A Basic Writing Adjunct Program and the Challenge of Student Diversity.* Urbana, IL: National Council of Teachers of English, 1993.

———. "Stimulated Recall in Research on Writing: An Antidote To 'I Don't Know, It Was Fine'." In *Speaking About Writing: Reflections on Research Methodology*, edited by Peter Smagorinsky, 163–181. Thousand Oaks, CA: Sage Publications, 1994.

Doheny-Farina, S. "Writing in an Emerging Organization." *Written Communication* 3 (1986): 158–185.

Durst, Russel. *Collision Course: Conflict, Negotiation, and Learning in College Composition.* Urbana, IL: National Council of Teachers of English, 1999.

———. "The Development of Analytic Writing." In *Contexts for Learning to Write: Studies of Secondary School Instruction*, edited by A. Applebee, 79–102. Norwood, NJ: Ablex, 1984.

Dyson, Anne Haas. *Multiple Words of Child Writers: Friends Learning to Write.* New York: Teachers College Press, 1989.

———. *Social Worlds of Children Learning to Write in an Urban Primary School.* New York: Teachers College Press, 1993.

———. *Writing Superheroes: Contemporary Childhood, Popular Culture, and Classroom Literacy.* New York: Teachers College Press, 1997.

Ede, Lisa, and Andrea Lunsford. "Audience Addressed/Audience Invoked: The Role of Audience in Composition Theory and Pedagogy." *College Composition and Communication* 35, no. 2 (1984): 155–71.

———. *Singular Texts/Plural Authors: Perspectives on Collaborative Writing.* Carbondale: Southern Illinois University Press, 1990.

Eiler, Mary Ann. "Process and Genre." In *Worlds of Writing: Teaching and Learning in Discourse Communities of Work,* edited by Carolyn B. Matalene, 43–63. New York: Random House, 1989.

Fahnestock, Jeanne. "Accommodating Science: The Rhetorical Life of Scientific Facts." *Written Communication* 3, no. 3 (1986): 275–296.

———. and Marie Secor. "The Rhetoric of Literary Criticism." In *Textual Dynamics of the Professions: Historical and Contemporary Studies of Writing in Professional Communities,* edited by Charles Bazerman and James Paradis, 76–96. Madison: University of Wisconsin Press, 1991.

Faigley, Lester. "Names in Search of a Concept: Maturity, Fluency, Complexity, and Growth in Written Syntax." *College Composition and Communication* 31, no. 3 (1980): 291–300.

——— and K. Hansen. "Learning to Write in the Social Sciences." *College Composition and Communication* 34 (1985): 140–149.

Fisher, Alec, and Michael Scriven. *Critical Thinking: Its Definition and Assessment.* Point Reyes, CA: Edge Press, 1997.

Fishman, Andrea R. *Amish Literacy: What and How It Means.* Portsmouth, New Hampshire: Heinemann, 1988.

Flower, Linda. "Writer–Based Prose: A Cognitive Basis for Problems in Writing." *College English* 41, no. 1 (1979): 19–37.

———. "Cognition, Context, and Theory Building." *College Composition and Communication* 40, no. 3 (1989): 282–311.

———. *The Construction of Negotiated Meaning: A Social Cognitive Theory of Writing.* Carbondale, IL: Southern Illinois University Press, 1994.

———, and John R. Hayes. "A Cognitive Process Theory of Writing." *College Composition and Communication* 32, no. 4 (1981): 365–387.

———, Elenore Long, and Lorraine Higgins. "Learning to Rival: A Literate Practice for Intercultural Inquiry." In *Rhetoric, Knowledge, and Society,* edited by Charles Bazerman. Mahwah, NJ: Lawrence Erlbaum, 2000.

Foertsch, Julie. "Where Cognitive Psychology Applies: How Theories About Memory and Transfer Can Influence Composition Pedagogy." *Written Communication* 12, no. 3 (1995): 360–383.

Freedman, Aviva. "Show and Tell? The Role of Explicit Teaching in the Learning of New Genres." *Research in the Teaching of English* 27, no. 3 (1993): 222–251.

———. "The What, Where, When, Why, and How of Classroom Genres." In *Reconceiving Writing, Rethinking Writing Instruction,* edited by Joseph Petragalia, 121–144. Mahwah, NJ: Lawrence Earlbaum Associates, 1995.

——— and Ian Pringle. "Writing in the College Years: Some Indices of Growth." *College Composition and Communication* 31, no. 3 (1980): 311–324.

———,, Christine Adam, and Graham Smart. "Wearing Suits to Class: Simulating Genres and Simulations as Genre." *Written Communication* 11, no. 2 (1994): 193–226.

Geisler, Cheryl. *Academic Literacy and the Nature of Expertise: Reading, Writing and Knowing in Academic Philosophy.* Hillsdale, NJ: Lawrence Erlbaum Associates, 1994.

Gick, Mary L., and Keith J. Holyak. "The Cognitive Basis of Knowledge Transfer." In

Transfer of Learning: Contemporary Research and Applications, edited by Stephen M. Cormier and Joseph D. Hagman, 9–46. San Diego: Academic Press, Inc., 1987.

Gilbert, Steven W. "Systematic Questioning: Taxonomies That Develop Critical Thinking Skills." *The Science Teacher* 59, no. 9 (1992): 41–46.

Gott, Sherrit P., Ellen Parker Hall, Robert A. Pokorny, Emily Dibble, and Robert Glaser. "A Naturalistic Study of Transfer: Adaptive Expertise in Technical Domains." In *Transfer on Trial: Intelligence, Cognition, and Instruction*, edited by Douglas K. Detterman and Robert J. Sternberg, 258–88. Norwood, NJ: Ablex, 1993.

Greene, Stuart. "Making Sense of My Own Ideas." *Written Communication* 12, no. 2 (1995): 186–218.

———. "The Question of Authenticity: Teaching Writing in a First–Year College History of Science Class." *Research in the Teaching of English* 35, no. May (2001): 525–569.

———. "The Role of Task in the Development of Academic Thinking through Reading and Writing in a College History Course." *Research in the Teaching of English* 27, no. 1 (1993): 46–75.

Greene, Stuart, and Lorraine Higgins. "'Once Upon a Time': The Use of Retrospective Accounts in Building Theory in Composition." In *Speaking About Writing: Reflections on Research Methodology*, edited by Peter Smagorinsky, 115–140. Thousand Oaks, CA: Sage Publications, 1994.

Grimm, Nancy. *Good Intentions: Writing Center Work for Postmodern Times*. Portsmouth, NH: Boynton/Cook Publishers, 1999.

Gunn, Victoria A. "Transgressing the Traditional? Teaching and Learning Methods in a Medieval History Access Course." *Teaching in Higher Education* 5, no. 3 (2000): 311–321.

Hagge, John. "Early Engineering Writing Textbooks and the Anthropological Complexity of Disciplinary Discourse." *Written Communication* 12, no. 4 (1995): 439–491.

Hall, Deborah C. "Developing Historical Writing Skills: A Scope and Sequence." *Magazine of History* 2, no. 4 (1987): 20–24.

Hallden, Ola. "On the Paradox of Understanding History in an Educational Setting." In *Teaching and Learning in History*, edited by Gaea Leinhardt, Isabel Beck and Catherine Stainton, 27–46. Hillsdale, NJ: Lawrence Erlbaum Associates, 1994.

Harris, Joseph. *A Teaching Subject: Composition Since 1966*. Upper Saddle River, NJ: Prentice Hall, 1997.

Harris, Muriel. "Writing Center Theory and Scholarship." In *Theorizing Composition: A Critical Sourcebook of Theory and Scholarship in Contemporary Composition Studies*, edited by Mary Lunch Kennedy, 364–371. Westport, CT: Greenwood Press, 1998.

Haswell, Richard H. *Gaining Ground in College Writing: Tales of Development and Interpretation*. Dallas: Southern Methodist University Press, 1991.

———. "Documenting Improvement in College Writing: A Longitudinal Approach." *Written Communication* 17, no. 3 (2000): 307–352.

Hays, Janet N. "The Development of Discursive Maturity in College Writers." In *The Writer's Mind: Writing as a Mode of Thinking*, edited by Janet N. Hays, P. A. Roth, J. R. Ramsey and R. D. Foulke, ???–???. Urbana, IL: National Council of Teachers of English, 1983.

Heath, Shirley Brice. "Rethinking the Sense of the Past: The Essay as Legacy of the Epigram." In *Theory and Practice in the Teaching of Writing: Rethinking the Discipline*, edited by Lee Odell, 105–131. Carbondale, IL: Southern Illinois University Press, 1993.

———. "Toward an Ethnohistory of Writing in American Education." In *Writing: The Nature, Development and Teaching of Written Communication*, edited by Marcia Farr Whiteman, 25–45. Hillsdale, NJ: Lawrence Erlbaum Associates, 1981.

———. *Ways with Words*. Cambridge: Cambridge University Press, 1983.

Herndl, Carl C., Barbara A. Fennel, and Carolyn R. Miller. "Understanding Failures in Organizational Discourse: The Accident at Three Mile Island and the Shuttle

Challenger Disaster." In *Textual Dynamics of the Professions: Hisotrical and Contemporary Studies of Writing in Professional Communities,* edited by Charles Bazaerman and James Paradis, 279–395. Madison, WI: University of Wisconsin Press, 1991.

Herrington, Ann. "Teaching, Writing and Learning: A Naturalistic Study of Writing in an Undergraduate Literature Course." In *Advances in Writing Research: Vol 2. Writing in Academic Disciplines,* edited by David Jolliffe, 133–166. Norwood, NJ: Ablex, 1988.

Herrington, Anne. "Writing in Academic Settings: A Study of the Contexts for Writing in Two College Chemical Engineering Courses." *Research in the Teaching of English* 19 (1985): 331–361.

———. and Marcia Curtis. *Persons in Process: Four Stories of Writing and Personal Development in College.* Urbana, IL: National Council of Teachers of English, 2000.

Himley, Margaret. "Genre as Generative: One Perspective on One Child's Early Writing Growth." In *The Structure of Written Communication: Studies in Reciprocity between Writers and Readers,* edited by M. Nystrand, 137–157. Orlando, FL: Academic Press, 1986.

Hobson, Eric H. "Writing Center Practice Often Counters Its Theory. So What?" In *Intersections: Theory-Practice in the Writing Center,* edited by Joan A. Mullin and Ray Wallace, 1–10. Urbana, IL: National Council of Teachers of English, 1994.

Horn, Robert E. "Information Mapping." *Training in Business and Industry* 11, no. 3 (1974): 27–32.

Hull, Glynda, and Katherine Schultz. "Literacy and Learning out of School: A Review of Theory and Research." *Review of Educational Research* 71, no. 4 (2001): 575–611.

Hunt, Kellogg W. "A Synopsis of Clause–to–Sentence Length Factors." *English Journal* 54 (1965): 300–309.

Jacott, Liliana, Asuncion Lopez-Manjon, and Mario Carretero. "Generating Explanations in History." In *International Review of History Education: Learning and Reasoning in History,* edited by James F. Voss and Mario Carretero, 294–306. London: Woburn Press, 1998.

Johns, Ann M., ed. *Genre in the Classroom: Multiple Perspectives.* Mahwah, NJ: Lawrence Erlbaum Associates, 2002.

Jolliffe, David A. "Discourse, Interdiscursivity, and Composition Instruction." In *Reconceiving Writing, Rethinking Writing Instruction,* edited by Joseph Petragalia, 197–216. Mahwah, NJ: Lawrence Erlbaum Associates, 1995.

Kaufer, David S., and Patricia L. Dunmire. "Integrating Cultural Reflection and Production in College Writing Curricula." In *Reconceiving Writing, Rethinking Writing Instruction,* edited by Joseph Petraglia, 217–238. Mahwah, NJ: Lawrence Erlbaum Associates, 1995.

Kaufer, David, and Richard Young. "Writing in the Content Areas: Some Theoretical Complexities." In *Theory and Practice in the Teaching of Writing: Rethinking the Discipline,* edited by Lee Odell, 71–104. Carbondale: Southern Illinois University Press, 1993.

Kiniry, Malcolm, and Ellen Strenski. "Sequencing Expository Writing: A Recursive Approach." *College Composition and Communication* 36, no. 2 (1985): 191–202.

Klooster, David J., and Patricia L. Bloem. *The Writer's Community.* New York: St. Martin's Press, 1995.

Kovac, Jeffrey. *Writing across the Chemistry Curriculum: An Instructor's Handbook.* Englewood, NJ: Prentice Hall, 2001.

Kuhn, Deanna. "A Developmental Model of Critical Thinking." *Educational Researcher* 28, no. 2 (1999): 16–25.

———. "Thinking as Argument." *Harvard Educational Review* 62, no. 2 (1992): 155–178.

Lajoie, Susanne P. "Transitons and Trajectories for Studies of Expertise." *Educational Researcher* 32, no. 8 (2003): 21–25.

Langer, Judith A. "Children's Sense of Genre: A Study of Performance on Parallel Reading and Writing Tasks." *Written Communication* 2, no. 2 (1985): 157–187.

————. "The Effects of Available Information on Responses to School Writing Tasks." *Research in the Teaching of English* 18, no. 1 (1984): 27–44.

Larson, Richard L. "The 'Research Paper' in the Writing Course: A Non-Form of Writing." *College English* 44, no. December (1982): 811–816.

Latour, Bruno, and Steve Woolgar. *Laboratory Life: The Construction of Scientific Facts.* Princeton, NJ: Princeton University Press, 1979.

Lave, Jean, and Etienne Wenger. *Situated Learning: Legitimate Peripheral Participation.* Cambridge: Cambridge University Press, 1991.

LeFevre, K. *Invention as a Social Act.* Carbondale, IL: Southern Illinois University Press, 1987.

Leinhardt, Gaea. "History: A Time to Be Mindful." In *Teaching and Learning in History,* edited by Gaea Leinhardt, Isabel L. Beck and Catherine Stainton, 209–255. Hillsdale, NJ: Lawrence Erlbaum, 1994.

————. "Weaving Instructional Explanations in History." *British Journal of Educational Psychology* 63 (1993): 46–74.

Lunsford, Andrea A., and Lisa Ede. "Representing Audience: 'Successful' Discourse and Disciplinary Critique." *College Composition and Communication* 47, no. 2 (May) (1996): 167–179.

MacDonald, Susan Peck. *Professional Academic Writing in the Humanities and Social Sciences.* Urbana, IL: Southern Illinois University Press, 1994.

McCarthy, Lucille Parkinson. "A Stranger in Strange Lands: A College Student Writing across the Curriculum." *Research in the Teaching of English* 21, no. 3 (1987): 233–265.

McLaughlin, Daniel. *When Literacy Empowers.* Albequerque: University of New Mexico Press, 1992.

McLeod, Susan H. "Cultural Literacy, Curricular Reform, and Freshman Composition." *Rhetoric Review* 8, no. 2 (1990): 270–278.

Medway, Peter. "Writing and Design in Architectural Education." In *Transitions: Writing in Academic and Workplace Settings,* edited by Patrick Dias and Anthony Pare, 89–128. Creskill, NJ: Hampton Press, Inc, 2000.

Mikulecky, Larry, Peggy Albers, and Michele Peers. "Literacy Transfer: A Review of the Literature." National Center on Adult Literacy, University of Pennsylvania, 1994.

Miller, Carolyn R. "Genre as Social Action." *Quarterly Journal of Speech* 70 (1984): 151–167.

Miller, Paul, Bausser Jaye, and Fentiman Audeen. "Responding to Technical Writing in an Introductory Engineering Class: The Role of Genre and Discipline." *Technical Communication Quarterly* 7, no. 4 (1998): 443–461.

Miller, Susan. *Textual Carnivals: The Politics of Composition.* Carbondale: Southern Illinois University Press, 1991.

Moffett, James. *Teaching the Universe of Discourse.* Boston: Houghton Mifflin Company, 1983.

Neff, Joyce Magnotto. "Capturing Complexity: Using Grounded Theory to Study Writing Centers." In *Writing Center Research: Extending the Conversatiohn,* edited by Paula Gillespie, Alice Gillam, Lady Falls Brown and Byron Stay, 133–148. Mahwah, NJ: Lawrence Erlbaum, 2002.

Nelson, Jennie. "Reading Classrooms as Text: Exploring Student Writers' Interpretive Practices." *College Composition and Communication* 46, no. 3 (1995): 411–429.

————. "This Was an Easy Assignment: Examining How Students Interpret Academic Writing Tasks." Center for the Study of Writing, 1990.

Newell, George E., and Peter Winograd. "Writing About and Learning from History Texts: The Effects of Task and Academic Ability." *Research in the Teaching of English* 29, no. 2 (May) (1995): 133–183.

Odell, Lee, Dixie Goswami, and Anne Herrington. "The Discourse-Based Interview: A Procedure for Exploring the Tacit Knowledge of Writers in Nonacademic Settings." In

Writing Research: Methods and Procedures, edited by Peter Mosenthal, Lynn Tamor and Sean Walmsley. NY: Longman, 1983.

Paul, Richard W. "Dialogical Thinking: Critical Thought Essential to the Acquisition of Rational Knowledge and Passions." In *Teaching Thinking Skills: Theory and Practice*, edited by Joan B. Baron and Robert J. Sternberg, 127–148. New York: W.H. Freeman and Company, 1987.

Pelikan, Jaroslav. *Scholarship: A Sacred Vocation.* New York: Association of American University Presses, 1984.

Pemberton, Michael A., and Joyce Kinkead, eds. *The Center Will Hold: Critical Perspectives on Writing Center Scholarship.* Logan, UT: Utah State University Press, 2003.

Perkins, David N., and Gavriel Salomon. "Teaching for Transfer." *Educational Leadership* 46, no. 1 (1989): 22–32.

———. "Are Cognitive Skills Context–Bound?" *Educational Researcher* 18, no. 1 (1989): 16–25.

Perl, Sondra. "The Composing Process of Unskilled College Writers." *Research in the Teaching of English* 13, no. 4 (1979): 317–336.

Petraglia, Joseph, ed. *Reconceiving Writing, Rethinking Writing Instruction.* Mahwah, NJ: Lawrence Erlbaum Associates, 1995.

Polanyi, Michael. *The Tacit Dimension.* Garden City, NY: Doubleday & Company, 1966.

Porter, James E. "Intertextuality and the Discourse Community." *Rhetoric Review* 5 (1986): 34–47.

Premack, David. "Some Thoughts About Transfer." In *The Teachability of Language*, edited by Mabel L. Rice and Richard L. Schiefelbusch, 239–262. Baltimore: Paul H. Brookes Publishing Company, 1989.

Prior, Paul. "Response, Revision, Disciplinarity: A Microhistory of a Dissertation Prospectus in Sociology." *Written Communication* 11, no. 4 (1994): 483–533.

Rafoth, Bennett A. "Discourse Community: Where Writers, Readers, and Texts Come Together." In *The Social Construction of Written Communication*, edited by Bennett A. Rafoth and Donald L. Rubin, 131–146. Norwood, NJ: Ablex Publishing Corporation, 1988.

Rogoff, Barbara. "Developing Understanding of the Idea of Communities of Learners." *Mind, Culture, and Activity* 1, no. 4 (1994): 209–229.

Rose, Michael. *Lives on the Boundary.* New York: Penguin Books, 1989.

Rose, Mike. "Remedial Writing Courses: A Critique and a Proposal." *College English* 45 (1983): 109–128.

Rose, Mike, and Malcolm Kiniry. *Critical Strategies for Academic Thinking and Writing.* New York: Bedford/St. Martins, 1998.

Russell, David. "Activity Theory and Its Implications for Writing Instruction." In *Reconceiving Writing, Rethinking Writing Instruction*, edited by Joseph Petraglia, 51–77. Mahwah, NJ: Erlbaum, 1995.

———. "Rethinking Genre in School and Society: An Activity Theory Analysis." *Written Communication* 14, no. 4 (1997): 504–554.

———. "Where Do the Naturalistic Studies of WAC/WID Point? A Research Review." In *WAC for the New Millenium: Strategies for Continuing WAC Programs*, edited by Susan H. McLeod, 259–298. Urbana, IL: National Council of Teachers of English, 2001.

Ryan, Leigh. *The Bedford Guide for Writing Tutors, Third Edition.* New York: Bedford St. Martins, 2002.

Salomon, Gavriel, and Tamar Globerson. "Skill May Not Be Enough: The Role of Mindfulness in Learning and Transfer." *International Journal of Educational Research* 11 (1987): 623–637.

Schryer, Catherine F. "Records as Genre." *Written Communication* 10, no. 2 (1993): 200–234.

Scribner, Sylvia. "Studying Working Intelligence." In *Everyday Cognition: Its Development in Social Context*, edited by Barbara Rogoff and Jean Lave, 9–40. Cambridge, MA: Harvard University Press, 1984.

Selzer, Jack. "The Composing Process of an Engineer." *College Composition and Communication* 34 (1983): 178–187.

Shemilt, Denis. "Adolescent Ideas About Evidence and Methodology in History." In *The History Curriculum for Teachers*, edited by C. Portal, 39–61. New York: Falmer Press, 1987.

Slevin, James F. "Genre Theory, Academic Discourse, and Writing within Disciplines." In *Audits of Meaning*, edited by Louise Z. Smith, 3–16. Portsmouth, New Hampshire: Boynton/Cook Publishers, 1988.

Smagorinsky, Peter, and Michael W. Smith. "The Nature of Knowledge in Composition and Literary Understanding: The Question of Specificity." *Review of Educational Research* 62, no. 3 (1992): 279–305.

Smit, David W. *The End of Composition Studies*. Urbana, IL: Southern Illnios Universtiy Press, 2004.

Sommers, Nancy. "Revision Strategies of Student Writers and Experienced Adult Writers." *College Composition and Communication* 31, no. 4 (1980): 378–388.

Sommers, Nancy, and Laura Saltz. "The Novice as Expert: Writing the Freshman Year." *College Composition and Communication* 65, no. 1 (2004): 124–149.

Spear, Karen I. "Thinking and Writing: A Sequential Curriculum for Composition." *Journal of Advanced Composition* 4 (1983): 47–63.

Sperling, Melanie. "Uncovering the Role of Role in Writing and Learning to Write: One Day in an Inner-City Classroom." *Written Communication* 12, no. 1 (1995): 93–133.

Sperling, Melanie, and Sarah Warshauer Freedman. "A Good Girl Writes Like a Good Girl." *Written Communication* 4, no. 4 (1987): 343–469.

Stahl, Steve A., Cynthia R. Hynd, Bruce K. Britton, Mary M. McNish, and Dennis Bosquet. "What Happens When Students Read Multiple Source Documents in History?" *Reading Research Quarterly* 31, no. 4 (1996): 430–456.

Sternberg, Robert. "What Is an Expert Student?" *Educational Researcher* 32, no. 8 (2003): 5–9.

Sternberg, Robert J. "Abilities Are Forms of Developing Expertise." *Educational Researcher* 27, no. 3 (1998): 11–20.

Sternglass, Marilyn S. *Time to Know Them: A Longitudinal Study of Writing and Learning at the College Level*. Mahwah, NJ: Lawrence Erlbaum Associates, 1997.

Stockton, Sharon. "Writing History: Narrating the Subject of Time." *Written Communication* 12, no. 1 (1995): 47–73.

Swales, John M. "Other Floors Other Voices: A Textography of a Small University Building." In *Rhetoric, Knowledge, and Society*, edited by Charles Bazerman, ???–???. Mahwah, NJ: Lawrence Erlbaum Associates, 1998.

———. "Re-Thinking Genre: Another Look at Discourse Community Effects." Carleton University Conference on Genre: Unpublished Paper, 1992.

Teich, Nathaniel. "Transfer of Writing Skills: Implications of the Theory of Lateral and Vertical Transfer." *Written Communication* 4, no. 2 (1987): 193–208.

Tosh, John. *The Pursuit of History: Aims, Methods and New Directions in the Study of Modern History*. New York: Longman, 1984.

Toulmin, Stephen E. *The Uses of Argument*. Cambridge: Cambridge University Press, 1958.

Trimbur, John. *The Call to Write*. 2nd ed. New York: Longman, 1999.

Voss, James F. "Issues in the Learning of History." *Issues in Education* 4, no. 2 (1999): 163–209.

Walvoord, Barbara E., and Lucille P. McCarthy. *Thinking and Writing in College: A Naturalistic Study of Students in Four Disciplines*. Urbana, IL: National Council of Teachers of English, 1990.

Wiggins, Grant. "Creating a Thought-Provoking Curriculum." *American Educator* 11, no. 4 (1987): 10–17.

Williams, Joseph M. "Afterword: Two Ways of Thinking About Growth: The Problem of Finding the Right Metaphor." In *Thinking, Reasoning, and Writing*, edited by Elaine P. Maimon, Barbara F. Nodine and Finbarr W. O'Connor, 245–255. New York: Longman, 1989.

Wineburg, Samuel S. "Historical Problem Solving: A Study of the Cognitive Processes Used in the Evaluation of Documentary and Pictorial Evidence." *Journal of Educational Psychology* 83, no. 1 (1991): 73–87.

———. "On the Reading of Historical Texts: Notes on the Breach between School and Academy." *American Educational Research Journal* 28, no. 3 (1991): 495–519.

———. "The Cognitive Representation of Historical Texts." In *Teaching and Learning History*, edited by Gaea Leinhardt, Isabel L. Beck and Catherine Stainton, 85–135. Hillsdale, NJ: Lawrence Erlbaum Associates, 1994.

Winsor, Dorothy A. "An Engineer's Writing and the Corporate Construction of Knowledge." *Written Communication* 6, no. 3 (1989): 270–285.

———. "Engineering Writing/Writing Engineering." *College Composition and Communication* 41, no. 1 (1990): 58–70.

———. "Genre and Activity Systems: The Role of Documentation in Maintaining and Changing Engineering Activity Systems." *Written Communication* 16, no. 2 (1999): 200–224.

———. "Invention and Writing in Technical Work: Representing the Object." *Written Communication* 11, no. 2 (1994): 227–250.

———. "Ordering Work: Blue-Collar Literacy and the Political Nature of Genre." *Written Communication* 17, no. 2 (2000): 155–184.

———. "What Counts as Writing: An Argument from Engineers' Practice." *Journal of Advanced Composition* 12, no. 2 (1992): 337–147.

———. *Writing Like an Engineer: A Rhetorical Education*. Mahwah, NJ: Lawrence Erlbaum Associate, 1996.

Witte, Stephen P., and Christina Haas. "Writing as an Embodied Practice: The Case of Engineering Standards." *Journal of Business and Technical Communication* 15, no. 4 (2001): 413–57.

Woodman, Harold D. "Do Facts Speak for Themselves? Writing the Historical Essay." *New England Journal of History* 45, no. 1 (1988): 39–45, 48.

Young, Kathleen McCarthy, and Gaea Leinhardt. "Writing from Primary Documents: A Way of Knowing in History." *Written Communication* 15, no. 1 (1998): 25–68.

INDEX

ABOUT THE AUTHOR

Anne Beaufort is associate professor in Interdisciplinary Arts and Sciences and coordinator of writing-across-the-curriculum at University of Washington, Tacoma. Her Ph.D. in Education (Stanford University) focused on language, literacy and culture, and she has done ethnographic research in both higher education and workplace settings on the ways in which adults can improve their handling of the writing process and write effectively in a range of genres. Her first book, *Writing in the Real World: Making the Transition from School to Work*, received an NCTE award for best technical/professional communications book.